DROPPING NAMES

Dropping Names

The Delicious Memoirs

of

Daniel Curzon

l'Aleph

Daniel Curzon

Dropping Names

Published by *l'Aleph* – Sweden – www.l-aleph.com

l'Aleph is a Wisehouse Imprint.

ISBN 978-91-7637-573-0

© Wisehouse 2014 – Sweden – www.wisehouse-publishing.com
Without limiting the rights under copyright reserved above, no part of this publication may be reproduced, stored in or introduced into a retrieval system, or transmitted, in any form or by any means (electronic, mechanical, photographing, recording or otherwise), without the prior written permission of the publisher.

A neurosis is a secret we keep from ourselves.

PREFACE

These memoirs were written in 1986. I'm leaving them pretty much as they were when I first wrote them. They are altered with relevant changes: deaths, fame, etc. in the later Updates.

I believe they say a lot about an era.

(June, 2004)

In these memoirs I intend to refresh my own memory about interesting people I have met, no doubt many of them included because of their name recognition. Let's face it. Do you want to read about a lot of nobodies? If I seem to drop names, you have only yourselves to blame, you see. If you haven't heard of some of them, you will, my dears, you will.

For I anticipate that these people will become even more "important" as time passes and this period achieves more charm as a literary and cultural age. I hope so. I wouldn't want to expend all this effort for naught. And you wouldn't want to read these pages because they're full of mere gossip, would you?

If I misremember details or make unfair judgments, please be kind. Or don't be kind. There can be no defamation here, for everything is the truth.

Maybe I will even uncover a truth or two about myself that I'm not aware of. The horror, the horror!

CONTENTS

Preface	7
Joyce Carol Oates	15
Lily Tomlin	21
John Steinbeck	23
Christopher Isherwood	24
Don Bachardy	30
Tennessee Williams	35
Dan Turner	37
Joyce Carol Oates	45
Frank Corsaro	49
Harvey Milk	52
Harry Britt	55
John Rechy	57
Tommy Kirk	60
Senator Milton Marks	63
Robert Patrick	65
Tom Ammiano	68
N. A. Diaman	70
Allan Estes	73
The Kuchar Brothers	77
Curt McDowell	80
Marion Eaton	82
Joyce Carol Oates	84
Arthur Bell	91

Arthur Evans	*93*
Vito Russo	*95*
Samuel Steward	*97*
Roger Austen	*100*
Herb Caen	*105*
John Preston	*107*
Edmund White	*110*
David Lamble	*113*
Richard Hall	*117*
Joyce Carol Oates	*121*
John Gardner	*124*
Philip Levine	*128*
Randy Shilts	*131*
Sally Gearhart	*137*
J. E. Freeman	*139*
Del Martin & Phyllis Lyon	*142*
Lester Cole	*145*
Harvey Fierstein	*148*
Armistead Maupin	*150*
Dean Goodman	*156*
Rita Mae Brown	*163*
C. D. Arnold	*165*
Felice Picano	*169*
William Dickey	*174*
John Gilgun	*176*
Walter Allen	*181*
Leland Mellot	*184*

Stephen Sondheim	*187*
Arthur Bressan	*191*
Robert Chesley	*194*
Robert Peters	*203*
Simon Karlinsky	*204*
Donald Allen	*206*
John Embry	*212*
Billie Young	*217*
Joseph Hansen	*221*
Paul Monette	*223*
Jeanne Barney	*226*
Bruce Billings	*227*
Andrea Gordon	*231*
Herbert Gold	*236*
Peter Robins	*238*
Tim Wolfred	*240*
Terrence Davies	*242*
Christmas Leubrie	*244*
The Angels Of Light	*251*
James Broughton	*271*
George Birimisa	*273*
Miss America	*274*
Doug Holsclaw & Leland Moss	*279*
Sean Penn	*284*
Terrence McNally	*287*
Suzy Bright	*289*

Romanovsky And Phillips	*291*
Frances Fitzgerald	*294*
Harold Norse	*298*
Sister Boom Boom	*300*
Robert Ferro	*305*
Joseph Torchica	*307*
Judy Grahn	*309*
Quentin Crisp	*310*
Jon Sugar	*314*
Daniel Curzon	*323*
Update – 1989	*326*
Update – 1992	*335*
Update – 1994	*345*
Update – 1999	*347*
Brave New World	*349*
A Double Standard	*350*
Since Then	*353*
Update – 2001	*355*
Daniel Curzon	*368*
Another Time	*371*
Update – 2004 – I	*376*
Lillian Faderman	*376*
My Lawsuit About The Hate Site	*382*
Ann Shay	*383*
Update – 2004 – II	*388*
Ann Shay	*396*
Update – 2014	*400*

Foster Corbin	*400*
Aaron Fricke	*400*
Michael Joseph Arcangelini	*408*
Lady Malet	*410*
Paul Sagan and Bill Neville	*416*
Zack Johnson	*419*
Charles Kruger	*421*
Joyce Carol Oates	*424*
John W. Gettys	*425*
Daniel Curzon	*425*

JOYCE CAROL OATES

Met Mrs. Joyce Smith in 1962, when she came to teach at the University of Detroit, where I had been teaching for a year myself. Mrs. Smith later turned into Joyce Carol Oates, but then that wasn't all she turned into. But more of that later.

I believe it was at registration that she and I first talked. Faculty had some responsibilities in that regard in those days. There she sat a tall, wispy, big-eyed, hyper-vigilant Madonna in her early twenties. She was a little less than three months younger than I.

I was just trying to make pleasant conversation when I asked her about the school where she'd been enrolled the previous year, Rice University, some miles from Beaumont, Texas, where her husband had gotten his first teaching job after they'd met and married at the University of Wisconsin. "I hear it's a good school," I said.

"No, it's not," Mrs. Smith said.

"Oh?" It hadn't been my intention to argue the point, and I was struck by the snappish answer. I made a few other efforts at pleasant conversation, all of which were rebuffed with an iciness that made my teeth chatter. I certainly was not inspired to seek out this brittle Olive Oyl-like woman for another word.

However, it turned out that our offices at the university

were next door to each other, and so we kept bumping into each other. One day we even had lunch together at the school's cafe. Either I was more personable that day or Joyce's defenses were down, because she was friendlier.

Now that I think about it, she became friendlier when I made some off-color joke that she was offended by. I apologized right away when she grew huffy. She had a Victorian, iron-maiden quality that one dared not upset. Another time she was petulant in her office about someone else, and I excused myself until she should feel better. She came hurrying to my office, all apologies. Maybe you had to get Joyce's respect by not surrendering to her stiff, snotty side.

Somewhere along in here Joyce called me one night at home, a home I shared with my parents. It was *my* home, though.

She wanted to know how I taught comedy to my classes. She was supposed to teach Moliere or something and said she hadn't any ideas. I was so naive and pre-sexual in those days that it never entered my mind that she was calling for anything except notes on comedy. But of course it was just a ploy, appealing to my male vanity to "help" her with my vast knowledge, when of course she probably could have taught me a thing or two. On the other hand, comedy never was Ms. Oates' strong suit, was it, and so it's possible I did suggest some helpful ideas about "discrepancies" or whatever.

Soon we were having long, very long two- and three-hour-long conversations on the telephone just about every other day. What did we talk about? I don't know. Literature, life. Sometimes she made me almost stammer because she seemed so intelligent. I was pretty sure she was smarter than I was. But, then, smart doesn't equal kind or nice, does it?

Joyce and I started going out together. Her husband, Raymond Smith, was having emotional troubles, compounded by drinking problems. He didn't like to go out much, but Joyce did. So she had selected me as a presentable young man a little stocky maybe, with a beard when men didn't have beards, but tall and possessed of a car and we went to plays and concerts and readings, as well as for drives out to the rich suburbs of Detroit, to look at all the fancy houses, houses that Joyce always noticed as being empty in the day time. All that wealth and no one there. It wasn't too long after that she succeeded in getting a fancy house of her own, followed by even fancier ones. I never cared about money or houses in those days, but then I was a fool. Joyce wasn't. She was also lucky since she wrote what she wanted and got paid handsomely for it. Once, as we were walking around the campus, we saw a man gibbering to himself, obviously mentally disturbed. "I get paid for doing that," Joyce smiled.

Another time Joyce gave a paper on the writer Borges just off campus. Many of the faculty attended, including one priest who asked Joyce a very long, convoluted question, which she answered with a very convoluted response. Afterwards I asked her how she'd been able to answer so well. Her reply: "I didn't know what he asked, so I answered the same way. It doesn't matter what's said, only how it sounds. Besides, he just wanted to show off by asking a question."

I remember having wonderful conversations. I also remember being bored with our relationship after a few years, because we had said everything we had to say to each other.

Well, not really. That was to come later.

What I resent to this day in that relationship was that Joyce Carol Oates was never willing to let me share my sexual side with her -- I mean talking about it. Granted, this was a period when the taboo about homosexuality was horrendous, but you would think a sophisticated writer like Joyce, a woman with a good mind and a wide background in reading, would have been more open to talking about our secrets. But no. Anytime I even hinted at my secret Joyce would let me know that such information was unwelcome. Once, later, I wanted to send her (or perhaps actually sent her) a poem of mine that had been published. Since it was about cruising a public park, Ms. Oates, sniffing, said she didn't care to know about such "vulgarity."

Of course she didn't mind flirting with her own vulgarity, which was of an adolescent variety. Joyce had severe problems with her adulterous yearnings. It's in all her work, as you know. I resented that she, as a heterosexual, could flirt with her secrets in my presence any old time she pleased, while I, as a queer, had no right whatsoever to air my problems. One time in particular she told me about a handsome book salesman who had taken her out to lunch and then had asked her to run away with him. She was positively thrilled. This may have been because she saw herself as a "brain" and sort of unpretty, and here was this sexy man giving her the chance to "change her life completely." Of course her common sense dictated that she not drop her security with Mr. Smith, however incomplete the marriage, and run off to God knew what. Yet she was tempted. She was often tempted.

I don't think Joyce knew for a long while that I was gay,

even after I finally took matters into my own mouth at age twenty-six, yes, twenty-six. She would say things like, "Dan, what you need is marriage." That was supposed to make me more mature. It didn't make her more mature, but she seemed to think it would work for me.

I do believe Joyce was in love with me, or at least infatuated, and for quite a few years. I think she would have married me if I'd asked.

We were friends for about nine years altogether, and during a good part of that I felt a lot of pressure to be her "boyfriend." It was a come-hither-oh-but-I-don't-mean-that attitude on her part that was not at all easy to live with. She made overtures, which I chose not to see, but if I said something "intimate," then she would get huffy. By "intimate" I mean such things as the time I told her that her lipstick was on crooked, and she got hysterical: "You don't respect me! You don't respect me!" How can you respect somebody who gets hysterical because you tell her that her lipstick is on crooked?

Another time she had a book jacket photograph taken. It showed her in a highly artificial, made-up pose I think it's on the back of her first novel, *With Shuddering Fall*. She said, "Don't I look pretty?" And I said, "Yeah, it doesn't look like you." Well, it didn't! She didn't like that remark either and threw a tantrum. But she wasn't pretty then. I think she got prettier later. I once watched her and her husband approach a movie theater lobby where I was waiting for them, asking myself, "What do they look like, objectively?" I concluded that they were not a handsome couple. She got skinner later, probably through guilt over her sexual fantasies, or realities. Joyce was always one of those people who may or may not be attractive. Everybody noticed her eyes; they were fascinating, no doubt about it. In a creepy kind of way.

Her biggest confession to me was after we'd seen Bunuel's *Belle Du Jour,* about a woman who is a prostitute by day and married by night. Joyce admitted, with great trepidation, that she had fantasies in which she was abused by men throwing mud on her and the like. I recall telling her that wasn't so awful, trying to make her feel better about herself. Maybe she's gotten modern now, and far from feeling bad about such fantasies, brags about them, just like everybody else.

I don't want to be like Hemingway in *A Moveable Feast* and use the sexual peccadilloes of my former friends as something to "accuse" them with, especially not the way Hemingway did, since apparently he was fighting his homosexual side so viciously he sneered at sexual irregularity every chance he got. Nor do I want to sound as bitchy and unbalanced as Truman Capote does in *Conversations with Capote*. I just want to tell the facts as I perceived them, not tinged too much with anger and the desire to get in zingers against the figures of my past. But I'm no Mr. Nice Guy either.

More about Ms. Oates by and by. Lots more.

LILY TOMLIN

She wasn't famous when I met her, but I think Lily Tomlin is probably the first celebrity I ever met. That was back in 1959 in Detroit, when I was a junior at the U of D. I met her because she was a friend of chubby, funny Jimmy Savedes, who was my friend. Jimmy and I were in Shaw's *St. Joan* at the college theater, and Lily came to see him play the part of the Dauphin. She was still Mary Jean then.

Earlier he had told stories of their exploits together, most of which I've forgotten, but I do recall him telling of the two of them going into shoe stores and trying on umpteen shoes, with absolutely no intention of buying anything, one time exasperating a clerk so much that he told them they should be gassed. "Orally, nasally, or anally?" Lily said immediately. It was the daring and the quickness for the 1950s that seemed so impressive at the time. Such rudeness, no doubt without the attendant cleverness, is commonplace now. (No, I hope not to include too many such old-fogey comments.)

I met Lily after one of the performances, when a bunch of us went to a rib house to eat. I remember her as tall and bony, dark-haired, long-faced. I don't recall any specifics, but the general impression she left with me was aggression. Since I didn't particularly relish being the object of other people's sharp wit, I can't say that I "liked" her. I can't say that she liked me either. At least she never called me after that! Indeed, the two attempts when I sent her notes and/or copies of my books backstage after she became a Star went unacknowledged. I'm sure all kinds of people did the same, presuming on as casual an acquaintance as mine was. She also had a reputation for being surrounded by a bevy of Amazonian women, who no doubt protected her from unwanted reading material. I always thought her friend Jimmy Savedes had as much talent and wit as Lily Tomlin, but he chose to become a teacher in Detroit and she chose to go to Hollywood. Such is show biz and such is life. (One of the silliest things I ever did in my life is tell Jimmy Savedes I did not want to be friends any longer. I was pissed that he would not call before driving up and asking if I wanted to go out. He also honked his horn, a sign of plebeian behavior. I found out that I had no other friends.)

JOHN STEINBECK

When I was writing my Master's thesis at Kent State in 1961 on John Steinbeck's work, I decided to write him a fan letter, wishing him immortality. Lo and behold, he wrote me back! Imagine my delight at receiving a letter that summer when I was all alone in the house, working night and day so that I could finish and go back to Detroit and teach college English.

The letter was handwritten on yellow foolscap paper, sent from Sag Harbor, New York. Steinbeck wrote that he didn't much want immortality, that he'd settle for a gun and couple of hunting dogs. He also said he was usually surprised by the theses on his work that he'd seen: the writers saw things he didn't and ignored things he thought were important. What I remember most is that Steinbeck had some spelling errors in his letter. I guess I was surprised that a noted writer couldn't spell. But he could write with great versatility!

Soon after, he won the Nobel Prize, and not long afterwards he died. I published several articles on Steinbeck and kept his letter proudly, but now I can't find it. I left it in a large book at my parents' home in Farmersville, Illinois when they retired. My mother loaned out one of my books while I was gone, and I have a feeling it may have been the one with Steinbeck's letter in it. A friend of a friend once xeroxed it for his collection, but I can't find the original. I've searched high and low. It's possible that it's in my garage in a box somewhere, my lost relic. There are times when I'd like to hold it in my hands, a talisman for my own writing doldrums. Or to sell it when things get really tough!

CHRISTOPHER ISHERWOOD

In 1974 I attended the annual conference of the Modern Language Association in New York, where Christopher Isherwood was the most celebrated speaker on a panel, a panel on homosexuality, the first ever such panel. Of course I didn't know the man, but he was much talked about because his *Berlin Stories* had been converted into the very successful musical *Cabaret* and the movie with Liza Minnelli.

At a smaller afternoon session Isherwood appeared, to discuss with interested parties various subjects of literary concern. Somebody – not me – asked him what he would teach if he taught a Gay Literature course. His response was that he had just read an admirable novel called *Something You Do in the Dark*, my book. I was thrilled. (Yes, I had sent him a copy.) He said some nice things about my book as I sat there. Finally I called out, "Thank you!" and he realized that the author was in the audience. For some reason I had to leave right then, for a job interview, I think. When I came back, I learned that Isherwood had said more nice things behind my back when he knew I was gone. I have never been an active seeker-outer of the famous and only bother if they fall into my lap, but I wasn't about to let die that opportunity to be an equal. I introduced myself to him after the session and said, "I teach in Fresno at Fresno State. Perhaps I could come and visit you in Santa Monica sometime." Isherwood then was in his seventies, with an elfish quality: short, with bushy eyebrows, a cheery demeanor. I recall him being most gracious to me and inviting me to visit.

Immediately I wrote him a letter and asked if he would mind writing out his remarks about my first novel. He did, and the quotation appeared on several editions. I even gave his name as a reference for a Guggenheim Fellowship, which I didn't get. I probably should have asked Isherwood's permission to give his name as a reference, but I didn't, out of ignorance about proper protocol. I came from a mother who went to the fourth grade in the "hollers" of Tennessee and a father who went to the seventh grade in the flat farm country of Illinois. And I guess I was afraid his kind words would go to waste if I didn't get them written down. I'm glad I did.

When I got to Isherwood's house I met Don Bachardy, his lover of many years, a man thirty years his junior. This was in 1974, and to be truthful I didn't know who Bachardy was, knew nothing about his drawings. He was slim and attractive, his hair just then going white. He had adopted Chris's British accent.

Isherwood and Don were a lovely couple. I was pleased at how thoughtful they were to each other. I guess they'd had their troubles over the years, but when I knew them they seemed idyllic. By that, I mean they didn't squabble, pick at each other, upstage each other, or any of the other things I've seen long-term couples, both gay and straight, do. Isherwood was a charming conversationalist: wryly amusing, self-effacing. I was beside myself with the glamour of it all – little Danny Brown from Detroit visiting such a famous writer! And here was this famous writer getting into the back seat of his car as he, Don, and I started off to dinner. Then here was Christopher Isherwood lying on the backseat under a blanket! I soon understood why. Don drove very fast, even recklessly, and the only way Chris could bear to drive with him was if he couldn't see where they were going.

Lying down, Isherwood would tell anecdotes about people he'd known, like Gore Vidal, Truman Capote, John Gieguld, and others, making me positively lust with envy. I hadn't known I was such a celebrity freak, or maybe it was that I'd never considered it possible for me to be in such company. Little working-class boys from Detroit didn't travel in these realms of gold.

About Gore Vidal I recall Isherwood saying, in his rather high-pitched, British voice, "I do wish Gore would stop claiming to be bisexual. I dare say he was in an orgy once, many years ago, and there may have been a woman present in the room in a corner!"

About Capote he said, "Truman is the stuff of which legends are made," and told the story of Capote's being asked to autograph someone's penis in a restaurant, when supposedly Capote looked at it and said, "Perhaps I can initial it."

Even then that story struck me as too good to be accurate, and I said so, but it was still exciting to hear because most anecdotes in life are so dreary, so un-clever. I'm sorry I never got to meet Capote, although he does seem to have been a mess at the end there.

Chris also told a story about visiting his old friend Somerset Maugham when the man was in his nineties. Here was Maugham in his villa in the south of France attended by a younger lover who saw to his every need, and who had done so for many years, and yet Maugham spent the luncheon complaining that nobody had ever loved him. He wasn't the least bit lovable, was indeed obviously loved, and still he couldn't see it.

Halfway through the luncheon Maugham leaned toward his lover and gestured at Isherwood and Bachardy and whispered too loudly, "Who *are* these people!" Ah, senility. I never spotted any in Isherwood, although I did catch him in a television interview not long before he died, and ten years after we had fallen out. He seemed to be fading, and I felt bad.

Chris, Don, and I visited eleven times. I counted. We would usually go to dinner and a movie. I never stayed overnight at their house. But after the first or second visit I felt a compulsion to make myself available to them sexually. Not that I really was inclined to have sex with them, but I thought it might be polite. Chris had complained in his MLA talk that when he went to gay bars men wanted to talk about his books but nothing more. I've always feared sexual deprivation in old age, and so I wanted to make Isherwood happy. Besides, everybody had sex with everybody else in the Seventies! I was thirty-six then, but looked much younger. Many considered me good-looking.

I sent them a valentine with a note about the possibility of a three-way, holding my breath about their response. I got a nice note back, telling me they were pleased with my offer but that it wasn't necessary. I breathed a sigh of relief, as I'm sure they did too, that our relationship could remain on a friendship level instead of turning into a sexual one, friendship always a guarantee of much greater longevity, don't you think?

We went to see Hitchcock's *Rope* one time, and all of us agreed it was homophobic, besides being boring. Chris and

Don loved movies and would go see almost anything.

Sometimes a fan would come up to Chris and Don as we stood in lines. There would be a few compliments, usually too effusive, and then there would be nothing left to say and the fan would disengage himself. It made me think just how much I wanted that kind of fame for myself, if it was ultimately so empty.

Isherwood irritated me one night at dinner, though I didn't let on, when he complained about "these people with their tragic sense of life!" I took it personally, even if it wasn't meant that way, because my writing till then had been pretty heavy. I thought it was easy for Isherwood to put down the tragic vision since his own life had been pretty nifty, from upper-middle-class birth to Santa Monica icon status. I also thought that his writing lacked depth. It seldom grappled with the harrowing sides of experience and thus was ultimately rather thin. Of course I didn't say this aloud, knowing no writer likes to be criticized.

It was surprising for me to learn, but I guess good for me, that even Christopher Isherwood had had rejections. He and Don and written an adaptation of *The Beautiful and Damned* that got nowhere, although they may have been paid something for it. Even for the rights to *Cabaret* Chris said he hadn't received that much, about $45,000 at that time despite the immense success of the Oscar-winning movie.

I didn't tell him I'd told my beginning creative writing class at Fresno State that I'd been to visit Christopher Isherwood and not a single one of them knew who he was, at least not until I identified him as the author of what had become

Cabaret. I thought that was shocking, and still do. It's amazing what it takes to penetrate the consciousness of the mass-culture, unless of course you're a pop singer or a basketball player.

DON BACHARDY

Don Bachardy I got to know apart from Isherwood because he asked to draw me. Posing was tiring, but at least Don liked to talk while working.

He had done portraits of many famous people, from Stravinsky to Bette Davis, and always had them autograph their pictures. To be included in this illustrious gallery was a treat for me; however, later I realized that Don liked to draw just about everybody he met, and that subdued the compliment a bit.

Don had to be careful about Chris's ego and not stealing too much attention. I had asked them both to sign a copy of a book, and Don said he'd better autograph just his drawing on the cover and not the inside, lest Chris be upset.

He also told me that Auden and Isherwood had been sexually intimate, if not quite "lovers," and that he felt that there was probably more love going from Auden to Isherwood than the other way.

He said, too, that he and Chris continued to have a sexual relationship even then, though the specifics as to days, times, and particular sex acts were not spelled out. Pity. Even with all the candid biographies coming out these days there are many things we don't ever learn about people, even people we know well. How do they keep it going?

Bachardy drew me three times and painted me in acrylics two or three times. You had to pay for a visit there with posing, but I didn't mind really, stiff joints and all. Once he asked me if he could draw me in the nude -- me, not him, in the nude. I was reluctant because of my foot phobia, but when he agreed I could keep my socks on, I said yes. I was in pretty good shape then, and Don made my dick seem bigger than life-size. When I asked him about it, he said, "I just drew what I saw." That was nice.

Unfortunately he didn't like the finished portrait, something about the perspective and said he wasn't going to have it photographed or reproduced. I think he said he would store it at Bekin's, where it may be to this day, for all I know. Don was willing to sell his drawings, but since he wanted $600 there was no way I could afford a picture of myself in those days.

I used one of his drawings of me with a beard for the cover of *The Misadventures of Tim McPick*, one of my novels. (Original title *Queer Comedy* alas, ahead of its time for my literary agent). I didn't ask Don's permission because I thought I had it when he sent me a nice black-and-white glossy of the drawing. I learned years later from Dan Turner that Don was a bit ticked off with me for not asking permission. But I had sent him a note saying it was to be used.

One time Don was drawing me and we talked about John Rechy, who had written some sections of his book *Numbers* about a pair of effeminate men very similar to Chris and Don. Bachardy said they felt betrayed. "One doesn't quite trust a person after something like that, does one?" he said. I took that as a warning that I was not to reveal information about him and Chris in any of my books.

I myself have never understood that reluctance to be

written about. I think it's flattering, even when what is written is not flattering. It wasn't till many years later than I read *Numbers*. I didn't think the portrait Rechy did of them was so awful. There *was* a certain amount of prissiness about their behavior.

My friendship with Chris and Don disintegrated because of a couple of incidents that I thought were favors to them.

An editor for *In Touch* magazine somehow learned that I had met Chris and Don and wrote me, asking if I would like to write an article about them. I thought about it and decided I would do a kind of *House Beautiful* piece -- you know, about their lovely home in the canyon, their paintings, their glamour, how I had come to meet them, etc. I wrote it up, revealing nothing that I thought they wouldn't want revealed, not even as much as I've said in this memoir, and was about to send it to the magazine, when it dawned on me that maybe they would object. So I sent the article down to Santa Monica.

I got a telephone call from Don, asking me not to publish it, not because of anything it contained but because "we make a distinction between friends and journalists." My word! Talk about a cultural gap. That struck me as insufferably 'upper-drawer.' Naturally I did not send the article anywhere, not wishing to lose the friendship. About six months later an interview with Chris and Don appeared in the magazine, by somebody else, a mere journalist, I guess.

I can understand you might not want everything you say in private to be taken down and used against you, but writers also usually like publicity of an innocuous kind, to help sell their books. I know I do. I thought then, and now, that I was helping the two of them.

Then another thing happened that turned out badly, despite the intention. A friend of mine, Roger Austen, had a TV talk show on PBS in San Francisco. He asked me if I could ask Isherwood to ask Tennessee Williams if he would like to appear on Roger's show to discuss his recently published *Memoirs*. Roger had tried and tried to get to Tennessee through his agent and other sources, to no avail. I hesitated to ask, but then Chris, the last time I had visited, had said he thought that people should get behind Tennessee and help him promote his new book. So I sincerely thought I would be helping out two friends.

Thus I wrote to Isherwood and asked if he could ask Tennessee to be on the show, which I assured him was legitimate and which would be widely seen. I put in a plug for Roger Austen, too.

Well, I got my letter to Chris back with his message written between my lines: "I never ask favors of my friends. That's how I keep my friends."

But But *But!* I wasn't asking for any favors! I was doing a favor! I was incensed but wrote Chris a placating letter trying to explain what I had done. I got back a postcard saying something like, "Oh, that's all right. I often have to say no."

Say no? But you'd asked people to help promote Tennessee's fucking book! How dare you put me into some beggar category!

Needless to say, being as proud as I am, the friendship didn't survive much past this episode. I think I saw Don and Chris a few times after that from a distance. I did ask him a question from the floor when he spoke in San Francisco. So I saw them on the stage somewhere, but I made no attempts to renew the friendship or to visit. We obviously had different notions of what friends are permitted.

When Chris died in 1986, I sent Don a note expressing my sorrow for his sake and telling him to persist, because grief would pass. He was good enough to write back and say he would get over the pain because Chris wouldn't want him to mourn.

I regret the misunderstanding, or whatever it was, but that makes a better memoir than "Chris and Don were just marvelous every minute I knew them!"

TENNESSEE WILLIAMS

My one in-person contact with Tennessee Williams occurred in San Francisco when Dan Turner (a collaborator of mine on several musicals) made an attempt to renew his friendship with Tennessee, for whom he had worked for three weeks as his private secretary. It seems they had separated on less than ideal terms, and Dan Turner was attempting to get on Tennessee's good side again. He somehow found out that Tennessee was going to attend a show that night, and so we made plans to attend the show, too. Turner's plan was to run into Tennessee casually in the lobby. "Oh, hi, Tennessee. It's me – Dan Turner. How are you?" That kind of thing.

Well, Tennessee came to the show all right, late, wearing a huge, oddly-colored fur coat. I mean huge. During the intermission, Dan and I strolled in the lobby, but no Tennessee. We kept waiting and waiting. Finally Dan went back into the theater. I did not go, not wanting to be pushy about meeting the great man.

When the second act started, I asked Dan what had happened. Had he talked to Tennessee? He said he'd finally gone over and said hello. But Tennessee had been rather cold and had not made Dan feel he wanted to see him again. Naturally I was curious about this famed person sitting a few rows behind us, so I turned around while waiting for the lights to dim. Tennessee Williams noticed me staring at him and stared back -- no, glared back as if to say, "What the fuck are you gaping at! Have I, famous though I be, no right to my privacy!"

Right, Tennessee, you're right. But then if you don't want people to stare at you, you shouldn't dress like an oversized dead bear! I would have stared even if you weren't Tennessee Williams. . . . Rest in peace, honey.

DAN TURNER

Dan could have written his own memoirs about the famous people he knew and slept with. Some Very Big names in the theater and movies. I told Dan that, because of his AIDS, he might have wiped out most of the American entertainment world.

Dan had the two things it took to get into that world: looks and drive. I saw a photograph of him when he was about thirteen. What an ugly boy then: big ears, glasses, nerdy-looking. Something happened, and Dan became one of the handsomest men I've ever known. He had a Tom Selleck-like face, a body he worked on at the gym. He had a way of standing very close when he talked to you, exuding all this sex appeal -- well, at least when you first met him. Later Dan's personality had a way of snuffing out the sex appeal. Simply put, he talked too much. His lovers must have given up when they couldn't get a word in edgewise. He and I never had any sexual relations whatsoever.

I confess a certain amount of jealousy of Dan, especially as I got older and less sexy, because men were always hitting on him. You couldn't go anywhere without male eyes turning toward him, blazing lust engulfing him. Male drunks would even rub their crotches and practically rip his clothes off. One of Dan's worst traits was that he too was always cruising. He'd be talking to you, but his eyes would roam everywhere. He annoyed any number of people with this trait, but I never knew it to stop, even after he got AIDS.

Dan Turner's greatest quality was his thirst for life, something he had long before he had a life-threatening illness. I've never known anyone who tried to do more things or who knew more people than he did. He'd be writing a play, acting in one, directing one, serving on some committee, hosting an out-of-town visitor, writing music, gardening, running off to a cocktail party, ushering, and more, all at the same time. He didn't want one tiny scrap of life to escape him.

Of course the other side of this was that Dan was always late. Indeed, I can't remember him ever being on time for anything. He'd arrive a half hour late for an appointment always surprised that he hadn't been able to squeeze four meetings and a love affair into the previous hour and get to you on time.

I met Dan in early 1977, when he auditioned for my evening of satirical skits called *Sex Show*, which I had decided to produce and direct myself. It had been fifteen years since I'd done any theater (in college), but I decided, after sending the skits out, that the best way was just to do them myself. I think five people auditioned for five parts. Dan Turner came with a handsome boyfriend with an I.Q. of about fifty-seven. But that boyfriend was gone before the show opened, I believe. For whatever reason Dan never kept boyfriends for very long. It was one of his greatest burdens. But as soon as one was gone, another took his place.

I was rusty as a director. In fact, I'd never had much experience, and even less taste for it. I hate finessing people, coddling them to get them to do what you want. But directors have to do that. I must give credit to Dan Turner for getting other people to work on my show, even more actors after some of the original cast members dropped out. I got into trouble because I was trying to parcel out the roles in the skits according to who could do the individual parts the best. I didn't want to let on to the actors what I was doing because I didn't want to hurt their feelings, and so I looked unsure of myself as a director. I also used to go to rehearsals and create the blocking then and there instead of having it prepared in advance. I have to give credit to Dan Turner for helping a lot with getting that show in shape, and it turned out very well, got excellent reviews, and played with several casts in three different theaters in San Francisco for six months. Dan was the only actor to stay with the show for the entire run. He was always easy to work with, not temperamental, accommodating, talented. Yet I remember one time when he was slightly ill and said he wasn't going to perform. I spent the entire afternoon with him, coaxing him, convincing him that he should go on. It was a bitch, but he finally consented. It was occasions like that one that made me stop directing.

Dan directed another play of mine, an hour-long one-act called "Beneath the Surface" which Earnest Players did as a midnight show. It had a cast of twelve, which was constantly changing during rehearsals, rehearsals held in my garage, by the way. It's a play about minorities trapped on a subway train together and how all their prejudices and hatreds come out as they compete for air. Needless to say, this play (1979) was ahead of its time; it didn't flatter minorities, and so some people in Earnest Players were offended by it. We went on with the rehearsals, with a million problems, casting Chinese actors as American Indians, whites as blacks and on and on, when suddenly director Dan Turner says he has to leave for a twelve-day visit to Texas, twelve days in the middle of a short rehearsal period!

The assistant director took over, but he wasn't forceful enough, and I thought the production was going to collapse.

Under-rehearsed and unsentimental, we got a negative review from a certain Carl Driver, who complained about the subject matter but also the fact that the director directed the horde of actors to exit in two different directions at the end, when they were all supposed to be going to the same place. (I hadn't caught it either.)

It wasn't really Dan's fault, but during that same production one of the actors playing the White Man went on stage drunk. He said all his lines v-e-r-y s-l-o-w-l-y, throwing the play off. The actress playing the Lesbian ad libbed something about him not having so much trouble as a white man if he wouldn't drink so much. He walked over and slapped her and ad libbed, "Who asked you, bitch!" It was the only time I ever screamed at an actor after a performance. We gave him a second chance in a benefit at a nifty club called Chez Jacques, and he got drunk there too.

Dan Turner directed another one-act of mine, "Your Town," a spoof of the nuclear family. He did an excellent job with that one, and we got good reviews, even though we performed in a converted mortuary.

Probably our most successful one-act was "Beer and Rhubarb Pie," which Theatre Rhinoceros did (1979). It had the threat of sex and appealed to audiences a great deal. We even made a videotape of the show in Dan's house. It made a star, at least in San Francisco, of Thomas-Mark, who in 1986 was unfortunately killed while learning to ride a motorcycle. I think we were the first show where the lead took off his shirt.

God, what we started!

Dan was very chatty about his three weeks as Tennessee Williams' private secretary, saying that the two had never had sex although he realized that Tennessee had seemed to expect it, though he hadn't pushed. He'd hired a male prostitute once and watched while Dan and the prostitute had sex.

I'd try to get Dan to tell me details about the celebrities he'd had sex with, but he was always very discreet. I managed, however, to put two and two together. One time, for example, Edward Albee, then at a definite low point in his career, spoke at Stanford, and Dan and I drove down to hear him. I thought Albee gave a good speech, but at the press conference afterwards he was an arrogant prima donna. I asked him a question, meaning to point out how he was coming across: "Mr. Albee, isn't it true that you have a reputation for being difficult to deal with?" Albee seemed rather surprised at the question and denied being a prick.

Naturally, Dan Turner had to stay afterward and talk to "Edward," whom he'd met before at a dinner party in Hollywood. I refused to go, not the least bit charmed by Albee's behavior at the press conference. So Dan went alone. About half an hour later he came back to where I was waiting not patiently and said, "Do you mind if I don't go back to San Francisco with you? Edward has asked me to drive back with him." Well!

Of course I "let" him go back with Albee, who I learned, by a lot of prying, asked Dan to accompany him the next day while he visited some classes at Stanford. Then they spent the night together. I wanted to know the details, but Dan was a model of discretion.

I don't mean to steal Dan Turner's stories, in case he ever does write his memoirs. He's jotted things down in his journals for years, but if he doesn't get around to writing them out they may disappear forever. I'll try to confine myself to his episodes with which I had some personal connection.

I always thought Dan's greatest talent was his ability to write music: wonderful, singable songs. I told him he was spreading himself too thin, trying to be a Renaissance man. The only conceited thing I ever heard him say was: "I do more with my left hand than most people do with two." He wanted to be a writer more than he did a musician. And he got better in his plays, the more he wrote. But the first works he showed me were pretty weak, decidedly amateur. He reminded me of myself when I was a kid, trying clay modeling, painting, singing, anything to get some attention.

Dan was not a trained musician; he played by ear. But he had that one thing that many people in music don't have, the ability to write great melodies. We eventually got around to writing some musicals together.

The first one was called *Comeback*, which, to this day, has not been produced. It started off as a play about a face lift for an older woman, and developed into a musical drama about a male cabaret performer having a sex-change. This was in 1978, long before *La Cage aux Folles* or *Victor, Victoria* or any of the other things about such subjects. We even wrote a song called "Just As I Am" long before Jerry Herman wrote "I Am What I Am." We did umpteen versions of the script. Since we were inexperienced, we wrote that first musical backwards; that is, we wrote many of the songs first and tried to squeeze them into the plot. We also collaborated on the lyrics, which took forever, and to my mind they were not as good as when I did the lyrics myself. We had staged readings and fund-raisers, and yet somehow that show still is unproduced. At one of the staged readings, at the Berkeley Stage Company, we had to sit on the stage and ask for audience reactions. One lady piped up to say, "If you're not careful some people might think your show is about a transsexual." Even the leading lady, Lynn Eldredge, a gifted singer and actress, apparently was mystified by the part she had just performed so well, because her comment from the audience was, "What's the difference between a sex-change and a transvestite? Which was I?"

Years after this Dan and I were still re-writing this musical, this time with the help of David Welsh, an actor-producer who had always liked the show. We went to Welsh's little apartment every day for two weeks, hashing out the new storyline. What a terrible way to write anything -- a committee, one in this case where the actor-producer was getting duns on the telephone since he was trying to raise money for another show and was promising this, that, and the other thing to everybody who called him or that he called. We'd hear him tell lies to them, one right after the other. At the same time Dan Turner had had a shot of interferon that morning for his AIDS, and it was evidently an overdose, for he developed a high fever and chills. We kept on with the re-writes, nevertheless. Of course nothing came of that version either. Dan always, always remained optimistic and sure that Success was just around the corner.

In between we wrote *No Mince Pies*, a musical about Oliver

Cromwell and the rise of the Puritans (later called O*liver Cromwell and the Boys*). We started it right after Ronald Reagan's first election in 1980, because it seemed to me there was going to be a rise in conservatism, a prediction that came true, making the musical more relevant as books and magazines began to be censored, mandatory drug tests began, and other signs of neo-Puritanism reared their heads. The parallels to the days when it was forbidden to eat mince pies became clearer. In the summer of 1986 Dan and I managed to get a college workshop production, with ten days' rehearsal, of this musical. It promised to be a disaster, but came together and really pleased the audience, despite the fact that we had to divide up the cast into singers and actors in order to get competence where we needed it.

Our biggest musical to date has been *Cinderella II*, which was first produced in the summer of 1984. I'll tell more of that hit with the backstage horror stories later on.

JOYCE CAROL OATES

Trying to think of some nice things to say about Ms. Oates. There must have been some or we wouldn't have been friends for so long. I promise, though, not to be too goody-goody in what I say.

I must give her credit; she was never egotistical about her writing as her career began to take off. If anything, she lived as though at any moment it might all be taken away by the gods. She would dip into a cup of flavored yogurt and say, sincerely, "This is what life is all about." All that mayhem cascading upon mayhem in her work is no doubt her genuine world view.

One time Joyce and her husband came to my house for dinner. My mother prepared it. I remember all of us sitting around, my fourth-grade-in-Tennessee-educated mother, my reticent father, me, and the Smiths trying valiantly to have something in common. It was not a success, and I always remember my mother thereafter referring to Joyce as "snooty." Joyce always felt tremendous guilt about her own family, her not very educated folks, her retarded sister, her grandmother. I think she and I felt a lot in common because of our backgrounds. We were trying to escape our semi-literate pasts and always had ambivalent feelings about where we came from and that we desperately wanted to escape being like. This and our commitment to writing gave us a bond.

It was Joyce Carol Oates who taught me how to be Machiavellian. She was very much a physical coward; still, she wouldn't hesitate to do things to enemies if she thought she wouldn't get caught. For instance, she used to write letters to the campus newspaper signed with the names of students that she didn't like or who had given her trouble. She'd wait until just before grading time to criticize the students' teachers. Since the letters were signed by the "students," there was a good chance the students might suffer when the irate teachers decided on the grades.

When Joyce started reviewing for the *Detroit News*, she sometimes wrote reviews of books she hadn't read, notably Andy Warhol's book entitled *A*. Why? Because she didn't like what Warhol stood for. Oates was always a closet conservative. One time she had to review a James Purdy novel. Knowing that he was a queer and not liking the book, Joyce found an especially awkward passage and quoted it, saying, "This is Purdy at his best." Such behavior shocked me in those days. But I've learned a lot from Ms. Oates, I must admit. A major thing is that homophobia runs deep in some people.

She also carried a gun, terrified of being assaulted or molested. Well, it was Detroit, after all, so she wasn't totally paranoid. She kept the gun in her purse and often patted it, until it became sort of a way of her threatening me subtly. I wonder what she's packing these days. I always thought she'd wind up shooting her husband one day, when he got "fresh."

One of her nicest qualities was that she seemed to care a lot about her students, at least the smart students. She'd have them over to her house and spend time talking with them in her office. I never had that much rapport with my own students. I was witty and pleasant but basically distant. Now there are some who would possibly suggest that Oates was just trying to pick their brains in order to get ideas and details for her stories, but not everything she did was selfish. Not everything.

Just recently I sent a story about Oates to the magazine at the college in Windsor, Ontario where she taught after she left the University of Detroit. Gene McNamara, the editor, and a former friend of Oates', sent me a story that he had written about her, published in *Chicago* magazine. His story tells of this woman writer who ransacks every English Department she visits to get cruel details about people and exhibit them in her books. Since I think writers have every right to do that, that aspect of Joyce didn't and doesn't bother me. But she did get incensed if you tried to do it to *her*. She could sure dish it out; she just couldn't take it.

I can recall many times when she would write a story about someone we both knew and then gloat and say, "Oh, boy, is he/she going to be mad!" Once I talked her out of portraying the daughter of Clyde Craine, the University of Detroit English Department head, as someone who didn't look like either a man or a woman. I'd become friends with this person and knew she would read the story and be very hurt, because she was boyish-looking. Joyce finally changed it to a fat girl. But, you see, to Oates' conventional mind being androgynous was not a plus but a horrible deformity. How ironic, then, that she should show up on a Modern Language Association panel on "Androgyny" a few years later. A lot she knew!

She has used me too, or parts of me, in some of her work, although whether I've been in her stuff since 1972 I can't say. Lord, how can I read all of her stuff! She writes faster than most people read. She's written two novels and a piece for *TV Guide* since I wrote this section of my memoirs!

There definitely was something about Joyce Carol Oates that made people react strongly to her, one way or the other, usually the other. Some people have that quality to make you notice them, loathe them. She has her fans, obviously, too. Some of us can barely get arrested, and Oates has always had people eager to publish her, to interview her, along with all those others who would like to see her hands tied for a few years so that she won't write anything else. If the tragedy of most American writers is that they've burned out young, with too little output, Ms. Oates' problem has got to be that she's already turned out more product than any other human being can ever possibly read, or want to, even a professor. I can see it now, a future doctoral dissertation: *Oates: The Tragedy of Not Knowing When to Stop, or Less Is More*. But the real problem isn't just volume; it's the way she repeats herself.

FRANK CORSARO

Frank Corsaro directed Oates's play at the Actors Studio about 1965. He had also directed many operas as well as *Night of the Iguana,* which turned out to be Tennessee Williams' last big hit. I met him because Joyce and I drove in my car from Detroit to NYC for the opening. Some ironies abound here. For one, she didn't like the theater, thought it slow and overly obvious. She'd shown me the play and asked my opinion, and I'd encouraged her to send it to her agent, who got it to Corsaro. She'd also forgotten that she'd made the father in the play black and the daughter white as a joke. When we got to NYC, Corsaro and the others talked in hushed tones about the "significance" of the mixed racial theme. Joyce and I made mouths to each other behind their backs.

Frank Corsaro was then in his forties, I'd say, slight, slender, intense. He had appeared as an actor in *Rachel, Rachel,* a Paul Newman-Joanne Woodward film. He had good words to say about them but nothing except ill-feeling toward Bette Davis, whom he'd directed in *Iguana.* According to Corsaro, Bette was a bitch on wheels, demanding, overblown. He seemed sorry he'd worked with her. He wasn't the least bit reluctant to bad mouth her to strangers, either.

When we watched Oates's play, I had some suggestions, but who was I? And Corsaro didn't exactly invite me to be play-doctor. But he should have asked somebody for advice, because the play got devastating reviews. It was one of the few times I felt sorry for Joyce, because she'd been thrust into the big time against her will.

She and I both felt out of place among the bigwigs of NYC. We had dinner at her publisher's apartment one evening, overlooking Central Park. A couple of wine snobs were the other dinner guests, and they ooed and awed, bragged and pontificated about wines so much that Joyce and felt like strangers from the planet Detroit. Neither of us drank alcohol then and thought we were caught in some kind of bizarre religious ceremony. All this brought us closer together, being rubes in the big city. But we weren't as provincial as her publisher, who asked us in all seriousness if we had television out in Detroit. That's right, she hadn't been out of NYC in a coon's age.

When we went out to lunch with magazine editors, we pretended to be cosmopolitan, though we weren't making it. I constantly got hiccups while eating, and I remember being given suggestions on how to get rid of them by any number of embarrassed editors. There I was, my thumbs stuck in my ears, lifting a glass of water with my fingers to try to kill the hiccups, or holding my breath, or leaving the table when the noises got too awful. Oates was a much more delicate eater than I and somehow managed to be understanding through all this even though I was probably making those editors wonder what kind of companions Oates kept.

Joyce also visited some of her old sorority mates on that trip. She felt great affection for them, and at the same time felt sorry for their lives, for instance, the one who kept dating Persian men, even though they abused her; the heavy one who couldn't get a husband. Joyce had a husband back in Detroit and a young, nice-looking escort with her in NYC! Take that!

I recall Joyce being unable to sleep at her friend's apartment because the friend snored during the night. So Joyce had sat up reading Mary McCarthy's *The Group* all night. She was dismissive of it.

Despite the problems, that trip was a highlight of both our lives up to then. What a different world the world was when one was feted and petted and treated like somebody special!

HARVEY MILK

Around 1975 some gay politicians decided to hold a meeting in Fresno, where I was then teaching at the state university there. Some would come up from L.A. Some would come down from San Francisco. All I had to do was stay where I was. I wasn't exactly a politician, but I had written some books, stories, and articles on controversial gay subjects, so I attended.

The two people I recall most vividly from that day are Harvey Milk and the Rev. Ray Broshears, both now deceased. Harvey wasn't St. Harvey then; in fact, he hadn't even been elected to the Board of Supervisors in San Francisco, but he was extremely articulate and charismatic as he spoke from his seat at the conference. I was turned on by him, to be honest. Maybe he looked especially good in contrast to the Rev. Broshears, who was a self-ordained, self-appointed gay leader, besides being a total crackpot, blackmailer, and meddling moron. Harvey Milk could out-argue him and do it with humor and deftness.

I spoke with Harvey at the end of the day, hoping for a more "personal" get-together, but it was not to be. He jumped in a car and headed back to S.F. immediately after the meeting. Of course I'd see him from time to time passing out flyers or waiting for a streetcar when I visited the big city. I never introduced myself again.

On May 21, 1979 I participated in what has come to be known as White Night, the night when several thousand people marched to San Francisco City Hall to protest the lenient sentence that Harvey Milk's killer got, a mere seven years for killing two men. Mayor Moscone had also been gunned down.

Until around ten P.M. the crowd didn't do much except listen to speeches and mill about, but then people started throwing stones and breaking the windows in City Hall. The cops with their riot gear and weapons were in a threatening group near the front door, but that only exacerbated the conflict. I remember Cleve Jones, one of the march organizers, later founder of the AIDS quilt, shouting through a megaphone to us in the crowd as things began to heat up: "Go home! Go home!" I didn't throw any stones, but I yelled, "No, *you* go home!" The least we had due us was a riot, so I incited others all I could. Harvey Milk had stood for gay legitimacy, and now his cold-blooded killer was getting off with barely a slap on the wrist because he was an ex-cop, because it was clear, once again, that queers were considered disposable scum. There was no question that symbols were involved in all this, and it was time for gays to stand up and prove that they could be as angry and "masculine" -- God save the mark! -- as the rest of the men who were screwing up the world with excessive testosterone. Quite frankly, I wanted to see some blood, and not gay blood, for a change.

People soon started tearing the cement trash containers apart and throwing the chunks at City Hall and at the cops. Finally the cops charged us, lobbing tear gas. I remember running across the mall with others to a pool to get some water to wash our burning eyes with. The cops pulled back.

Someone managed to set one of the cop cars that were parked in front of City Hall on fire, and then nine cars in a row on a side street went up, one after the other, their sirens howling, set off by the flames. It was spectacular, and I was right there in the middle of it, thank god.

When the fire trucks arrived, the crowd blocked their access so that the police cars continued to burn and burn. I saw men bleeding from being hit on the head by irate cops, on the far side of the burning police cars. Communist agitators were yelling for revolution; media journalists were interviewing members of the crowd, including me; vandals were starting to emerge from wherever they lurk to capitalize on the situation and break windows of nearby businesses. I myself was shoved by a cop. The riot went on for a couple of hours, until I finally got back to my car and drove home, dazed and thrilled. Even then I knew it was one of the most exciting nights of my life.

HARRY BRITT

Now, I knew Harry Britt before he was Harry Britt, as I told him in person once. Harry Britt, in case time is not good to his reputation, was appointed by Mayor Dianne Feinstein of San Francisco to take Harvey Milk's place on the Board of Supervisors after the assassination.

I first encountered Harry at a Gay Atheists meeting at the home of Tom Rolfsen. He was an aide to Harvey at the time, and a former minister. Former ministers make good atheists, though Britt downplayed his lack of religion later on because it's not good politics.

Harry was starting to get heavy even in those days; he got positively fat later on. He wore glasses, had curly, dark hair, and looked like somebody's uncle.

I always thought Harry didn't get his fair shake as a politician because he had to dwell in the shadow of St. Harvey Milk. He was a good speaker, progressive, and very hardworking. He had an annoying habit that may have made others dislike him: he would continually look over the shoulder of the person he was talking to, to the next person he meant to talk to. The result was that you never felt he was talking to you. You want to have the illusion at least that you have the ear, or the eye, of someone you're talking to, right?

Harry came to a party at my house once, but of course he left within twenty minutes to go to another party or another meeting. In those days he made very little money as a Supervisor, had one ugly suit, and took public transportation everywhere. But he wasn't a good mixer, the way Harvey Milk was, and for all his efforts I don't think he inspired admiration, certainly not devotion.

One time I attended a meeting somewhere conducted by Harry. I spoke with him afterwards and offered him a ride.

There was some kind of sexual tension present, on my part as well as on his. He put his hand on my leg and left it there in a manner that means only one thing. I must say I toyed with the idea of having a fling, or at least a sexual episode, with my city Supervisor, but for some reason I didn't. Perhaps it was because I thought it might be a fiasco or somehow get out of hand or create that barrier that often arises after two men have had sex but don't want to continue having it. I hope I didn't hurt Harry's feelings. He took a lot of flak being in the public eye, and he deserved all the orgasms he could get.

JOHN RECHY

John Rechy's *City of Night* was the first gay book I ever read, probably about 1964 or so. That's where I learned that men sometimes had sex in parks or in YMCA's. I owe my first sexual experiences thus to John Rechy. I won't say that my arrest by a Vice Squad plainclothes cop in a Detroit park is likewise due to him, but that arrest led to my radicalization in the realm of sexual liberation and the writing of my first novel, *Something You Do in the Dark*, the first gay protest novel. (The original Putnam press release said: "It is ... a scathing indictment of society and the terrible methods it uses to haunt and harass some of its members.") So I owe a lot to John Rechy.

I'm also grateful to the man because he called me once, years later, when I happened to be in the bathtub, to tell me that I was a good writer. He did it because my friend John Rowberry, an editor of a magazine, had told him I was depressed. As so often has been the case during my writing career I was having difficulties. I thought it was terrific of Rechy to bother to call.

But the times I've seen him in person have been few and far between. He had a book signing at the old Walt Whitman Bookshop at this same time and actually gave me a free copy of his book *Rushes*. Unfortunately he didn't look too good that day. His years were showing, especially in his loose chest and bad teeth, and yet he continued to dress like the hustler he had been in his youth.

One time I had Rechy as a panelist at the American

Booksellers Association get-together in Los Angeles. I was the moderator. This must have been about 1978 or '79. When he came into the room, dressed in his tight, tight pants and his tight, tight shirt, open to the navel, everybody stared at him. I've always been amazed at people who aren't afraid to attract such attention, usually hostile, by their appearance.

Rechy obviously delighted in his looks. But what was happening was that he was losing his physical charms and still playing the role of sex god. I have no objection to people looking as good or being as sexy as possible for as long as they can, but there must come a point when one must face the inevitable, if not gracefully, at least realistically, unless one is willing to become a grotesque like Mae West, a painted, garish seductress in her mid-eighties!

In a book review I said that Rechy had better watch himself or he was going to wind up as the world's first seventy-year-old hustler. I confess I felt awkward after putting that in print, wondering if Rechy had seen it. If he had and was still nice to me afterwards, then he deserves even more credit as a good person than I've given him already.

He didn't stay after his panel presentation, and so he missed my attempt to call attention to the plight of the writer of serious fiction. I took out a gun and held it to my head and said I was going to blow my brains out right there on the podium to make my point. The audience just stared at me. Only Paul O.M. Welles, one of the panelists, and my friend, attempted to stop me. It wasn't a real gun, but I guess it was convincing. Welles was the only person, other than my roommate, who would talk to me after that. I guess I looked like some kind of nut. I did it because I thought then, and still think, that you can sit there for those thirty or forty years writing your wonderful little works of art and nobody gives a damn. But stab your wife or do something else newsworthy or provocative and suddenly you're interesting – and commercial.

What I admired in Rechy's writing was that he was honest. He did not glamorize the dark cruising world that he inhabited and wrote about so frequently. He knew that he was trapped in an underworld of compulsive sexual behavior and told it just like it was, with all its orgasmic glories and all the emotional hollowness as well. I hope Rechy finds loving sex someday. He's had the other.

TOMMY KIRK

Soon after I arrived to teach at Fresno State University in August, 1974, I received a letter from a certain "Thomas Kirk," who said he wanted to make a movie of my 1971 novel *Something You Do in the Dark*. I wasn't sure if this person was the same Tommy Kirk who had been a child star in umpteen Disney movies and a teenager in the "Spin and Marty" series on the old *Mickey Mouse Club*. But a call to Hollywood confirmed that this indeed was the case.

I was staying with Jim Frey of the English Department until I found a place of my own, and we decided to drive down to Los Angeles together to meet with Mr. Kirk. I was on top of the world because I had escaped from the U.S. military in Asia (which was trying to fire me for trying to teach something gay), even though the position at Fresno was merely a one-year replacement, and because I'd won the job over two hundred twenty-five other applicants, despite complaints from the Affirmative Action Committee. I was a white male. Being a gay male didn't count except against you, of course.

Well, we drove down to Hollywood and were to meet Tommy Kirk at the Gold Cup, a restaurant that looked rather seedy for the meeting place of such a high-level movie deal. I learned later that the Gold Cup was notorious as a hustlers' hangout. But we all know we have to put up with the colorful quirks of movie personalities, right? When Mr. Kirk had wondered on the telephone how we would recognize each other, I had said, "Oh, I'm sure I'll recognize you!"

Well, I didn't. I had figured out that Tommy Kirk had to be in his early thirties about this time, but I didn't see anybody in the restaurant who looked like that fresh-faced, crew-cut kid of my memories. There was a sort of chunky youngish man with thinning hair and dark sunglasses sitting at the counter half a dozen stools away from me. This person also had been looking around. I am proud to say that when I approached him I had the cool not to say, "Didn't you used to be Tommy Kirk?"

My traveling companion, however, almost as soon as we were seated in a booth, said, "What have you been doing lately, Tommy?" This is *not* the question you ask of an actor who obviously isn't at the top of his career. Tommy glared at Jim and said, "I made a bike movie. I did summer stock in Kentucky."

Now he wanted to star in a movie based on my book, maybe even direct it himself. When I asked why my novel rather than some other, he said because he identified with the hard times of the gay hero. He also strongly implied that he'd been fired by Disney because he was gay. Apparently drugs played a part as well, although this was not discussed. It came out in a newspaper article I saw afterwards.

He said he had a producer who was interested. I said I'd like to write the screenplay and maybe play a small signature part, if possible. I gave him my agent's name and address. It seemed obvious to me that we had a winner here. Headlines all over the world would read: FORMER DISNEY CHILD STAR WINS OSCAR IN DRAMATIC ROLE AS HOMO-SEXUAL.

But then I heard no more. My agent heard nothing. I wondered what was going on. I had my suspicions because as Jim and I were leaving the restaurant that day in Hollywood, I noticed Tommy, who had left a few minutes earlier, was paying his bill in pennies, counting them out one by one for the impatient cashier. Tommy Kirk, where *are* you now?

SENATOR MILTON MARKS

After I moved to San Francisco in June, 1976 I began to meet more prominent people. One of these was California state senator, Milton Marks. Before he converted to the Democrats, Senator Marks was in the uneasy position of being a Republican representing a very liberal section of the state. As a consequence, he had to make forays into all sorts of communities, including the gay. Poor man, it must have been difficult for him.

On several occasions I saw the good Senator, a rather haggard-cheeked gentleman in his fifties, out on Castro Street, flanked by two assistants, trying valiantly to make contact by shaking hands with his constituents. I was accosted by this triumvirate and offered a rather tentative "handshake" from the haggard one in the middle. "This is Senator Milton Marks!" the assistant said. The Senator grunted, as if on cue. I had the feeling that Senator Marks, possibly stuffed, had been wheeled out to do his political duty, but why should I, or anyone, be expected to vote for a man who stuck out his hand at me, shook mine with two weak little fingers, and then was wheeled away to wherever they kept him stored between visits?

What did he stand for, what was he against? He just existed? If anything, this approach, devoid of any content, probably cost the good Senator more votes than it earned him.

The Senator also sent letters of congratulations or proclamations to everybody, for any reason. I'll bet corpses got them for dying. It must have worked, though, because the man had great name recognition.

Later I was solicited by telephone to give my endorsement when he was running for re-election. I was surprised and said, "Oh, I don't give political endorsements." The aide said, "But you're a friend of the Senator's, aren't you?" Friend? He didn't know who I was from Adam! Politics, you can have it.

ROBERT PATRICK

Bob Patrick, author of *Kennedy's Children* and innumerable other plays, came to San Francisco in the late 1970s because Theatre Rhinoceros was doing one of his works. Indeed, it did a whole string of his plays under the artistic directorship of Allan Estes.

Patrick won my heart immediately when he spoke after one of the performances because he recognized me in the audience and informed the crowd: "You are privileged to have Daniel Curzon in your midst." I couldn't have said it better myself!

I should point out that I was not on good terms with Allan Estes at that time, and when Robert Patrick praised and sought me out to go have a snack with him afterwards, leaving Estes and the other Rhino people to sit by themselves, I was making new enemies even as I was making a new friend.

Bob Patrick was then a thick, melon-faced man, not exactly a movie star in looks but not as ugly as he complained he was. He objected strongly to the emphasis on attractiveness among gay men, but he liked the cute ones, too. All men do. They can't help it.

His play "T-Shirts" is a comic diatribe about this "looksism" problem for the unattractive. I wrote my own one-act "Last Call" as a companion piece, an answer to Patrick's, but an affectionate one.

Patrick was brilliant, for all his physical problems. He had that glimmering, diamond-hard verbal facility certain New Yorkers have, especially born-again New Yorkers. (Bob was from Texas originally.) I'll bet Oscar Wilde was re-incarnated in this man. I felt like a shy, little hick in his presence. So I ventured that a friend of mine, meaning Dan Turner, had had sex with Edward Albee, in order to make myself seem more sophisticated. "I'm reasonably non-plussed!" Bob replied.

Fortunately he was warm and curious as well as brittle, and we liked each other, I could tell. He filled me in on the machinations of Broadway types, and I recall him very distinctly saying, "To be a Broadway producer *is* to be a crook!" Producer Alexander Cohen had tried to buy *Kennedy's Children* outright from him for a paltry sum after it was a hit.

Patrick had the halo of genius about him more than anyone else I've ever known. He also had a gift for making enemies, as I do, and I'm sure he caused any number of people headaches when they had to work with him.

He toyed with moving to San Francisco and being my roommate, but changed his mind when he found out that he wouldn't be able to sit in the bathtub hour after hour writing his plays.

He wrote reviews of my books in *Christopher Street* and other publications, always glowing ones. I felt flattered and vindicated in what I was doing because I knew that Bob Patrick was smart and an artist, besides. (They don't always go together, by the way.)

After many stunning productions, and quarrels to match, Patrick set off, leaving New York City behind him. He took a bus trip across the country -- my idea of Hell. But when he came through S.F. on his way to L.A. and we had dinner together, he seemed contented, or at least more subdued, than the previous time I'd seen him.

I must have struck him as an alcoholic because I finished off his carafe of red wine after he had just a few sips and didn't want any more. He wasn't drinking or having sex. He said he'd never expected sex from his actors because it was a lousy way to cast a play anyway. He seemed to earn his living by going on these cross-country excursions, directing his own plays or giving seminars on theater to folks out there in the great heartland. He seemed to enjoy it.

Then he decided to stay in L.A. Fuck New York and all the problems that went with it! So Bob set up shop and produced and directed some plays at a coffeehouse down there. What energy he had! I hate the minutiae of rehearsals in getting a play mounted; he jumped right into the fray time and time again.

I got letters from Bob from Southern California, one asking for a copy of my neo-Shakespearean play. But I never heard from him on that, and the next thing I knew he was back in NYC putting on plays there again! I should have known. They always go back there, don't they?

I love Bob Patrick, but something tells me that he probably won't live a long life. He must be about fifty now. There's something in some people that reads "hard, gem-like flame" and "Beware! Quirky genius at work!" I hope I'm wrong, but, however long he lives, I think Robert Patrick is one of the most talented writers of our time. I'm honored to have been in his midst.

Tom Ammiano

Back in 1975 I drove up to San Francisco from Fresno to attend a meeting of some gay activists with media representatives, the latter on the defensive because of their bigoted, usually minimal representations of gays in the mainstream. A microphone had been set up in the center of the room to allow angry speakers to address their complaints to those on the panel.

The voice I recall the best from that day is that of Tom Ammiano, who was a public school teacher then and has gone on to become a well-known stand-up comedian and politician since. The voice was squeaky and high, yes, downright "nelly," and I admit I was unliberated in thinking people like that contributed to the negative stereotypes about gay men. Why couldn't they sound more masculine? Why didn't they control their wrists better? Well, to be honest, I'm not exactly a fan of strident nelliness even today, but I've come a long way from thinking that "butch" is necessarily better than "fem." And Tom Ammiano no doubt contributed to my growth.

When you think about it, you never hear effeminate male voices in broadcasting or public speaking of any kind, truly a form of censorship. So when you do hear such things no wonder they strike the ear as bizarre. With Tom Ammiano, the voice and the mannerisms that turn off many people in life are the very things that make him so alive and interesting on stage. I've noticed that's often true in show business.

It's people like Ammiano and Lea DeLaria, the bulldyke comedian, who have led the way for alternative ways of being, probably out of revenge for the way they've been treated. At this point (1986) gay and lesbian comedians have not broken through the way black and other ethnic comedians have. The prejudices are still prevalent, as Ammiano has told me more than once. But Ammiano is so funny, eventually his pioneering will pay off, hopefully not just for those who follow him but for the man himself. You see, I'm an optimist!

I can't say that I've ever been comfortable with Ammiano in person. We've exchanged mild pleasantries; he'd seen a play of mine; I'd reviewed him in a newspaper column I had, and so on. I always feel uncomfortable with people I have to review when I meet them on a social level, because it's hard to be objective about people you know personally. I also harbored a bit of resentment toward Tom because I was once asked to speak in Alaska; then he was asked instead of me!

We've run into each other at meetings, on the street, on radio shows. We never fall into each other's arms. We are groundbreakers together, trying to open up paths usually closed to the likes of us, but there is no real friendship. One time I did a rave review of *Wrists*, one of Ammiano's shows. During the run, I happened to be at the theater one evening. But when I heard that Tom was coming up to the lobby, I realized he might notice me. So I hid. I didn't want him to feel beholden to me, nor did I want to feel that I'd have to say I liked his shows thereafter for the rest of my life.

Sooner or later gay comedians like Tom will be co-opted by the larger culture, for good or ill. It may be nice to get part of the action and reduce homophobia, yet it may not be much of a gain to become homogenized and safe.

N. A. DIAMAN

Another person I met at that same media conference was N. A. Diaman, the writer. He was a slender, Greek-looking fellow with a pronounced stutter. No, more than a stutter; he virtually could not talk. I'm happy to report that he had therapy along the way and eventually was able to speak much more normally, with just occasional long pauses in the middle of sentences.

I accepted a satire from Diaman for the literary journal I was editing out of Fresno, *Gay Literature*. So I was a bit taken aback, later, when Diaman turned down a story of mine for a journal he was editing, a story called "Virility," which was included, down the road, in the anthology *On the Line*, edited by Ian Young.

And there in we come to the differences between us. To Diaman's mind, my story was too "negative." He was of the school which said literature about gays and lesbians had to be "positive." To my mind, that meant reducing our variety and energy to a kind of pretty-pretty public relations pap that might get some laws passed but would be dismissed in years to come. I was too proud to argue the point with him, however.

Diaman brought out a number of his own books under his own imprint, something I was forced to do myself at times when I'd written something nobody seemed to want right then. I wasn't about to be one of those writers who slit their throats because they can't get into print. So I admired N.A. Diaman for having the guts to self-publish. Since he had that terrible stutter, it was twice as hard for him to promote his work, I'm sure. I don't think he was taken seriously by many. I was embarrassed by some of the mannerisms of his writing. The first books were all in lower-case type, as though his typewriter were broken. And the works were so gay-lib gooey that I couldn't relate to them.

Diaman showed up everywhere book signings, parties, you name it. Several times we were reviewed together. He called me once when a publisher in Brazil expressed interest in a book of his and of mine too, because it was reviewed nearby. Nothing ever came of it.

We also were reviewed together by Patricia Holt of the *San Francisco Chronicle* one time. Holt was one of those raving feminists that got into positions of power in the 1970s and 1980s because of the women's movement but who will leave little of permanence in their contributions to literature. Holt referred to the books by Diaman and me as "amateurish." I was outraged and wanted to kill the woman, not just for dismissing a book that others had called a "major contribution to American letters" but for stultifying Political Correctness.

I tried to gas myself in the garage after that review, but luckily or unluckily I couldn't get my car inside because of all the junk stacked in the way. Diaman, the next time I saw him, seemed to shrug off Holt's nasty words. I couldn't tell if he was just less sensitive than I or just less able to articulate his feelings.

After vowing never again to let anyone have that much power over my concept of myself, I took it upon myself to attack the women-first "aesthetics" of Ms. Holt and her whole liberal, leftist bag of third-rate clichés that no doubt made her a rotten creative writer who couldn't get her own simple-minded crap published and forced her to write newspaper reviews encouraging real writers to write like her. (Once the Scott Meredith literary agency wrote in to the *Chronicle* say that Ms. Holt had attacked it because she'd tried for years to get that agency to represent her, but it wouldn't because she wasn't any good. I have to give Holt credit for at least printing the letter.)

N. A. Diaman continued to show up everywhere, like the ghost of gay lit. He must have had a private income of some sort. At least I never could figure out how he earned his living. He was always passive. I wondered if he seethed with hidden passions. But even his books were gentle. Maybe he's writing his memoirs right this minute, killing us all off, one by one.

ALLAN ESTES

Allan started Theatre Rhinoceros in 1977 and gets credit for starting gay theater in San Francisco, yet his production of "The Madness of Lady Bright" *followed* my production of *Sex Show* at the old Gay Community Center. I didn't see that first production, but I did catch Rhino's next bill of one-acts. What I saw so appalled me by its stunning amateurishness that I helped found a new theater group, Earnest Players, meant to be devoted to gay theater of higher quality. Who needed a lot of bad actors in inept productions!

That conflict infuses most of my subsequent relations with Allan Estes. He was a very young man, in his early twenties, when we first met, vaguely nice-looking but beset with poor hygiene and quite a few moles. Little did I suspect that this man had a Vision about gay theater and the energy and single-mindedness necessary to bring it off.

Even as the years went by, I found myself often embarrassed by Theatre Rhinoceros productions, especially since it had become the only gay theater in San Francisco. The level of professionalism was low, and yet we who were reviewing plays were expected to write glowingly of gay theater even when it didn't glow. Frankly I didn't think such poor productions did gays any good whatsoever in the eyes of the rest of the world. I didn't even see how it could make gays feel good about themselves since there was absolutely no art in evidence, only the correct politics.

All this was at its worst when Rhino would have its noisy claque sit in the back and laugh at everything, hoping to inspire the audience to do the same. It even yucked at C. D. Arnold's subtle poetic plays as if they were burlesque.

At one point Allan Estes did agree to put on my "Beer and Rhubarb Pie" at Studio Rhino in 1979. With its strong erotic element, it was a notable hit. I heard later that Estes said I had originally written it as a "stroke story." That showed the gap in sensibility between us, since I've written only one "stroke story" -- and that one for money when I was desperate -- in my whole life. I began to feel greater and greater contempt for Allan Estes, an emotion I could barely keep out of my reviews. I should mention that I praised the hell out of anything that was good, but I wasn't about to be Estes' adjunct publicity hack.

An ethical dilemma was created thereby, because I was submitting plays for possible production to Theatre Rhinoceros. I had no intention of saying in my reviews anything less than what I really felt, but Estes was committed to making his theater a success, and no goddamned reviewers like me were going to stand in his way.

He actually told the editor of the paper that I was reviewing for that his theater wouldn't be buying as many ads until the level of the reviews of his productions "improved." Another time Theatre Rhino ran an ad containing a quotation from Penni Kimmel about how wonderful one of the productions was, when in reality the words were written about her expectations for a *forthcoming* production.

I couldn't tell if Estes didn't know he was doing bad theater or simply thought bad theater appealed more widely than good theater. I remember attending a Rhino party once after

I'd given a so-so review to a so-so production. Estes and his cronies wouldn't talk to me. Another time Estes wrote me a letter saying that his theater would never do my plays as long as I continued to bad-mouth his theater in my reviews.

Well, that seemed a bit too much to me, and I sent a copy of Estes' letter to the Board of Directors of his theater, which was largely a rubber stamp. But I understand Estes was cautioned at least not to put such corrupt sentiments into letters. I entered into a long series of telephone conversations with Mike Zimmerman of the Board, who tried to placate both sides.

Estes was going to make a video of "Beer and Rhubarb Pie," and we even signed a contract, but nothing ever came of it. So Dan Turner and I did a video ourselves. It was left half-finished.

Estes had a genius for raising money, and I'm sure he saw me as an enemy standing in his way. I hate people who criticize my work, so I understand his feelings. But then again I felt he was doing smelly work, usually with lots of male nudity to no point except to titillate his audience. I felt I was writing well, and he should be producing me!

One time Rhino got a bad review from a writer in the *Bay Area Reporter*. I saw Estes and his cronies going around to bars and other places where the paper was available for pick-up and taking away all the copies they could get their hands on, to destroy them. How's that for dedication! If only as much trouble had gone into the productions!

Theatre Rhinoceros had a reputation for drugs in those days. Some of the staff apparently was paid off in such. Some said that much of the profit of the theater went up people's noses. I know from first-hand observation that there indeed was a lot of excess in the air. I have it on good authority that Estes didn't detect his own case of AIDS for a long time because he was coked up so much he didn't notice or pay attention to the symptoms. He was dead within a month of his diagnosis, still under the age of thirty.

Theatre Rhinoceros was mostly a male theater for a long time, but Estes started doing outreach to women, at about the same time that lesbian separatism was easing up and many women were willing to work with men again. Eventually women took over some of the key positions on the staff of Rhino, including Artistic Director. I personally have benefited from Allan Estes' death, not to put too fine a point on it, because I was able to become part of the playwrights group after he was gone. I was never able to be the cheerleader for his theater that he wanted, but I think I did contribute some good material to *The AIDS Show* and to other bills, things that probably would not have been included had he lived.

I think I'm expected to conclude with some sort of generous memorial statement about Allan Estes, but I think that would be hypocritical. Doric Wilson, when I finally "met" him online in a theater chat-group, had even crueler things to say about Mr. Theatre Rhinoceros.

THE KUCHAR BROTHERS

I forget exactly when I met the twin brothers George and Mike Kuchar, but it was in San Francisco in the 1970s. One of them was heavy; one was thin; one was outgoing; one was withdraw. Both were filmmakers.

They made underground films with titles like "I, An Actress" and "Kiss Me When I'm Naked." Then again some of their films were more serious. They influenced John Waters a lot with their campy, pseudo-evil, don't-you-love-schlock approach to movies. Waters found Divine, and the rest is history, as they say.

But George and Mike didn't have any commercial instincts themselves whatsoever. Besides, they moved to San Francisco from New York City, thus taking themselves out of the "mainstream" and getting considerably less attention thereafter.

They lived just a few blocks from me in S.F.'s Mission District, but we saw each other only occasionally, usually through Dan Turner, who had acted in some of their films. Their apartment was a monument to bad taste. It contained posters of *Godzilla* movies, and worse, plus statues of the Sacred Heart of Jesus and other religious camp, artifacts of culture at its worst. They loved it.

I myself have a limited tolerance for camp humor, but it obviously pleases people who like mockery. George seemed to make some money from film festivals and the like and got to travel often. His idea of a good time was to go to Oklahoma and film the wild thunderstorms.

George was the heavy-set one, heavily into junk foods. I ran into him once at our bank, and we had dinner together in a sleazy, plastic-seat place on Mission Street. George ordered a meal with mounds of potatoes and extra bread and butter and stuffed himself. I was trying to keep my weight down and gave him a few words of advice on eating habits. But he said he didn't mind being overweight and dressed in ragtag clothes. Muggers were afraid of him that way! Actually George had some money because he taught filmmaking at the Art Institute. He merely dressed like a bum.

One time I needed an unattractive man for a part in my one-act "Last Call" at the One Act Theater, directed by Ed Decker. I asked George, who had acted in a number of movies, if he would audition for the part. He seemed a little hurt that I thought he qualified as "unattractive," and thus I learned to describe the character as one "who thinks of himself as unattractive." Few actors think of themselves as ugly. Well, George came and read, and it was a disaster. His thick Bronx accent and his stage presence just weren't right for the part, and I felt terrible, because he'd put off a trip in order to try out. He was great on film but not on the stage.

He was wonderfully funny, though, in person as well as on the screen. I went with him once to Marin County for a film festival screening of one of his movies. He spoke first, convulsing the audience with that accent and ironic, witty remarks.

Mike was the skinny one, with a straggly, patriarchal beard. He was also much more introverted than his brother. So I guess they weren't identical twins. Mike did a lot of illustrations for comic books; very talented that way. He even designed the cartoon cover for my novel *Superfag*. He seemed to keep out of the spotlight most of the time and wasn't funny like George. He was hung like a horse, though. One time I ran into Mike in the 21st Street Baths. This was before AIDS reared its ugly head. Mike and I got to talking in my little cubicle, and I intuited that he might want to have sex. Since we'd met socially, I knew it was hard to overcome that barrier, to add a sexual dimension to the relationship. I'm usually very reluctant to initiate sex, especially in such a situation, but I thought I'd be brave. So I touched Mike's penis as he stood up, admiring it. It was a moment when he could have followed up on my overture. But he chose not to. The funny thing is I didn't feel rejected. I didn't do it out of lust. I did it to prove to myself it's possible to overcome friendship taboos among men. It didn't quite prove that, though, did it?

I remember watching some of their films at their apartment one night, thinking how lucky I was to be in San Francisco having such experiences so that I could write about them in my memoirs some day.

At the same time I lamented the fact that the artistic community in S. F. wasn't really all that close. Sometimes I wanted us to interact more. I've long known that biographers love to write about groups instead of individuals: the Beats, Bloomsbury. Other times I thought I needed the time to be alone in order to write. Eventually the Kuchars and I drifted apart, even from that limited contact, even without having had sex!

Curt McDowell

Another underground filmmaker I knew was George Kuchar's lover for a time, Curt McDowell. He and George did *Thundercrack* together, that zany underground classic.

Curt was a little crinkle-faced guy who loved sex, as you can tell from his films. He thought nothing of approaching strange, handsome men on the street and asking them if they'd like to be in a movie. Most of them were willing. Curt didn't seem to resent one-sided sex, the way I would have.

I first met him in 1977, when he came to see *Sex Show*. But it wasn't until he saw my one-act "The Birthday Girl" at the One-Act Theater Company in 1982 that we had much to do with each other. He decided he wanted to make a video of it. So we got Channel 25 to let us have "community access," got the actors to agree, got tapes and cameras, and filmed about five minutes of the forty-five minute play. It turned out that Curt, experienced filmmaker that he was, was unsure of the video equipment, and we just could not get rolling despite four or five hours in the studio. The tapes even disappeared later, when I foolishly left them at the studio.

Curt lived in virtual poverty, without a telephone. He had made some films in the '70s that he was unable to even get developed until the '80s because he didn't have enough money. Finally he got a NEA grant for about $10,000 and was able to finish some of his films.

Then he got AIDS. I happened to be at a critics' screening

at the Roxie Theater the very day Curt was waiting in the box office for a taxi to take him to the hospital for tests. He said he had been exhausted for some months, not like himself at all. I wished him well, as we all do, but wishes aren't sufficient.

I went to visit him in the hospital, where he was very lively despite the severity of his diagnosis. He had a big brown spot on his nose, which probably was from the intravenous feeding, but it could have been a KS spot. Because I didn't want to call attention to it, I didn't ask.

What I remember is how Curt had decorated the walls around his bed, making his environment as attractive, as interesting as he could. He also took Polaroid shots of all his visitors, including me, and showed them to everybody. I envied his ability to overcome his environment instead of accepting it stoically, as I tend to do.

MARION EATON

Ms Eaton was visiting Curt at the hospital the day I went. She had starred in several of his movies, and they were very close. At the time she was in her early fifties, a thin, mildly raucous woman who had once been wealthy and now had fallen on hard times. For years she'd been married to a rich man and then had lived with another rich man, acting in plays and films as she chose. Then the man she lived with got addicted to cocaine, and other women, and Marion left him.

She had to move from Marin County splendor to S.F. so-so. She was a terrific actress, as is evident in several Curt McDowell films, such as *Thundercrack*, where she does a lot more than use a cucumber as a dildo. I was so impressed by her talent that I asked her to be in my play "The Birthday Girl" at the One-Act Theater, playing the part of my lover's mother in a play about drug addiction in which I had changed the sex of my lead character and written him as a woman. Marion was great in the mother's part.

She did a staged reading of another play of mine at the Julian Theatre, and again she was splendid. We even started rehearsing a monologue of mine for a monologue festival, but Marion backed out at the last minute, because she had been accepted into Equity, the actors' union, and thus couldn't perform without being paid.

She thought Equity was the beginning of her real career, especially after she was cast in a touring production of *Nuts*, but the play, despite a long run in Los Angeles, did not do well in S.F. and closed quickly.

And so it went. Marion couldn't get a paying job, and when she tried to take non-paying ones Equity would intervene and tell her to stop. She'd never had to work before, but after the age of fifty she found it necessary to start working as a waitress. I'd see her from time to time, but as is typical in the theater we didn't meet as much as when we'd been working on a project together.

She had a little studio apartment on Guerrero St. that I visited a few times. Marion would tell tales of the black man she'd slept with, of the gay men, then how she was falling in love with her female therapist. Such catholicity of taste! She was putting all her mental problems into her journals, filling page after page.

I'd see her at plays occasionally, and we'd talk. She'd laugh and talk in her croaky-throated, slightly spacey way, and I'd worry about her. But I didn't know what to do, since I was so poor myself. I thought she was a major talent being wasted.

Not so long ago my lover's apartment mate decided to get an apartment on his own. He mentioned that it was at No. 2 Guerrero. I said, "Oh, that's where Marion Eaton lives. You'll be neighbors." He said that some woman had been evicted for not paying her rent, thus freeing up the apartment he had taken. "I hope it isn't Marion's place that you got!" I said. About a week later he said he'd looked at the old name near the bell and yes it was Marion Eaton's. So the woman who had played my lover's mother was displaced by the man who had been my lover's lover before me. It had modern overtones, and yet mostly it smacked of the Victorian age, a woman destitute, proven talent going to waste, because the system was defective in some essential way.

JOYCE CAROL OATES

I'm told I must not forget the good side of people. Believe me, I'm trying. About Ms. Oates, for instance. Can you picture her playing pool? Well, it's true. Joyce Carol Oates and I used to play, back in Detroit, and not just a few times. She wasn't bad either.

We also played lots of tennis. Maybe she harbored a grudge during our later problems because I always beat her. Possibly I should have been a "gentleman" and let her win a few times, but I've always considered women absolute equals, and that means not letting them win just so they'll feel good.

We'd play tennis, then stroll through the park. I had to be careful, however, of describing that wet stuff on our foreheads. Joyce didn't like to use words like "sweat." Once she even rebuked me for saying I was "full." Nice people, you see, weren't "full." They were "finished." Please!!

I also couldn't get her to play miniature golf. One time she consented to go with me; we got as far as the course, only to have her back out at the last minute. It was somehow beneath her image of herself, I suppose. She could write stories about girls forcing menstrual blood down their legs in front of seminarians, but if anyone asked her point blank about what such things meant, Oates would hyperventilate and/or cover her face and refuse to answer. I saw her with my own eyes shriek when asked such questions by the assistant in Joyce's agent's New York office.

In 1972, during my second year in London, Joyce and her

husband, and their Mercedes, came over to stay for a year. I just re-read one of her letters to me from that time, in which she said I simply had "to be there!" I had written her that I was having financial troubles. My first novel had been published by G.P. Putnam, but it had sold only 1800 copies. A French translation, then a Dutch, plus US paperback rights were sold, but the sums I received were not enough to live on. I had no other source of income, except an occasional class for the University of Maryland on a military base. I tried to get a job in a British school, tried very hard, but they weren't hiring Americans, or at least not me. I was literally short on food.

Now you'll have to decide for yourselves who was right and who was wrong in the events leading up to the severing of my friendship with Joyce, but let me spell out what I believe happened.

Our by now mutual agent, Blanche Gregory, had asked Joyce if she would give a blurb for the dust jacket of my novel. I had not asked Joyce myself because I knew that the world of homosexuality that I portrayed in that book made her very uncomfortable. So I suppose she thought she was doing me a huge favor by agreeing to the blurb, any blurb. Never would I expect someone to endorse a book publicly unless the person truly liked the book. Joyce had led me to believe that she admired mine, even if she wasn't exactly a gay rights advocate. Hah!

Of examples of her earlier behavior that had made me reluctant to enlist her in the cause for my particular kind of sexual liberation let me give just two. When I gave her my very first novel, never published, it was my way of coming out to her, in a time when the subject was considered not just criminal but disgusting. Joyce didn't talk to me for six months. Then when we did get back together, we went out to lunch one day. Something had gone out of the relationship, my availability as a fantasy sex object, I suspect. As we were getting up to leave, I helped Joyce on with her coat. Men still did that in those days. She looked down at my hand holding the coat, then reached up and flicked my fingers away with withering disdain, as if to say, "Oh, who are you trying to kid? You're not a *real* man!" I know you'll find it hard to believe, but such insults of "queers" were commonplace then.

When she and her husband arrived in London and took their Mayfair flat, she was rolling in dough, with a National Book Award and foreign rights and movie sales in her ledger, while I was almost broke. As you recall, 1971 was still not a year in which homosexuality was fashionable. It was such a great taboo that the most one could hope for was a male audience willing to read about an unspeakable subject. Indeed it was so unmentionable that Oates and my housemate in London urged me to use a pseudonym on my book lest I suffer the consequences. Thus I chose the name Daniel Curzon instead of my legal one, Dan Brown. I saw the name on a movie theater marquee and seized it, knowing that was one sure way to keep my name in lights.

(How odd that Dan Brown later became a best-selling writer – it just wasn't this Dan Brown!)

Well, anyway, I was poor and desperate with a book about queers as my approach to fame and fortune, and Joyce was now rich. She'd done two screenplays for Joanne Woodward, plus re-writes, and received around $50,000, plus lots of other sales. I remember Joyce complaining about supporting fifty

"Welfare families" with her taxes.

Maybe I shouldn't have asked her for help, but we were so close, and other writers had helped each other, hadn't they? Sherwood Anderson had gotten Faulkner's first novel published without even reading it! I thought maybe Joyce knew how to get my book reviewed in the *New York Times*. (To this day I have not been reviewed in the *New York Times*.) If not that, then maybe she could get me a review in the *Detroit News*. After all, my book was set in Detroit and concerned the Vice Squad, and yet it hadn't even been reviewed in the hometown newspaper. And the only reasons for that were the troublesome subject matter and the times. Joyce was reviewing books for both publications.

(Must be careful here. I can feel myself getting angry. Down, spleen, down!)

I was cautious with Joyce, my so-called "best friend," because she didn't offer to do anything. I hinted; she ignored. The Zeitgeist then was how shall I say it? as if I were asking her to help me write about having sex with dead babies.

We had lunch one day and I spoke of my publishing problems and my financial expectations. Putnam had turned down my next two books. Joyce wanted to know if I had enough money to last for the year she'd be there. "After that, I don't care what happens to you!" This was meant to be a joke, so I laughed.

I didn't expect her to support me or even buy my book, but I did expect her to do something for me as a friend. Even if she hated my book I would think trying to help would have been mandatory if she had a speck of generosity in her soul.

Since then, other writers, even people I've barely known, have done far more for me than my "best friend" ever did, without my even having to ask them.

I had not had the nerve to ask Joyce directly for assistance at the luncheon, until she wrote in my copy of her new novel *Wonderland*: "To Dan, with gratitude for our friendship and admiration for your writing." So I wrote her a letter detailing my problems and asking for some literary assistance, like getting more coverage for my unpopular but breakthrough novel. She'd written reviews of books she hadn't even *read*, so it couldn't be the ethics of it that she was worried about.

To give her the benefit of the doubt, let's ascribe Joyce's reaction to bigotry about homosexuality, rather than to a rejection of a friend asking for help. I have to believe that she would have helped me, or any other friend, if the subject had been anything else. Nobody's that stingy! I hadn't asked her for money, only for some contacts. If she felt she couldn't write a review herself, then maybe she could put in a word with the right people. Maybe I was really just looking for a gesture of love for her queer friend.

What did she do? She wrote me back a hurt, offended letter, saying that I had destroyed our friendship. She added: "Nobody helped me with my first book!" That's not even true. I appeared on a radio show in Detroit to plug her book when other people didn't know who she was. I should have called and tried to smooth things over, but I was too vulnerable that way. I wrote back, explaining my position, apologizing for having made it awkward for her. What did the noble lady do? She returned my second letter unopened. On the back she wrote: "I have agonized over this for many minutes, but I have decided to return your letter unopened." Many minutes . . . indeed.

Years later I mentioned this episode in an interview in *The Advocate*. Joyce saw it somehow, and bothered to write a long letter justifying herself, saying that I had become violent and abusive in my second letter. How would she know? She didn't even open it! Since then, she's written things trying to show that I was the guilty party and she was all frail innocence. No, both of us were "guilty" of wanting things to be different from the way they were. The fact that Joyce felt obliged to answer me indicates that she still feels some guilt about her actions. She's also transferred the hysteria from herself to the other party. She's probably read too many Joyce Carol Oates novels!

If she didn't like my writing she could have told me, in the nicest way she knew how, and I would not have requested so much as a bookmark from her. But, no, she said she admired it. Maybe I should have been smarter and spied the reservation in her praise, even in the blurb —"Engrossing, powerful, and disturbing" —and not have tried to get help where it was so unforthcoming. After all, a blurb is a blurb is a blurb. But I was unable to sell many copies of my first book, or sell a new book, or get a job. I didn't know anybody else to turn to. A decent person would have said, "Dan, are you struggling? Can I loan you some money? Pay it back when you can. You have been so good a friend to me – and I probably saved that much since you always paid my tips."

From her perspective, I guess she thought she had already exceeded the bounds of duty and good taste by lending her name once to a rather sordid subject matter. Besides, she didn't have time to help a friend; she had to finish her novel about a doctor eating a cadaver's cervix.

Ah yes, why couldn't I just go on being the charming, witty luncheon companion, the date that made it so easy for her to get around in her busy social life? Why did I have to go and spoil it all by writing about That and then asking her to cheer for it? I mean, don't people like that kill themselves; they certainly don't ask for favors! No, Ms. Oates was certainly not ahead of her time on this subject. She was just an old fart in a young body. I don't want to whine about homophobia, but homophobia, I do believe, was the principal obstacle to decency here.

ARTHUR BELL

One time I wrote to the late Arthur Bell when he was a noted columnist for the *Village Voice* to see if he might give a plug to one of my novels. He wrote back, magisterially: "I don't do plugs."

All right, that's fair. His choice. I was not upset, and when his royal presence came to San Francisco I was gladly introduced to him at a party by Edward Guthmann, an ambitious young journalist who had plugged Arthur Bell and received assorted lumps for his efforts. (Guthmann is now a film reviewer for the *San Francisco Chronicle*.)

Bell must have been in his mid-forties then, but he looked older. I assume his health was not too good. At least he gave off an air of unwholesomeness. He was short, with a bad limp and bug eyes. He affected, or really had, a bored air as if he'd done it all, heard it all. I mentioned that William Como, the editor of *Dance* magazine and *After Dark*, had liked one of my books and taken me to lunch when he visited S.F. I inquired if Bell knew him, because he was a nice man. "Oh, I suppose so, if you like capes!" was Bell's tart response about Como's clothes. He said some other things equally nasty, and I can't say that I warmed to him.

Later I gave him and Guthmann a ride somewhere, and I was invited to join them for a drink, but I declined, mainly because Bell was so brittle, so hardcore New York. I wasn't willing to cozy up or kiss his butt or whatever I was expected to do. If I'd been truly unethical in the promotion of my art I guess I would have tried to milk that contact, if that's the right metaphor. I'm just sorry I didn't go have the drink. I'd probably have more dirt on Arthur Bell to share with you. It's gossip when you're alive; it's literary history when you're dead.

ARTHUR EVANS

When I learned that Arthur Bell and Arthur Evans had been lovers in NYC before Evans moved out west, I couldn't believe it. True, Evans had a bad leg, like Bell, but he was good-looking, and the most anyone could say for Bell was that he was a frog trying to be a queen.

Evans is someone I've been trying to avoid for years. He was the leader of a gay liberation group in the early days of the movement, but he came to it from a leftist perspective that didn't just leave me cold, it left me sizzling with anger. These activists made the world take note of gay oppression – good! But when it came to literature they demanded agit-prop poster crap that even Stalin would have found inartistic.

When I was starving in London, I managed to sell some articles to *The Advocate*. Arthur Evans frequently had articles in the same issues, on the same pages. He wrote of the coming revolution of the masses and other nonsense. I come from the masses, and they aren't the least bit like middle-class leftist politicos think they are. Evans' roseate, foolish hopes and predictions for the world's future drove me up the wall. I hear Arthur became disillusioned later when things didn't turn out the way he'd hoped. Well, for god's sake, what did he expect!?

Various people tried to introduce me to Arthur Evans over the years, and I always avoided him. One time Dan Turner and I were in a bar when he came in. Dan went over to talk to him. I went in the other direction. I am constitutionally unable to hide my feelings.

He ran a Volkswagen repair shop, to show that gays could be mechanical and "of the people," I imagine. I already knew that. His shop was called the Buggery. Ah, the times, they are a-changin'!

Arthur came to see my evening of skits called *Sex Show* and booed at one that showed a lesbian mother in as bad a light as it does her ex-husband. That was Politically Incorrect, you see. Lesbian mothers are never bad. Only straight, white men are bad, at least in the world of Arthur Evans, and he was going to make the rest of us say the same, whether we wanted to or not.

He'd also put up notices on telephone poles and elsewhere as the "Red Queen," agitating for some cause or other. Once in a while one of them was even legitimate. I based a fascist radical character in one of my novels (*The Y*, never published) on Arthur Evans, because he symbolized for me the enduring struggle between the artist, who wants to tell the truth as he sees it, and the ideologue, who wants the artist to do what he's told.

Years later, he started writing conservative letters to the editor complaining about the drug addicts in the Haight. It figures.

VITO RUSSO

First saw Vito Russo on panels at various Gay Academic Union conferences and the like. This was before he started doing his *Celluloid Closet* film demonstrations. Vito was thin, bespectacled, and suffering from excessive New Yorkitis. I developed a severe antipathy to his public persona: aggressive, know-it-all, coupled with excessive hugging of everybody as if the whole world was a close friend. (I think you should hug only those you really like.)

Vito even complimented me on a book of mine one time, so it wasn't that. He was just so self-righteous, unsubtle and taken with himself up there on those podia. He always assumed that New York was the center of the world, too, and since I had deliberately chosen not to live there with the attendant loss in prestige and contacts I resented his continuance of a mind set I wished to alter.

I would avoid him at parties, glare at him from across the room. I discovered later that he thought I did those things because I'd sent him a book of mine to give to Lily Tomlin, and he hadn't done it. Come on. I'm guilty of a lot, but not of that particular sin.

Then Vito started getting lots of attention for his film demonstrations. He probably even did a great deal of good in calling the movie world's attention to its egregious prejudices about gays. But I couldn't bring myself to like Vito because his sense of self-importance and cheap camaraderie still offended me. "Darryl, darling! How are you!" Kissy-kissy! Maybe I was envious of his social ease.

When his book *The Celluloid Closet* came out, I did a nice review of it and wrote and congratulated him on a terrific job. I thought it was time to bury the invisible hatchet. He wrote back a gracious reply.

Later I saw him backstage with the man who wrote the screenplay for *Making Love* and was introduced, but I wasn't invited to go off and have coffee with the chosen when they left, and I was ticked off. I thought I was pretty important by then, but I guess I wasn't. I've read enough biographies of artistic types now to realize that this craving for being noticed and sought out is not limited to me. Probably we wouldn't be creative if we didn't hope to get loved.

I would run into Vito here and there casually, especially after he moved to S.F. to be with a lover, who then died of AIDS. The last connection I had with him was when I was waiting outside the Castro Theater for a friend who was inside attending the Celluloid Closet presentation. It ran overtime a full hour and half. I kept waiting and waiting, yet I couldn't be too upset because I realized that Vito knew he might be giving the last show of his life; he wanted to say it all. We all do.

SAMUEL STEWARD

Sam Steward had a very diversified life, as a college teacher, as a writer, as a tattoo artist. He's also known as Phil Andros, and some modern-day revisionists have tried to elevate his porn stories, both soft and hard, into Art. I think Sam himself knew better. He'll be remembered for his terrific memoirs of personalities like Gertrude Stein, Lord Alfred Douglas, Andre Gide, and others.

When I finally met Sam it was after one of his talks in S.F. He said he hoped I wasn't mad at him because George Whitmore had praised some of his stories at the expense of some of mine in a book review. I had enough savoir-faire not to say what I really thought, mainly because Sam seemed nice. A nice writer, believe it or not!

When I finally went to visit him at his home in Berkeley, around 1979, I was struck by his depression. He sat in a room crowded with dozens, maybe hundreds, of clocks, all ticking away noticeably, calling attention to his mortality. Sam was in his seventies, lean, having hip trouble, and I'm afraid he wasn't a very good advertisement for old age. He was not living any golden years; he was bitter and unhappy with his career and even more so about his minimal sex or love life. I'm not sure that Sam ever had a lover, but sex was always very important to him, and there he was, still eager but without many sex partners to choose from. I felt uncomfortable being around him, not wanting to hear that what I had to look forward to were frustration and sadness as I got older.

Luckily Sam's fortunes took a turn for the better after that.

He wrote some new books and had some of his old ones reprinted. He even started getting visits from fans willing and ready to show him a good time – sexually but also by getting him out of the house.

One time I ran into Sam walking without his cane, his hip made new, as he was about to sign autographs for a long line of people, only some of whom were lined up for Sam. Most of them were for Armistead Maupin or Miss Manners, and Sam confided that he was nervous that nobody would come up for his books. I know the feeling and thus sympathized. Later he said he did all right.

I asked Sam if he'd ever spotted evidence of "genius" in Gertrude Stein when he knew her and if so in what did it consist. She seemed to me distressingly vague about the topics she and other "geniuses" discussed in her *Autobiography of Alice B. Toklas*. Sam just sort of pursed his lips and shook his head and said no; "genius" wasn't that palpably in the air. I had always wondered why Stein got so much attention, since few people really enjoyed reading her work. Yet they couldn't get enough stories about her and Alice. Some people have that "fame" talent, it seems.

I called him once, when I was feeling guilty about neglecting him, and he sounded fuzzy. I wondered if he was having an attack of some kind. He explained that one of his young men had given him a pill that had made him woozy in a good way. Not long ago I told a friend to ask Sam if he was getting any. The word back was: "Sure am."

His life isn't ideal, but Sam Steward seemed to get back at least a little of the attention he showered on literary types in the thirties. Only fair. Wonderfully, his life became the subject of a very well-received biography by Justin Spring called *Secret Historian*, published in 2010. We should all be so lucky. (By the way, I was criticized by some for misspelling "Steward" as "Stewart" in an earlier edition of this book. Far be it from me to be defensive, but even Gertrude Stein spelled his name wrong.)

ROGER AUSTEN

Been holding off on writing about Roger Austen either because of the way his life turned out or because of a tinge of guilt.

I met Roger when he did an interview with me for *The Sentinel*, a gay newspaper in S.F. That interview led to an offer from a reader of a house to stay in whenever I spent a weekend in S.F., so I owed Roger one.

He was in his early forties when we met, a thick-bodied man with horn-rimmed glasses, cigarette-stained teeth, a hearing problem, and a streak of conservatism two miles wide. I was a vegetarian then, and I can still hear his gay-accented voice saying with disgust, "You mean to tell me that chickens were meant to *live*?"

Austen was his pen name, lifted from Jane Austen. His real name was Roger *Asselstein*, a name which, as you can imagine, provided plenty of ammunition for the always sensitive youngsters of this world.

Roger tried to emulate the wry wit of those he admired, such as William F. Buckley, of all people, that pretentious, right-wing, eye-popping writer and interviewer. I asked him why he wanted to sound so affected. But Roger thought it was sophisticated to throw your head back and grit a pompous question through your teeth.

Roger, you see, had grown up in Yakima, Washington, raised by a Pentecostal mother. He had left home to have everything that was literary and established. He would have been in heaven having tea with Virginia Woolf's second cousin. He saw his task as the elevation of *The Sentinel* to a paper with class, going around the owner, who was virtually illiterate and using it merely for a political center of power.

Roger began working on a book on gay novels, a book that was eventually published as *Playing the Game*, about how writers until the 1970s had to disguise gay realities or else suffer the consequences. Roger and I drove down to Monterey one time in my car so that he could use some archives there.

I knew that Roger was attracted to me sexually. I'm sorry to say I wasn't attracted back, I used him as the model for the unsexy man in my title story of *Human Warmth and Other Stories*. I did feel sorry for Roger's sexual dissatisfactions. He complained often of how little sex he was getting, and this was in the hot and horny days of the mid-1970s. But it was not easy to feel sorry for him because he bitched so much about it, even in his book and theater reviews. And then, too, he would turn down or sneer at offers made by men he didn't find attractive. They were his equals, but he wanted his betters. His answer was to take long, long hot showers. "That's my sex life," he would say. "The water comforts me."

Roger is the one who wanted me to ask Isherwood to get Tennessee Williams to appear on his show on Public Television that featured gay people. I might add that there is no such show on now.

What I didn't mention before is that Roger's hearing was not at all good, to put it mildly, and so when he had to interview people on the air, he often did not know what their answers to his questions were. As a result, he couldn't follow up the answers with related questions and produce a natural flow to it all. Instead, he had to refer to his list of prepared questions. Actually he did quite well at disguising his deafness. He did seem stiff, though.

I had real problems with the fact that Roger went to review plays, taking me as his guest, without being able to hear a good many of the lines being said. He'd write up his impressions anyway. I mean, it's admirable to hire the handicapped, but deaf theater reviewers?!

He next wrote a biography of Charles Warren Stoddard, but he couldn't get it published, even though *Playing the Game* was well-received. I understand that he later wrote another book or parts of several. He also showed me a novel that wasn't bad. I thought it was a rotten state of affairs that he had so much trouble getting his research published since he was quite a competent scholar.

Our problems started when I asked Roger if he was going to include my *Something You Do in the Dark* in his history of the gay novel. After all, many people considered it the first gay protest novel, in the sense that it showed a man caught between his old self-hatred and his new sense of being a member of an oppressed group. (On the back cover archivist Jim Kepner said: ". . . Curzon's novel surpasses its predecessors in harsh, beautiful honesty, in liberated grasp of the subtle varieties of homosexual character, in anguished, unsentimental protest and in its spirit of nowness.") At first Roger said he was going to stop before he got to 1969, the date of the Stonewall Rebellion. Then he said he was going to add a last chapter in which he would catch up with all the post-Stonewall books.

He wrote up a few pages on my novel and showed them to me. They weren't exactly praise, but they at least acknowledged my book's existence. That's all I could ask for.

But when I got my early unbound reviewer's copy I looked in the index to see my name. There was a brief reference to my book on a certain page. But nothing else. I looked through the book for the part I had read and found nothing. Oh, I take that back. I did find many pages lambasting Patricia Nell Warren's books and other titles Roger didn't like. I thought surely there was an oversight about my book.

Naturally I called Roger and inquired sweetly what had happened. He replied that he had cut those pages out of the finished manuscript. I couldn't believe my ears. "You cut me out?" I said. And then I screamed into the telephone -- to aid his hearing, as my only motivation, I'm sure: "How dare you! I NEVER WANT TO SEE YOU AGAIN AS LONG AS I LIVE!" Then I slammed the phone down hard.

And I never did see Roger again. Oh, he'd be at a meeting or something, but I wouldn't acknowledge his presence. Please, please, I know I should have been wiser, kinder, whatever, but I wasn't. How could he cut me out after putting me in? It was only two or three pages. If it isn't evident by now, it will be by the time you finish these memoirs my writing is the most important thing in my life, and the only reason for putting up with Roger's unwanted amorous overtures and his right-wing politics was so that my work could get some exposure.

He hung around S.F. for a few more years, and I'd hear rumors about him. He couldn't get his other works into print;

he was even fatter. Finally he moved back to Yakima, Washington to live with his widowed Pentecostal mother, who considered him a sinner. Talk about nightmares. I assume he kept up with his hot showers.

He stayed there for a couple of years, I believe, still writing, until at last he moved to Los Angeles and went back to graduate school. Come to think of it, Roger had had a hard time in graduate school earlier, but here he was back trying again.

He didn't get an advanced degree, however, or publish any more books. What he did was drown himself. I hope he found some comfort at last. I hope the water was warm. I didn't even know he was dead for two years, and I cried a little, for Roger dead, for Roger deaf, for Roger ugly, for Roger frustrated, for all the drowning Roger Asselsteins of this goddamned world.

HERB CAEN

Can't remember when I first wrote to Herb Caen, the famous columnist for the *San Francisco Chronicle*, but I'm sure it was because of his snide anti-gay comments. There was hardly a day that he didn't put gays down. I'm not being too thin-skinned either. He never said anything good about us. I don't believe in phony PR about minorities just because they're minorities, but enough already! He saw us as outsiders with funny customs who had no redeeming qualities at all. Throughout most of the history of the world all we've had are put-downs!

So I wrote several letters telling him off. I heard nothing in reply. After a particularly obnoxious put-down, I wrote Caen again, saying that remarks like his contributed to the mind set that gays were fair game and thus led to things like the Harvey Milk assassination. I sent along a copy of my novel *From Violent Men*, about somebody trying to murder a figure similar to assassin Dan White. There is even a section in the book in which a columnist for a large paper, unnamed, is presented as ridiculing homosexuals as a group. Yes, I meant Caen.

When the letter marked "Caen" appeared in my mailbox, I was afraid to open it at first, fearing that he was planning to sue me or at least give me a good going-over. What he said was: "Aside from all that, this really is an excellent book." I must say I was disarmed by the flattery. I was hoping he'd say the same thing in his column, but he didn't. So I went out and ordered a thousand stickers with his quotation on them, to paste on the cover.

Didn't work too well. *From Violent Men* remains my least-selling novel. I suspect the title is off-putting to many, as is the cover with too much blood dripping from San Francisco City Hall. The book's cover was even shown on ABC's "Nightline," but virtually nobody has bought it. Maybe they burned out on the Dan White affair.

It seems to me that Herb Caen soon changed completely in the way he referred to homosexuals in his column. Teasing was one thing; constant disparagement was uncalled for. I attribute this change to the considerable number of open gays around here, not to the fact that overnight my novel changed him! But I do believe good fiction can alter perceptions of those considered outsiders, because it forces one to live through the same experiences and feelings.

Herb Caen wrote a column for a long, long time, keeping his fingers on the pulse of San Francisco. He was slow to change, and now homosexuals can hope to be as banal and ordinary as anybody else.

JOHN PRESTON

John Preston and I met the first time when he was the new editor of *The Advocate*. I stopped by to help insure my continuing contributions to the publication. He was very tall and thin with very short hair. We had a nice chat, and then he promptly returned several of my articles as not positive enough. All my writing career I have not been "positive" enough to suit lots of people. I've tried to pen a few upbeat things as a result, not wanting to be one-sided, but in my heart of hearts I guess I continue to have a jaundiced eye, if one can have an eye in one's heart. I assume that I will be admired for my honesty, if not now, then later on. Am I off the beam completely? Maybe they go on thinking you're too negative even after you're dead?

Anyway, my relations with John Preston became strained after I was cut off from *The Advocate*. But I didn't do anything unpleasant to him. I wrote elsewhere.

Then he quit editing and started writing books, lots of books, books with S&M themes, books with admirable drag queens, books about safe sex acts. I confess I read only the one about the admirable drag queen, which I found readable, if sentimental. Preston was being published by Alyson, which I thought didn't know nothin' about birthin' books! Or at least nothing about literature. They spewed out self-help books for horny teens, syrupy romances, and other disposable junk. The editor-in-chief once answered a review of mine, defending his books. To his mind books was books! Whatever happened to art? This editor did half-promise to re-publish my novel

Among the Carnivores sometime, but that was years ago. I knew it was to my advantage to praise the books Alyson did or to shut up about what I didn't like, but I couldn't seem to learn this lesson. As a matter of fact, I wanted them to change their policy. The company almost went broke publishing their wholesome trash. I imagine it would have gone broke even faster publishing quality material. So what is truth?

John Preston was sitting in the office of a magazine called *The Alternate* one time when I visited John Rowberry, who was the most generous and quality-oriented editor I ever dealt with in the gay press. He had told me that Preston had yelled at him over the telephone for running a review of mine about *Prick Up Your Ears*, a biography of Joe Orton. I liked the book, but I said the moral of it seemed to be: If you want to get attention for your plays, get murdered by your lover. I still believe extra-literary gossip and scandal have more to do with many so-called "literary" reputations than art does.

I grudgingly said hello to Preston. How I envied those who can sit down and chat up people who might be useful to them. I guess most people do this all the time, don't they, with bosses and relatives and whoever? When I'm mad at someone, I don't hide it very well. And I hate to kiss ass. I hate being hypocritical. I'm not bragging about this trait. It's probably a result of stupidity rather than any great virtue. But I develop animosities and then I can't smooth them over. I often wish I could, but I feel like a wimp when I lie.

A year or so ago I saw John Preston and Sasha Alyson at the American Booksellers meeting. I looked Preston right in the eye and could have talked to him. I could have talked to Sasha too, later at the Walt Whitman Bookshop party. But

I didn't. I went out of my way to avoid them.

EDMUND WHITE

Now I confess I did try to chat up Ed White through the mail once. He had published some books with a very noticeable "style" and was getting lots of press. I wasn't exactly an unknown myself, so I wrote him a friendly letter, ending with a mention that maybe we could correspond a bit, since future literary historians might be interested in the Gay Writers, the first openly gay set in the world's history. I thought it would be nice if we interacted somehow, to give the historians something to write about.

White wrote back a short letter giving me a charming brush-off. He said something like: "I'm sure everybody is looking forward to your new book!" I found out from a reliable source (Robert Prager) that he hadn't even read any of my books and didn't like what he hadn't read. I thought this rather odd coming from a man known to spend a lot of time cultivating literary contacts, attending readings, going to the proper parties, wheeling and dealing to get ahead. Now that I think about it, it was a double insult, since he didn't think I was important enough to cultivate. Hmm. The only time I saw Ed White in person was at a signing of his at the old Walt Whitman Bookshop. I expected to see a collegiate-looking man like the one on his dust jackets. Instead I saw a middle-aged man, very professorial, in a baggy suit. I vowed I would update my own publicity pictures. (But I haven't really.)

We both lived in the Midwest, even in Detroit, it turns out, during the same years. Only he went to fancy suburban schools. I lived in a working-class neighborhood and went to a nothing Catholic school. He majored in Chinese in college. Obviously we come from widely divergent backgrounds. I thought it significant that he doesn't even mention his city by name in *A Boy's Own Story*, while I have mentioned Detroit often in my books. Particularly in *Something You Do* in *the Dark*. My Detroit is working class, sordid and unappetizing. His world has elegance. I guess most people who buy books would rather read about elegance, and not about Detroit.

A Boy's Own Story is the only book of White's I could finish. In fact, it's an excellent book. But too many of his others have suffered from a constipated "style" that makes Henry James's later books seem like Dick and Jane. Some folks in NYC got it into their heads that Literature is equivalent to an overblown, pushy "style," to the exclusion of narrative, characterization, or depth. It's really a shame people in our time don't know how to read better. It's so easy to snow them with the trappings of literature, instead of honesty.

White's *Travels in Gay America* didn't suffer just from excessive "style" but from inadequate research. He stopped in ten cities for three days each and had the gall to pronounce judgments on the lifestyles of entire populations. Please spare us from such shallowness! The only believable part of the book is the NYC part, because White at least has lived there. When he says at least a third of the people in the arts there are gay, you trust him. Everything else is a New Yorker's glib and condescending trip to the "boondocks" to make a buck.

Caracole is a joke, an unreadable, bloated crystal mountain of lifeless "style." Somebody's got to say it. It's as if White and his cronies are trying to ape Nabokov, or Ronald Firbank, god help them! What we wind up with is dead books, airless mansions of Art. I hope Ed White gets over his "style" (as of 1986) and writes some more good books soon.

DAVID LAMBLE

I'm afraid I'm beginning to sound like an old sourpuss. I vowed that my life would be more lively than my parents' was. They sat in their little house in a tiny Illinois town, where playing shuffleboard in the local tavern was the height of culture, where conversations centered on diseases and food. I thought I'd be a literary celebrity by now. I'm not unknown, but I'm not besieged with invitations for speaking engagements, not even for dinner parties. (Perhaps if I ever returned the favor I'd get invited again?!) I'm reading about Henry James's social life, and frankly I'm envious. He just moved right in and kept right on moving. I attribute my inadequate social life among the upper echelons to a profound lack of money. I couldn't afford dinner parties even if I wanted to give them. (If I had plenty of bucks, though, I might have them catered.)

I have concentrated on writing what I wanted to write and expected the world to beat a path to my door. Alas, there are quite a few weeds in the path.

The fact that I was making $9000 per year (1986) in a community college, because the educational system has refused to hire me full-time, cannot be ignored in my personality development. I have been a pauper for over ten years, just barely getting by. I wouldn't feel so angry and revengeful if I had enough money to live on, enough fame to suit me.

I was about to write that maybe no amount of fame would ever suit me, but that's simply not true. I've had to struggle for every book I've ever written, for the qualified reputation I currently enjoy. I've always been convinced that I deserve much more. Why don't I get it? Perhaps this memoir will reveal it to me as much as to you. But, you see, I still keep expecting to be lionized any day now, lifted up to Major Literary Figure status. It may never happen; it may happen after I die; it might destroy my discipline if it did come, but I may dwindle into unbearable rages and pathetic hatreds unless I get more than I have at the moment. Maybe if I wrote about adultery? There hasn't been much written about adultery now, has there?!

Let me tell you about David Lamble. I do have some friends, and so far I haven't broke with David, and I've known him for many years.

David achieved a nice reputation as a radio show host, with ambitions to be a video and film producer. Already he has made a short film called *Bashing* and is about to edit a videotape of a short play of mine called "The Murder of Gonzago A Comedy." He is a model of tact and pragmatism. He wears thick glasses, likes nelly young men—a subject we constantly debate, since nelly young men do nothing for me except elicit an anti-erotic response.

Let me say unequivocally that David Lamble is the best friend I've ever had, and I've dedicated my new novel to him. Actually David has done many career favors for innumerable gay writers, artists, performers, and not only gay ones. Unlike me, he has built up a long list of people he has helped in one way or another. He calls it networking. In his case it leads to an utter scrupulousness about not offending the people he wants to network with. The few occasions where he has violated his own rules have cost him contacts he wanted, and he has revised strategies in consequence. On the other hand, I go on, feeling "honest" and making enemies by the carload.

The main thing I've learned from David is that maybe you can't say whatever you want in this world and get your way. (Though he doesn't get everything he wants either.) I think we get along because we complement each other. We can also talk freely. He opens up to me about many things. Believe it or not, I do have a capacity for listening, for sympathizing with other people's troubles.

David has done interviews with me, in the press and on his radio shows, promoted me and my work in a hundred ways. He even asked me to be his Critic at Large on KPFA-FM when I had a falling out with the censorious lesbian who edited my column in a S.F. newspaper. Let me say it loud and clear: I have nothing but warm feelings and eternal gratitude for all the help David Lamble has given me during the past few years.

David has only two faults. He's always late, although he's getting better about that since he realizes his lateness interferes with his networking, and he's cheap when it comes to tipping in restaurants. He's not as bad anymore, but he used to pick up the tips the rest of us had left on the table – on the sly. He did it for the same reason I don't have dinner parties. He makes very little in his job as a doorman. He was even working in a photocopy shop as a clerk this past summer! It's an outrage. Here is this gifted, energetic, kindly man just squeaking by, opening doors for klutzes in an apartment building when he should be getting paid $100,000 a year to do radio shows! He remains poor because his sense of integrity comes from doing the radio shows he wants to do, not the ones that pay well. And maybe he counts on "networking" too much, instead of just getting a good job.

RICHARD HALL

Another person I've admired is Richard Hall, the writer. I don't recall exactly when we met, but it must have been through Dan Dulaney Allen, his ex-lover.

Richard lived in NYC and I would see him when I visited there or he visited S.F. He was a nice-looking man, tall, with a mustache, who looked fifteen years younger than his real age. Besides his books, he was the book editor of *The Advocate* for a long time.

We would meet and discuss the current state of gay literature. I thought Richard's short stories were excellent. Later I had heated discussions with a friend of mine who didn't like Richard's work. I didn't see how he could like mine and not like his. Though of course Richard's work was much more "gentlemanly" than mine, both for good and ill. He also didn't write very much, because he said he was so fussy.

I helped Richard Hall get a publisher by deliberately introducing him to Don Allen, the noted Grove Press editor who started his own small press when he moved to S.F. I was overjoyed that it worked out, and thus *Couplings* and other books of Richard's saw print. He returned the favor to me a few years afterwards by telling Bettie Gershman of Knights Press that I was a good writer and that she should contact me. She did. Richard and I gave a reading together one time, arranged by David Lamble at a Sunday morning gay caucus held in a Unitarian church. Ah, liberation. Richard was a good public reader. We were a hit.

In general I'd say Richard inspired trust. He was always the soul of discretion about everything. I sometimes wished he'd loosen up a bit since he had a way of curtailing a good gossip session just when it was getting going. In fact, he never seemed to want to talk about one topic of any kind for very long.

For some reason Richard never quite fit into the NYC gay literary Establishment, centered on *Christopher Street* and *The New York Native*, if that's Establishment. So some of us on opposite coasts were closer to each other than people who lived in the same city. Eventually, Richard decided to give up his rent-controlled NYC apartment and move to S.F. He admitted he had always wanted to have a Broadway play, but when he at last realized he never would, he decided he'd no longer put up with the hassles of the big city. But he never quite got to S.F. He moved to Oakland, across the bay, and lived there for eleven months. We had one brunch and he came to a workshop reading of a musical of mine, but he was, as he said, "socially immobilized" living here. He called one day and said he was moving back to NYC. He said he couldn't stand flowers in February and missed his friends. So at the age of sixty he was going back to share a loft with a friend for a much higher rent.

Richard must have invested his money wisely, because he always seemed to have it. I believe he worked as an editor for a university publishing house for a good while, but all the time I knew him he didn't have to work.

He'd go to Puerto Rico for holidays. He seemed to like smooth-skinned brown young men. Once in my living room Beau Riley, another writer who couldn't quite get his career together, accused Richard of "exploiting" the poor youth of

Puerto Rico. He was very belligerent about it, but Richard maintained his usual cool. Who exploits who in such situations?

He did get angry, however, when Dan Dulaney Allen, his ex-lover, an ex-alcoholic, suddenly wrote a long diatribe against Richard and me about our writings, our personalities. He sent us both copies. It may have been from envy since Dan's work had all been self-published. I wasn't offended particularly. I probably asked if I could reprint it somewhere! Publicity is publicity. But Richard was incensed and stopped visiting his ex-lover. He felt betrayed. I tried to change his mind, but he was adamant.

But when Dan Allen developed AIDS, Richard came back into his life and actually was there in the last days, providing love, comfort, and wisdom. He even became the executor of Dan's estate when Dan died and arranged a memorial service at the Columbarium in S.F. for the cremated remains. I thought it was a perfect service, with some of us rising to tell anecdotes about Dan, sharing the many aspects of his life with the mourners. I've become quite an expert on funeral services of late, and this was one of the best.

Richard even contested Dan's "will," a will that was not found because Dan was such a scatterbrain. He kept it on the floor of his car, where it was kicked out several times and finally lost. But some reliable friends of Dan's testified that Dan had intended his house and savings to be put into a trust fund to provide scholarships for gay/lesbian students at City College of San Francisco, where he taught. Because the will wasn't found, Dan's born-again fundamentalist family in Texas was to get all the money. They certainly weren't going to give it to gay scholarships! They hated all of Dan's gay liberation activities. Good old Richard Hall decided to challenge the will, even though it meant the family in Texas sued him for a "frivolous" lawsuit. For many months he lived in danger of losing his own money for trying to save his ex-lover's money from the grasping Christian hands down south. Happily the judge ruled that the suit was not frivolous. So it appears that at least half of the money will go to the scholarship fund after all. Better half than nothing.

As I write this (1986), Richard Hall and I have been involved in a crisis with my publisher, Knights Press. Bettie Gershman changed her mind about publishing my novel *Shakespeare Lives!!* Chiefly because it isn't "gay enough." I was heartbroken and despondent and sent Richard copies of Bettie's letter and my reply. He called me, saying I shouldn't alienate Bettie, pointing out that there weren't too many publishers who signed their letters "Love." I didn't want to alienate her. I just wanted her to publish the book. I called Bettie and we agreed she'd ask Richard Hall and a few other readers to read the manuscript to see if it was "gay enough." (I won't dwell on the irony of not being "straight" enough for most publishers and not "gay enough" for this one.)

That's when Richard called to say he was going back east. He wouldn't have time to read the manuscript. He also thought it best if it were read anonymously. I appreciated the difficulty of his being put in the middle like that. I hoped he'd say, "Go ahead. Publish the damn thing!" just on general principles. Of course if he urged Bettie not to publish it, I would kill him and the obituary I'd give at his memorial service wouldn't be very nice at all. So it's probably good that he didn't have to make such an important decision in my life.

JOYCE CAROL OATES

After I left London to teach again on US military bases in Asia (late 1972), because no other jobs were offered, I didn't communicate with Joyce Carol Oates until 1974, when I went to the Modern Language Association conference – NYC, I think. I had some job interviews. When what to my wondering eyes should appear but Ms. Oates on a panel – on *Androgny*, of all things! I had to give her credit for saying things the feminists didn't like, and I sat marveling at the way she pounced on a questioner from the floor: "I'm not sitting up here so you can use me to ventilate your ego!" One tough prissy lady indeed.

At the end of the panel, a long line of fans waited to touch the hem of Ms. Oates' garment. So I thought I'd say hello. In my pocket I had a present for her, a box of rubbers. I didn't know what it meant exactly, but somehow it seemed appropriate. I made my way past the line of admirers and caught her eye. It was like one of her rape fantasies, where this horrible bearded male is coming after her. In fact, that's one of the reasons I did it, to twit her with a taste of her own medicine. When I got close, I held out the rubbers, saying, "Here's a present for letting me starve in London!" I pressed them into her hand, or tried to. Ms. Oates of Androgyny fame was aghast and pushed the back of her hand against the box, causing it to fly into the air. I wish it had come open and showered her with prophylactics, but all I can claim is that when the box landed one of the fans picked it up and tried to give it back to Ms. Androgyny of 1974. . . . I left. When I got back to Asia, I received a letter from Joyce telling me she had been surprised by the look of hatred on my face in NYC. (Nothing about whether she was enjoying the rubbers or not. I thought of sending her a note breaking off the friendship. I mean, if she can't even send a thank-you note for a gift! Jesus!) Then commenced a series of some six letters each, in which we spilled out all the resentments that had built up in our days together. I've kept the correspondence, which someday may be published as the "literary gold mine" that my new agent at that time called it. (For the curious, the letters are with my other papers in the Hormel Collection of the San Francisco Public Library.) Two highlights I recall: Joyce saying, "I can't sign this letter because you might be tempted to sell it" and me saying, "You seem to have gotten religion of late. Can menopause be far behind?" I did what I did for a complex of reasons. The ones I'm aware of myself are, first, my obvious sense of betrayal; second, a conviction that if Joyce and I were going to break up after being so close, she sure as hell wasn't going to kiss me off, no nicey-nicey, bland fadeout for me; third, life is dull and we owe it to history to do some things that are dramatic and lively; the very things people complain about as being too extreme are the things they write and talk about and that give life its power; fourth, I thought Joyce was bright enough to see that our feud was somehow a game we were playing, both genuine in its animus and false in its execution. I guess I didn't count on Oates's capacity to inflict real harm. She saw the world as this threatening monster, and she'd do anything sneaky to get back at people.

In this case what she did was get her agent, Blanche Gregory, my former agent, to put pressure on David Stewart Hull, my new agent, to withdraw as my representative. He was representing my novel *The Misadventures of Tim McPick* after

Ms. Gregory withdrew. I had sent him the "literary gold mine" letters (his phrase), *not* to sell them, just so he'd know what was going on. Whatever it was Oates and Gregory said to him, he caved in and dropped me flat. I no longer had a major NY agent, and the book thus *never* got to the best editors. I guess Oates felt good about that. It showed what power she had. This was also the time when she told the Placement Service at Wayne State University, where I'd received my Ph.D. in 1969, to remove the letter of reference she'd written for me.

JOHN GARDNER

Ironically enough, my first contact with writer John Gardner (a too-common name, don't you feel?) came about because Oates and I had sent submissions to his little magazine called *Mss*. At that time he was little-known, before *Grendel*, *The Sunlight Dialogues*, or *On Moral Fiction*.

Months and months had gone by, and Joyce and I had heard nothing, so we conferred and I wrote Gardner a note, asking about our work. I got back a notice that the magazine had changed addresses; it was now at some university. I wrote to the university and got no response. Finally Joyce and I agreed that I should query the department chairman to see if Gardner and his magazine were anywhere in evidence.

Just about then my short story came back from *Mss*. with some personal comments, while Joyce's novella was accepted. Soon after came a blistering, four-page, single-spaced letter from Mr. John Gardner lambasting me for daring to write to his chairman and thus get him in trouble. He had taken each of my innocently penned sentences and re-written them to show how I should have worded them to make them even more cruel. Cruel? I showed the letter to Joyce and we agreed that Gardner was a crackpot.

I wrote him back a gentle reply, telling him my heart was still beating fast because of his interpretation of my note. I'm sure I didn't mention it, but I was not pleased that he had said Ms. Oates was "a real writer" and how dare I drag her into this! He was correct about my story; it wasn't any good, but it had been Oates's idea to write the chairman!

Anyway, Gardner apparently didn't lose his job because of my note, and he went on to write some of the books that made his name. Funnily enough, he and Joyce became friends years later when she moved to the East Coast.

My next contact with Gardner occurred when he was selected to be the judge of the short story contest of *The Kansas Quarterly*, a magazine that by this time had published me. I couldn't believe my eyes when I read Gardner's preface to his choice of prize winners. This must have been about 1977 or '78. He said, quite snottily, quite without any sense that he was a bigot, that he wasn't giving a story with a gay theme a prize or not giving it a higher one because, "as everyone knows, homosexual stories are inherently inferior" and so were gay artists. Believe me, I am not making this up. Anyone can check the preface he wrote. This was so patently false that I was outraged. It was sentiments like this, expressed not only by Gardner but by editors and reviewers for *The New York Times* and the like, that made it so hard for gay artists to get their fair share of the pie unless they deliberately hid their orientation and wrote about straights and their problems exclusively. I hated having to be "defensive" all the time, but I had learned that queers didn't get anything but abuse and weren't likely to get anything else until they spoke up.

So I testily wrote to Gardner, saying that he obviously didn't know how many gay writers had contributed to the world's literature or that he hadn't read much openly gay literature or he wouldn't say such things; he also wouldn't dare say such things about Jewish writers or Irish writers as though their particular worlds weren't relevant to the human condition. How dare he deny gays the same right to describe their worlds and be given the same credit for universality!

Well, I got back a letter saying, "Yeah, I know you and your books, and I hate both." (Surprisingly, however, Gardner explained that when he had written his snotty words he'd been suffering from cancer and he hadn't been thinking clearly about the number of gay writers. He said pointedly, "But this is not an apology!" I was tempted to write back and say, "I had a hangnail when I wrote you, and I'm sorry.")

I forget what I wrote back. But Gardner convinced me what an uphill battle we openly gay artists were fighting, especially when it came to straight men. They weren't going to let us in if they could help it.

It was odd that Gardner who came out with a call for "moral" fiction, in a surge of neo-Victorianism, complaining about the cynicism and ugliness of so much modern fiction. (He bad-mouthed Oates, among others, for this.) Why? He didn't show much evidence of nobility of soul or graciousness or even plain old tolerance. How dare he demand "moral" writing. He wouldn't know it if he saw it!

I followed his career from a distance. I read *Grendel* and actually liked it, but I couldn't bring myself to read his later strained, trying-too-hard novels. I felt sorry for writers like Gardner because they had to stand on their heads and tell their stories sideways or upside down in order to give them some freshness. I was sure that my subject was quite fresh, however much people like Gardner and Oates didn't want to admit it into the mainstream.

When John Gardner died in a motorcycle accident at the age of forty-nine, I cannot say that I shed many tears. If anything, I saw his death as removing yet one more of the homophobic obstacles that had made it so difficult for "my people" to get their due. It might take the death of a whole generation, although I'm not so sure the next one is being raised with much less mindless bigotry.

PHILIP LEVINE

Poet Phil Levine was not on the committee when I was hired as an openly gay teacher at Fresno State in 1974. I probably wouldn't have been hired if he had been.

I never got to know him well, although we did attend some faculty meetings together. He was always off on one grant or another. I thought we might have some things in common since we were both from Detroit. I did hear him read his poems once, and he was an entertaining reader, a heavily tanned, lithe man with curly hair, not afraid to hawk his books to his audience after he read.

At one point we exchanged autographed copies of our books. I gave him *Something You Do in the Dark*, but then I didn't hear any more. Believe me, I had learned by that time not to query people too closely on their reactions. Usually if they like your work they seek you out to tell you. Levine was very silent.

From a distance I'd see him playing tennis, hear of his winning more grants and fellowships and guest professorships, and whatnot. Well, good for him, I thought.

Then I started hearing that Levine was bad-mouthing me to people in a position to hire me. They had asked him about me even though I hadn't given him as a reference. Apparently he had hated my novel and was going out of his way to keep me from being hired when I would have to leave Fresno State after my second year.

This was the same period when I was sending out applications listing my editorship of *Gay Literature* magazine, plus my having published stories in *Gay Sunshine* and the like. Several closet gays and even sympathetic non-gay friends on hiring committees wrote back telling me not to apply so openly, because various chairmen at E. New Mexico State and San Jose State, to name but two, were appalled that the "queers are trying to get in."

For Philip Levine to attack me seemed part of the heterosexual Establishment's devoted efforts to maintain the status quo. Of course he had a right not to like my work, but a friend of mine told me that he'd read a poem by Levine about a queer dwarf sitting on the poet's lap, making nasty overtures to him. So it seemed to me that maybe Levine had a particular problem with the subject matter that had a lot to do with his going out of his way to denounce my "gay-lib" novel.

Whatever the intricacies here, I decided to write him from San Francisco after I moved and ask him please not to badmouth my book anymore, since it was costing me jobs. (Maybe I forgot the "please.") The letter I got back I have been able to read only once, because it is so vicious. I obviously had touched a nerve in this aggressively macho guy that didn't want to be touched.

What we're dealing with here is a very complex issue, actually, because I'm willing to entertain the idea that someone can be pro-gay, anti-gay, or gay-neutral and still not like my work. Big of me, no?

But with a taboo-riddled subject like homosexuality and men in "fem" professions like writing poetry (or at least as so considered at the time in the good old USA) it's virtually impossible to separate such an extreme reaction on Levine's part from the subject. If he hated some novel about blacks would he go out of his way to see that the author didn't get a job somewhere? It would be no skin off his white nose.

Now I hate it when minorities always blame majorities for their problems: it's "racism," it's this-ism or that-ism. No, sometimes it's just the ineptitude of the individual members of the "minority"! But with homosexuality we're still at that very awkward stage where deep fears and irrational hostilities are inextricably bound up with the material itself. I think Phil Levine had real problems there. And they became my problems.

RANDY SHILTS

If life wasn't hard enough already, I had the "pleasure" of meeting Mr. Randy Shilts, boy reporter, some time in 1976 or '77. My own lover of the time was an alcoholic who had dyed his dark hair flaming blond, so maybe that's why I found Randy Shilts sexy and went out of my way to get to know him. He must have been in his mid-twenties, cherubic, bright-eyed.

I chatted him up at a party. But evidently I wasn't his cup of tea. At one point my second novel came up in the conversation, and Shilts launched into a vivid analysis of how ugly the cover was. I ventured to hope that he had gotten beyond the ugly cover to read the book. He hadn't. I had made the mistake of assuming he was a fellow writer because he was a newspaper reporter. How silly of me. He admitted later, somewhere, that he hadn't had any respect for "authors" until his own first book came out. Unfortunately he seemed to be a prime example of the young literate but totally unlettered generation. I let his comment about my ugly cover go. I thought it was ugly myself. I just hadn't been able to control the way it turned out.

Then during a discussion of politics in the kitchen at this same party, I asked the group what I thought to be a searching question about politicians: did they cynically know the evil things they did were corrupt or did they actually think they were right? Various people gave me their thoughtful answers. Randy Shilts snapped, "If you read the newspapers you'd know."

Was journalism truly the answer for life's psychological mysteries? Obviously the novelist (me) and the newspaperman (him) were at odds on the fundamentals. Again I didn't respond to the puerility of Shilts' remarks.

But then a little later, when everyone was discussing astrology, I said that I was at the tail end of Pisces but that I preferred to be Aries, because Pisces were said to be wishy-washy. Shilts's immediate reply as he looked at me was: "Aries are wishy-washy, too."

Now if there's one thing I've been in my life it isn't wishy-washy. I couldn't believe my ears. Shilts had gone out of his way to insult me three different ways in the space of an hour and half. What had I done to him? Was he this way with everybody? I went home from the party furious. I may not be able to command compliments, but I sure as hell resent gratuitous put-downs. I was doubly incensed because I'd been attracted to Shilts and he obviously hadn't been attracted back.

He also didn't seem to realize how difficult it was to get serious works of fiction published, gay serious ones even harder. Somewhere in the conversation he had said that he was going to write a "bestseller," without so much as an ounce of shame. I lost respect for him right then and there. Who the fuck but a hack wanted to write a bestseller?

I wrote him a letter care of *The Advocate*, where he was on the staff at the time, informing him that he had really ticked me off with his remarks at the party, but I wrote the whole letter ironically, saying I was forgiving him his callowness, aesthetic density, and rudeness because of his extreme youth. I learned from somebody that Shilts put the letter up on the bulletin board at *The Advocate*. Clearly the man had skin a foot thick.

Actually I liked this quality in gays when it came to dealing with the homophobic world because they could give as good as they got, but I was laboring under the delusion that gays were necessarily more sensitive than others. Shilts seemed about as sensitive as a whore's clitoris.

After that, I couldn't bring myself to talk to the man anymore. I'd see him everywhere, but I didn't want to have anything to do with him. One time we were at Channel 6 to do back-to-back interviews with the host. But we simply passed like ships in the night.

No doubt I'm too sensitive to slights. I wish I weren't. Sometimes I feel as though I'm all exposed nerve endings. As you can see, I've eventually learned to hit back hard. My mother always wanted me to do that when the other kids beat me up. I'm hope you're happy now, Ma.

I didn't speak to Shilts for years. His career zoomed. He became a major reporter for the *San Francisco Chronicle* and was writing a book about Harvey Milk for a major press. It would have been to my advantage to repair the connection. But that would have been brown nosing, no?

One day, though, I was asked to be one of three judges for the journalism category of the Cable Car Awards. Randy Shilts and Frank Robinson, the writer of one of the books that became *The Towering Inferno* movie, were the other two judges.

We met at the Patio Cafe, and that's when Shilts and I made up. Nothing was said about the past; we just proceeded to interact on a more or less friendly basis. Indeed, he invited me to stop by his place sometime and smoke a joint. Since I didn't like marijuana, nothing ever came of this polite gesture.

What I remember most distinctly from those awards meetings was that it was necessary to give some lesbians some prizes, whether their stuff was really better or not, because of the growing pressure for lesbian input into the "gay" movement. We managed somehow.

Shilts and I didn't exactly become great friends after this, but we would meet at various functions and chat. He had a gift for controversy, for getting his name into the papers. All I had a gift for, it seemed, was making enemies that kept my name out of the papers.

When Modern Times Bookstore announced that Randy would be having a signing for *The Mayor of Castro Street*, his non-fiction book about Harvey Milk, I went, knowing that book signings are often sparsely attended and wanting to support a fellow writer.

I was right. There were very few people there, and Randy seemed positively glad to see me. I even bought his book, a hard-cover edition, even though I had received a review copy for IGNA, the news agency I was running at the time. Randy wrote some nice things in the front of the book. At the same time I did an interview with Randy for my news agency, with his eager consent, by sending him some questions through the mail and letting him type up his answers.

He made some money from his book, but it didn't exactly head the "bestseller" list. I think this experience chastened him a bit. Naturally I hate to see people have a hard time -- no, I don't, not when it makes them understand the pains of life that others go through.

The sorriest I ever felt for Randy was when he was on a TV show about AIDS. It was produced by Russ Coughlin of Channel 7 and represented just about everything vulgar that Coughlin's idea of television represented. The panel consisted of Randy, a doctor, and an AIDS patient plus, via satellite, the Rev. Jerry Falwell. What a well-known religious fanatic was doing on a TV show on the medical aspects of a disease only Russ Coughlin would know. It was a good way to bring in "moral" questions, I suppose, and ratings. Poor Randy and the others were floored by Falwell, partly because his face was on a screen that took up three times as much space as theirs did, but also because Falwell was forceful, wasn't the least bit thoughtful, and kept saying his spiel. Shilts didn't come off well at all. Where was gay aggressiveness when we needed it?

I began to cool toward Randy again when he started on his bandwagon campaign in the *Chronicle* to close the bathhouses. Whether he did it out of a cynical capitulation to terrified public opinion in order to give a symbol that gays were doing something about AIDS or because he sincerely believed that closing the baths would halt AIDS, I don't know. I thought it might have had a lot to do with Randy's guilt about his own highly promiscuous days. I mean, in 1983 he and I had a book signing together at a Waldenbooks store on Polk Street. He solicited every single good-looking gay male customer who came to look at our wares. In fact, he made a date with one and "had" him later. A friend of mine who went to interview Randy one time was "had" as well. It likewise seemed rather shoddy journalism for Shilts to be stacking the deck against the baths, when it was the sexual behavior of people, not the locale, that put them at risk. One could pick up a trick in the baths and have safe or unsafe sex just as easily as one could at a book signing.

Shilts began to put on weight. He turned from cherub to chub. His soaring career took a downward turn. He had sold the movie rights to his book to Joe Hamilton, Carol Burnett's husband, and even got to write the screenplay, though devoid of mere experience in that field, but the screenplay was scrapped. Rob Epstein went on to make a film about Harvey Milk and win an Academy Award. This must have been a bitter pill for Randy.

He managed to get a TV weatherman as his lover, but the affair didn't last. I remember him complaining the lover would get in his face too much and hang on him all the time. I really felt sorry for him. Here he was in his early thirties, wealthy, famous, with a lover who hung on him all the time. No wonder he had to drink so much.

I'm sure I'll see Randy Shilts again. He spoke to me at the Berkeley Rep not so long ago, but I was in a cranky mood and didn't respond very enthusiastically. I've really got to learn to hide my emotions better. And it's becoming obvious that maybe some people aren't going to be around that long.

SALLY GEARHART

Tried to like Sally Gearhart because she did a lot of good for the Cause when she and Harvey Milk represented the gay/lesbian community in various public debates during the Briggs Initiative of 1977. Lisping Senator Briggs wanted to prohibit all gays from teaching in the schools. She was a speech teacher and sometime writer who practiced what she preached, a handsome woman in her forties, robust, professorial.

But when I attended a session of the Modern Language Association, in San Francisco in 1978, I believe, Sally and her lover delivered a paper to an assembly of academics that was a perfect example of how politics ruins literary appreciation. Whether they alternated reading sentences aloud or just took turns reading parts of the paper to us, I forget. This was the period when everything was considered "sexist" unless it led to equal parity in everything, unless of course women wanted to exclude men, as they often did. The paper was a purported literary analysis of various gay and lesbian novels that had been written in recent years. It soon became clear that Gearhart & Co. were only interested in scoring points for lesbians against gay men. Since my *Something You Do in the Dark* was one of the evil men's books they quoted to show how "awful" our sexual behavior was compared to theirs, I sat there with more than usual interest.

They cited a passage where I mention the hierarchy of physical attractiveness in male cruising, not something I'm especially proud of but a fact nonetheless. The women's novels, on the other hand, showed lesbians helping Rape Victims in the Snow, and the like, offered to the assembled scholars as evidence of superior literary accomplishments.

Unfortunately for Gearhart & Co. whenever they read a gay male passage, the humor, ironies and general command of fictional techniques became obvious in the appreciative response of the audience, while the Good Lesbian Fiction stank of self-righteousness and dull correctness, like some Victorian ladies' manual for proper behavior, which it was, only not Victorian. Alas, it was all too contemporary.

Gearhart & Co. read on, assuring us there was much more to their strenuous scholarly effort, although they wouldn't be presenting all of it. As Samuel Johnson said of *Paradise Lost*, no one ever wished it longer.

At the end I rose in the midst of some hundred or more people and spoke up, my voice quavering. "I don't think it's fair to cite one passage from my novel as though that sums up the whole book," was about all I could manage to get out. The times were such that anything lesbians said was better than anything a mere man might say. Some others did jump up to defend art vs. simplemindedness. Happily, this lopsided perspective has altered in the last few years. Sally Gearhart has, to all appearances, dropped out of public life. . . . Pity. Is that the word?

J. E. FREEMAN

The first time I saw Jim Freeman, the actor, was when he did a staged reading of C.D. Arnold's play "Dinosaurs," the same day we did my "Beer and Rhubarb Pie" at Theatre Rhinoceros. He was a tall, lanky fellow who looked like a psychopathic killer, but he was one terrific actor. As of this writing, he has been in the movie *Ruthless People*, has played the lead in *Hard Travelin'*, and seems to be about to have a major film and TV career.

But he's a strange dude. He started getting a reputation for backstage violence when he was connected with certain theater groups, once hitting a director over something or other. In fact he was being black-balled by some theater companies because of his behavior. I mentioned this fact in a creative writing class of mine at City College, without naming Freeman, and who should come up during the break and identify himself but Freeman's lover! I didn't think it wrong or even awkward to describe Freeman's antics. If anything, maybe the word would get back to him and he would get his act together.

He appeared in a number of plays in S.F. and was never less than good. But I remember seeing him in a C. D. Arnold play where he had to take his clothes off. He shouldn't bother.

I don't know what he thought of me, but one time I was rehearsing with a singer who was about to sing "The S&M Waltz," a song Dan Turner and I had written, at an after-theater club on Geary St. There was no microphone and so I could barely hear the singer and called out for him to project more. I must not have been loud enough myself, and the singer called back, wanting me to yell. Jim Freeman, whom I'd never been introduced to, was standing behind me, watching and listening. He gave me this psycho-killer smile and said, "Maybe he could hear you if you blew it out your ass."

Where had that come from? I hadn't been talking to him, seeking his advice, or anything else. I'd even been trying to be fairly quiet. How dare he say such a thing! "Who asked you?" I snarled. "Who the fuck are you!" He was bigger than me, and he has that flint-eyed look of his, so I was afraid of him, but I wasn't about to be treated that way by anybody. He gave me a placating grin, holding up his hands, even followed me around to apologize. (I think.)

I was disconcerted about it all, and later I began to wonder if his rude comment had been some kind of weird sexual overture. Don't want to be the type that sees everything as either a come-on or a rejection, but his remark was so completely off the wall I didn't know what to make of it except to tie it in somehow with his possible S&M tendencies. Maybe it had more to do with Freeman's long personal history of anger, which I heard about from the lover (now ex-) years later.

The maybe-not-so-odd thing was that on screen Freeman was mesmerizing. I was sure he'd always be cast as a heavy, but in *Hard Travelin'* he plays a good-hearted victim of the system. Who knows where he'll go in Hollywood, but he's the only person I've ever "known" who got even this far as an actor. He went to NYC, did a soap opera, came back to S.F. when the work dried up, was seen in a play, got a movie, then went to L.A. and started clicking. Hooray! I couldn't be happier for him.

Still haven't been introduced to him, though. We've even sat at the same table, too. (Do other people do this, or is it just me?)

Del Martin & Phyllis Lyon

Perhaps Del Martin and Phyllis Lyon were a handsome couple once upon a time. When I knew them, they weren't. Del was a big truck driver kind of woman, not your typical grandmother, although she was one. She had white hair, cut short of course, with a broad peasant face. Why is it so many dykes look like this? It must be in the genes. Seriously. Nobody would deliberately try to look like this!

Del and I were on a television program back in the mid-1970s when I wasn't too well known. She had done her book *Lesbian/Woman* by this time, and I learned how to market my books from watching Del. When her turn came, she didn't promote the book directly; instead, she held up the paperback version and mildly complained about the color used by the publisher. This allowed her to hawk the book without seeming to. It was very clever. I think she was complaining about the lavender or the pink color or some such, but it was evident that she was heavily into selling that sucker. By the way, doesn't that title *Lesbian/Woman* sound just like the 1970s?

Even by this time Del and Phyllis had become sort of resident lesbian royalty, if you can conceive of such a thing. They had been together forever, and longevity becomes nobility after five years in the gay community. They even got a plaque from the city. They had managed twenty years when I encountered them. Some unkind souls suggested that their togetherness sprang less from virtue than from their inability, with their looks, to find anybody else. Phyllis was a horse-faced woman with beaver teeth that seemed to get more crooked with each year; perhaps she chewed on the wrong things. (You're aware, aren't you, that I'm saying these things about them because I'm not supposed to? Lesbians can criticize gay men their emphasis on appearance, their promiscuity, their whatever. Men aren't allowed to criticize back.)

Anyhow, I met Phyllis on a plane as we were coming back from Florida after we had both spoken to a gay convention. We sat right next to each other for the flight, and I got to know a lot about her. She was more palatable in person than as a "spokesperson" for a cause. Even her looks ceased to be so emphatic after one adjusted to the shock. (Yes, yes, I know she couldn't help her face! But lesbians have often made a virtue of what is at best a misfortune.)

Phyllis came through on that plane ride as a woman-firster of the first water and the Second Coming. Women should be hired because they didn't have sex in the bushes; women stayed together, while men flitted about! Women! Women! Women! And on and on. What I felt was the moral fascism of the women's movement washing over me. From time to time various ideas, social, psychological, religious, or whatnot, achieve an ascendancy, and ideas that contradict or qualify these notions are labeled heresies, and it becomes all but impossible to speak up. For example, there was a media committee once that wouldn't allow lesbians to be portrayed as jealous. Come on now! Lesbians are just human beings, for god's sake.

In the times I'm describing the Collective Virtue of Women was a given. The inherent sexism, nastiness, and inferiority of men were fair game for endless castigation. One felt like a Protestant trying to argue with the Inquisition about the nature of morality. Only there was no room for other interpretations. Believe me, I had no trouble accepting the viciousness of men. I just didn't think women were exempt from the flaws of the human race and especially despised the censoriousness of lesbian feminists when it came to certain issues; they wouldn't let the opposing side express its opinions. Only the "proper" opinions, the Politically Correct opinions, were permitted expression. When it came to art, I found this limiting, false, and dangerous. I once made up a cartoon once showing two panels. In one was a pinch-faced, moralistic, old-prude Victorian bluenose. In the other was a pinch-faced, moralistic old prude modern-day lesbian feminist.

I got into lots of trouble because I would write and speak out when I thought lesbians were getting favored treatment, as they usually did in those days. They would demand such things as gender parity in all areas, when in fact lesbians did not constitute fifty percent of the gay population. They wanted power, and they took it. Since at times I felt they were taking it from me, after I had worked like a dog to overcome my working-class background and get a Ph.D. and to write my books and plays, I fought back.

LESTER COLE

Lester Cole was one of the Hollywood Ten, one of those screenwriters pilloried by Senator Joe McCarthy in the 1950s. I first met him at a meeting of the Bay Area Theatre Critics Circle in the late 1970s. He wrote reviews for *The People's World*. I was the Corresponding Secretary for the Critics Circle.

By that time Cole was quite elderly, frail, well into his seventies. One time I saw him fall as he tried to get into his seat at a theater. I believe he came to my house for the meeting, but it's possible it was held somewhere else. In any case, his car wouldn't start and I gave him a jump with my cables. He was very grateful. I'm sure he had no idea of me or my writing.

Dan Turner had taken a course in screenwriting from Lester Cole and said that he seemed rather homophobic. As an old guard Commie, what else! I felt sorry for his tribulations in the McCarthy era, but it was difficult to cheer when he belonged to an organization or had sympathies with a system that considered homosexuals "decadent" and fit for concentration camps. So I'm afraid I didn't read any of Lester's reviews, but I did see him at several more Critics Circle meetings. He seemed to be getting feebler and feebler. He eventually stopped coming.

Then I wrote some screenplays with Isabel Gilbert, a nurse/hypnotist who had also done some TV writing. Our mutual agent, Bertha Klausner, got us to collaborate. Well, Isabel suggested we show our first screenplay to Lester Cole. I knew him as that feeble, aging man, but I agreed, especially when Isabel said she'd pay for his critique.

So there we were, Isabel, who was in her mid-seventies, and I climbing the stairs to Lester Cole's second-floor apartment in the Portreo District of S.F. It was a three-room apartment of very modest furnishings; it did, however, have a view of the city. What crossed my mind was why Lester Cole lived in such relative poverty. Yes, he had been blacklisted and that had curtailed his income, and there were rumors of divorces and alimony, and all that, but what about all the money he had made before and after? You see, he did come back from the blacklist and wrote more movies, the last being *Born Free*. He had also written scripts under pseudonyms during the bad days. He must have gone through tons of money, and there he was living in a dump.

We talked of some of the scripts he'd written in the old days. Then we got down to business. He had read our script and made a number of suggestions, some of which were even good. He said our heroine would lose the audience's sympathy if we presented her as a snitch. So we changed that. We altered some other things as well. But some of his other comments were imperceptive, for Lester was getting on, alas, and he forgot what had happened from one part of the script to the next. I don't say this to protect the script at all. The screenplay was based on Isabel's concept and was merely a money-making project in my eyes. My ego wasn't tied up with it at all.

Strangely, Isabel seemed to go all girlish over Lester, agreeing with everything he said, even when he contradicted himself, talking too much, trying very hard to be vivacious. When we left, she said, "I wonder if Lester is married." He was surely in his eighties by this time, but hope springs eternal, I guess. (I found out at her funeral later that Isabel Gilbert herself had taken ten years off her age. So she was still out "cruising" in her mid-eighties!)

We also paid Lester to read our second script, or maybe it was the second draft of the first one. Whatever. That time I went alone to his apartment, because Isabel wasn't available for some reason or other. This time Lester served me tea, which he fixed in his tiny kitchen, shuffling about in his slippers, shrunken, getting bent over, but still lively. He broke a saucer and seemed rather downhearted. "I had that a long time," he explained.

He was making plans for a new novel, a new agent, and was seeking an experienced novelist to help him. This had come up the first time too, and Isabel had plugged me as a suitable expert, but none of this seemed to register on Lester, so I didn't push it. I just thought it both admirable and sad that he was struggling in his eighties to get an agent and a publisher.

Neither of the screenplays has sold as of this date, through no fault of Lester Cole's. He liked the idea of authentic hypnosis that we were writing about, but he said we'd have to convince an audience that it wasn't a bunch of mumbo-jumbo. Maybe we didn't succeed in doing that.

One day a couple of years later I read that Lester Cole was dead. Pity and fear came over me. Was this the meaning of life, doing piecemeal script reading in a semi-senile state to make ends meet, alone in a puny little apartment?

Well, at least he'd had a view.

HARVEY FIERSTEIN

Harvey and I were introduced in the lobby of Theatre Rhinoceros when my "Beer and Rhubarb Pie" was done again as a midnight show and his *International Stud* was on the main stage. Little did I suspect from the rather crummy production at Rhino that this play of Harvey's, along with two others, would go on to stunning success as *Torch Song Trilogy* and play on Broadway and even win a Tony for the author.

Nor did I suspect that he would then go on to be asked to write the book for *La Cage aux Follies* and become rich beyond avarice. Not bad for a drag queen under thirty!

I wish he had fallen deeply in love with me there in the lobby, but he didn't. Some people have a gift for making friends and/or contacts in the theater. I don't. I must give off these "stay away from me" vibes. Partly it's shyness. Partly it's a real "stay away from me" feeling I have for many people. Maybe I'm afraid of rejection, and so I reject others first?

Apparently Harvey was witty and delightful in person. That could only have helped his career, but when a couple of influential NY critics praised *Torch Song*, the rest was theater history. We live by and die by such chance.

His success made any number of us "upfront" gay writers ponder the question of why Harvey had hit it so big and we hadn't. Let me say it right out. I felt I'd been one of the pioneers in the field, but I wasn't becoming a millionaire because suddenly, briefly, gay was chic. Then again, my work wasn't exactly a laugh a minute, wasn't glamorous, and called for a strong stomach for the depressing sides of existence. These do not a Broadway musical make, my darling! (An opera maybe?)

Give 'em male couples yearning to be just like straights monogamous, one butch, one fem, wanting love, love, love above all other earthly pleasures. These a Broadway comedy make. I'm trying to control the jealousy here. I can't really expect to have a popular success if I refuse to write popularly, can I? Actually later on I wrote *Cinderella II* to be a popular success, and it was. But San Francisco success doesn't count for much actually.

I wrote Harvey a congratulatory letter upon his successes, commenting that somehow we both had survived Theatre Rhinoceros and calling him the "flan of Broadway," instead of the "toast of Broadway." He didn't write back. I really must learn how to compliment people.

But I didn't want to come off as a sycophant since I hadn't exactly sought him out when we had met in person. So what I did was bend over backwards to put him down a little bit in my letter. That would "equalize" us. Is this dumb or brave?

What I really felt was that he had been in the right place at the right time and was reaping the few windfalls that gay plays or books were ever going to wrest from the reluctant general public. I hope I'm wrong. I hope Harvey and all of us go on to achieve vast admiration for our work, and a few dollars, maybe. I just hope it doesn't come after we're dead, as is so often the case.

Now Harvey Fierstein has to live with that other problem of this life: what do you do for an *encore*?

ARMISTEAD MAUPIN

Another 'charmer' that I haven't gotten on with as well as I should have is Armistead Maupin. I have some charm of my own, believe it or not, and Armistead and I are often even said to look alike big-eyed, baby-faced and plumping out in our riper days. So what happened? He and I have certainly been thrown together often enough.

The first time was at the S.F. Jewish Community Center (late 1970s?), where some local authors were invited to be the half-time entertainment. I mean it. A bunch of singles was meeting there, and we authors were supposed to stand by our books and chat about them until such time as the singles paired off, got married, or got drunk. You see what I've done for my art?

Well, anyway, Armistead was there, dressed to the nines in whatever the fashion was at that time, pseudo 1930s, I think. He was just making his name then because *Tales of the City* was a big deal in the *Chronicle*. I have to confess I didn't read it in the newspaper, largely because I don't much enjoy fiction unless it's in book form. But Armistead had hit just the right note for a large audience.

(By the way, have you noticed the way writers who have large audiences always try to explain that that doesn't mean they are junk writers but have real art, while we writers who don't have large audiences always try to say we don't mind?)

Armistead picked up one of my books *The Revolt of the Perverts* just out, and said he'd been hearing a lot about me. I said, "Why don't we have a feud? That way we'll get more readers." I was joking, but I do think feuds have contributed to some famous people's fame. It wasn't too long after this that Armistead and I did have sort of a feud, whether he knew it or not.

Here's what took place. I got a crush on a man I met in a bar, and this guy met Armistead somewhere or other. Naturally they discussed me and my work, and the report came back that Armistead thought I should "lighten up" in my writing. Well, this was met with all the usual modesty and amiability of my personality. Fuck him! How dare that journalistic pop tart criticize my stuff! If anything, he should "heavy up" his oh-so-with-it writing.

Actually I sort of enjoyed his first two books, but I did think they were cream puffs with few redeeming literary qualities, just bon-bons for the masses.

I wrote a satire of Armistead (plus Rita Mae Brown, Ed White, and Felice Picano) for a California magazine to relieve some of my resentment. (Later included under the pseudonym of The Saint in a book of satires from Alyson). Then I lived in fear that Armistead would see the piece and challenge me to a duel or something. So far he hasn't. Maybe he's never seen the satire about trendy, trivial A-gays.

I'd keep running into Armistead, and he was always charming. The only time I've seen him upset was when a review of one of his books appeared in *The Sentinel*, the old *Sentinel*, when it was *the* gay paper in S. F. He was distressed, even though there was a long interview with him as well. The review, you see, of the book itself referred to it as "fluff." "So I guess I'm just a fluff writer!" he said with great indignation. What did he think he was – Dostoevsky? (My contemporaries really have got to read some more literary history.)

This was right in front of the Castro Theater. I recall it vividly. Armistead went on to mention that no less a personage than Gore Vidal had called to tell him he had enjoyed his book and to wish him well. Armistead said he queried Vidal on the East Coast reception to his book, which hadn't been all that favorable or widespread. Vidal: "Well, you have two things against you. You're on the West Coast and you're a faggot." (Little has changed in that regard.)

Armistead went on to great success at getting his name bandied about in the right places, such as in Herb Caen's column. Apparently an intruder once got into Armistead's house and some to-do occurred. Later on Caen said it had all just been a publicity stunt, engineered by Armistead and his housemate, Ken Maley, so Armistead lost a few points there, but not many.

I kept harboring this grudge against him because of what he'd said about my "heaviness". I mean, for god's sake, didn't he know, instinctively, somewhere down in his shallow little A-gay soul, that I was head and shoulders above him in talent, perception, and artful honesty? He didn't? Well, what was wrong with him then!?

Every time a gay writer was mentioned it was Armistead, rarely me. I ground my teeth. I didn't want to drive him out of the field. I simply wanted to be included. (I am reading a biography of Henry James right now, and I see that even the Master was envious of more popular writers of his time, writers now unread. Only I don't have the surety that I'll get into the pantheon of literary saints, the way Henry James is now, even though I truly believe that's where I belong. Maybe they'll put Armistead there and leave me out in the cold, bitching?)

There would be Armistead M.C. at the Cable Car Awards, the Gay Parade, even the welcome home for some goddamn hijacked passengers! Nobody ever asked me to be an M.C. I can even talk. I've taught college for years. I would go through these inner rages that I was being ignored and at the same time hate the thought that I might have to go out on a stage and "please" people. "Hi there! I'm your host tonight. Which part of my anatomy would you like to sample?"

I gave a reading once at a Unitarian church. I read from my 1982 *Gay Etiquette* book, which is funny. Yes, I managed to read some amusing sections, but I also read a part about gays in concentration camps that was a real downer and meant to engender guilt in my listeners. Not a good idea, Dan. (I think that's when I finally learned that when you deal with a live audience you must give it what it wants, not what you want. That's all there is to it. Unless you don't mind them glaring at you and avoiding you afterwards.)

Apparently none of these worries bothered Armistead Maupin, since he never even considered not pleasing everybody every chance he got. He gave readings at the Walt Whitman bookshop to overflowing crowds. (I did all right myself, filled it, with forty people.)

My lover, John, used to tease me by saying he wanted to meet Armistead because he would probably have more in common with him than with me, and they'd run off together. Thanks a lot, honey.

I ran into Armistead on the MUNI underground trolley one time when I was with David Lamble. Armistead and Steve Beery were going to a movie. David was personable and asked us if we knew each other. Armistead gave a big, friendly smile. I was sullen and withdrawn, mumbled something. Am I neurotic? I don't seem neurotic to myself, only when I write down what I do.

Armistead had his problems, too, it seems. He sold *Tales of the City* to cable TV, yet it still hasn't come out (as of 1986). He may also feel that he's trapped in the kind of book he has to write. He may wind up doing *Tales of the City* until the day he dies whether he wants to or not. Then, too, the *Chronicle* gave him a hard time with the last batch, something about the right of prior censorship, and so Armistead took his tales to the *Examiner*, which no matter how hard it tries just isn't read the way the *Chronicle* is. The *Chronicle* even said the name *Tales of the City* belonged to it since it owned the copyright and wouldn't let Armistead use the name in a rival paper. Class act.

The last time I saw Armistead was at Harold Norse's birthday party. Happy to see that he's even bigger than I am. Still fashionably dressed. I wore my best twenty-six-year-old sport jacket. I even made myself talk to him, though not well. It was a mixture of lingering resentment about his critique and apprehension that he'll bring up the satire I did about him. But, you know, I think I'll be better able to deal with Mr. Maupin the next time I see him. These memoirs are great therapy!

After all, why should I hold a grudge against Armistead and barely speak to him when my own lover of over six years feels the same way about my writing! I speak to him. I do more than that!

DEAN GOODMAN

Dean Goodman is better known in S.F. than around the country. But he was once married to Maria Riva, Marlene Dietrich's resentful daughter, so that alone should pique your curiosity. There are, in addition, other colorful aspects of Dean's personality.

I first met him in the mid-1970s when I went to his Geary Street apartment because he was a part-time editor for a magazine and I was trying to place some of my short stories, to no avail, since mine weren't jack-off stories, that bane of gay magazines that continues to drive out everything else, to this day. Dean used several pen names in writing his little profiles of naked porn stars; he used his own name for his acting career.

He was in his mid-fifties then, corpulent, and for a long while he wore a yellow-tinged white wig that did not fool anybody. Eventually this gave way to a realistic bald head and a big white beard.

Visiting with Dean that first time was Jack Wrangler, a gay porn star who later lived with Margaret Whiting, the singer. I don't recall that Wrangler said anything memorable, although he did do some stunning push-ups and side-to-sides right there in the living room.

Wrangler was there to star in the play Dean had written. I've forgotten its title, but this drama was to play a part in my own life a few years later. In the initial production apparently Dean made money; male nudity on stage was a rarity then.

It was Dean who invited me to join the Critics Circle when he was president, maybe four or five years after we first met. He managed to juggle several careers as actor, as critic, as ESL teacher. I always said he was very talented in a number of ways. His acting was particularly good.

But he got into some trouble and was ultimately reprimanded by the Critics Circle, when he got into a fight with Michele Truffaut of the San Francisco Repertory Company, whom Dean maintained had promised him a certain part. When the theater reneged, Dean wrote a letter saying he wouldn't be reviewing that company any longer. Some thought Dean was abusing his position as a critic, in effect threatening a theater, while Dean said he couldn't be expected to review objectively a theater that had done him dirt and the ethical thing was for him to avoid reviewing that theater. I sided with Dean.

When my "Beer and Rhubarb Pie" was a hit, Dean came to see it and may even have written a good review of it somewhere. But when Theatre Rhino wanted to re-open the show on the main stage, we encountered some problems when Dean decided to raid my cast for a new production of his old Jack Wrangler play! My turn had come.

I had heard about Dean's calls to Thomas-Mark and Richard Staven, my actors, offering them nice salaries if they'd leave my play to appear in his. Now actors have a right to be paid, and Rhino wasn't paying anything or not much in those days, but I thought Dean should have confined his recruiting efforts to actors who were not already committed.

Richard Staven and I talked on the telephone; he said he

was indeed considering leaving my cast for Dean's. I said, "Do you want to leave a hit for a bomb?" For Dean's play had not been favorably reviewed in the original Jack Wrangler production, big dick or no. Well, I got an irate call from Dean accusing me of bad-mouthing his play, which he insisted had been a tremendous hit, and this time around it would be even bigger since he had producer Jonathan Reinis behind him.

I went over to Dean's apartment, and we had a knock-down, drag-out "discussion" of the affair. Yes, Richard Staven was taking the bait, and that meant we'd have to get a new actor and rehearse the play all over again.

Besides defending his actions, Dean was dismissive of Thomas-Mark, who had decided not to take the part offered him and stay in my play instead. The way Dean told it, he hadn't really wanted Thomas-Mark anyway; besides, he was too huffy. The way Thomas-Mark told it, he had read the script and thought it poor. On top of that, Dean had made him audition in Dean's apartment, privately, asking him to take off all his clothes and strike poses while Dean evaluated his performance from various positions on the floor. It was a work of art requiring nudity, you see, so naturally Dean had to check the sightlines. Another actor I know also told me he'd "auditioned" for Dean one time, again in his apartment, alone, and had had to remove all his clothes. How ironic, then, that it was Dean who asked me to write a play for him, for an older man, showing somebody who had a full, rich sex life and who didn't have to worry about loneliness, as the stereotype about the older gay man would have it. I guess not if you're into auditions.

Anyway, Dean and I went around and around over what I

considered his theft of half my cast. The wrangle concluded with him saying that he would put on a quality production. With that same script? No, he was definitely making revisions in the script to get rid of its flaws. He'd also written a song for the new production.

When I went to see the play, it was pretty bad, and the reviews were deadly. It ran for three hours, had not been rewritten so that you could notice; the set, the direction were by Dean, plus his song, don't forget, which, by the way, he sang on a tape played at each performance. He had cast it with two pretty men in their twenties, who represented the younger gay generation, along with two muscular hunks in their thirties, who were supposed to represent the "older" generation unable to get much sex. The jokes were left over from the forties, knee-slapping, cornball humor that didn't fit the characters and was mere filler between the numerous nude scenes. A play with a potentially serious theme had been turned into a skin show.

I had even offered to attend some rehearsals and make some suggestions, but Dean didn't invite me. "I have forty years in the theater!" he intoned instead. Well, forty years weren't enough to save that turkey. It didn't even make money the second time around, or shouldn't have. I met one of the "younger generation" cast members managing the Waldenbooks store where I had my signing with Randy Shilts. Small world. He said he was still trying to live down that production.

I thought that would be the end of my relationship with Dean Goodman, but it wasn't. Somehow we got over that hump, and, as I say, later on he even asked me to write him a play. I wrote *Don't Rub Me the Wrong Way*, but he must not have liked it too much. At least he didn't produce it. I had a staged reading of it afterwards at the Phoenix Theatre with Dean starring and saw that it had some problems that needed ironing out.

I have used Dean as an example in my playwriting class, without naming him, of the kind of person who can be such an "expert" that he puts on blinders when it comes to his own work and won't take any criticism during the writing or rehearsal period. A little humility at that time can save a ton of distress later.

But I owe Dean a debt of gratitude for recommending my neo-Shakespearean play, *Henry IV, Part III*, to the American Conservatory Theatre when he was hired to act there. He was very impressed with the work and urged the new artistic director, Edward Hastings, to read it and put it on. Hastings did read it, liked it, and said he would keep it in mind "for the future." And there it stands as I write. Probably nothing will happen with it. A new Shakespearean play? Too avant-garde for the traditionalists, too old-fashioned for the avant-garde.

Dean also started acting with the Berkeley Repertory Theatre, and I gave him good reviews because I thought he deserved them. At sixty-five he was acting in the most prestigious companies in S.F.

Until that happened, however, Dean had sometimes produced himself, sometimes wound up acting in fly-by-night companies. By this time, with his strong sense of himself, he did not like to audition. He thought people should know his work. So he got into one of his casting snits with Andrea

Gordon, the twenty-eight-year-old, very pretty artistic director of Tour de Force, a struggling young theater company. Later I became the dramaturge for this theater myself and had my own troubles with Andrea Gordon.

Andrea and Dean got into a dogfight. This time I was sort of a mediator, or at least I heard it from both sides. Andrea felt Dean was temperamental. Dean felt Andrea promised too many promises to too many people. (They were both right.) Simon Levy, a man I had recommended to the Jewish Community Theater in Berkeley as a director, also found Dean terribly temperamental to work with as an actor and vowed he never would do so again. Dean was a lot like me, I can see now battles and feuds and hurt feelings. But he never brooded about his, as far as I could see. He'd go out to fight even harder.

The oddest thing I ever saw him do took place when Andrea Gordon, Dean, and I were all on relatively good terms and going to see a play together in Marin County. Dean and I were waiting in the car for Andrea when he suddenly went into this fit of nerves and anxiety about Andrea not paying attention to him or not acknowledging something he'd done. He was shaking, almost unable to speak, as if he were six years old and needed reassurance that he was a valued and important person. In his mid-sixties and still feeling those needs, and so nakedly? I saw that "artistic" types are a breed apart. I hoped I would never need to be needed quite so desperately. I also saw how you could manipulate people with egos that hungry.

Dean even ran for public office, the College Board, one of those elected offices that politicians in S.F. use as a stepping stone to higher office. He came out against the coalition of minorities and liberals, but he didn't win. The next time around he wrote a letter defending John Riordan, the reigning arch-conservative, and tried to downgrade the liberals again. The one thing you could say about Dean Goodman was that he didn't take a back seat to life.

RITA MAE BROWN

So far I haven't actually met Rita Mae Brown in person, but we did correspond once. After she reads this, she probably won't want to meet me anyway.

I invited her to be on the same panel at the ABA that John Rechy was on. After all, she had a name. She sent me a cordial note saying that she couldn't because she was finishing a book, *Southern Discomfort*, I believe.

That did not bother me. What bothered me was that Rita Mae Brown was so well-known as a writer. I thought she had written one decent book, *Rubyfruit Jungle*, while the others were embarrassing and, for me, unfinishable, if not downright unreadable.

I had discussed *Rubyfruit Jungle* with Elaine Noble, the Boston elected official, when she spoke at Fresno State and I, as faculty advisor for the gay students group, had given her a lift to the airport. She and Rita Mae were lovers at the time, and Elaine seemed intrigued by my comments on her lover's book, especially the negative ones. Hmm.

Why was Rita Mae Brown so famous? Randy Shilts called her "mediagenic," a word that made me gag, but I knew what he meant. She was physically attractive, slim, energetic, and not "dykey."

When *Rubyfruit Jungle* was picked up by Bantam, it became a bestseller, as did a number of her other novels. The style seemed to be lousy, with writing like "Hello, Tom, my older brother" and endless "She chuckled's" and "he stated's" and the like. Was great popularity dependent on having a tin ear yourself?

Sure, I knew why she was doing so well. I just didn't want to acknowledge the low level of taste in gay/lesbian readers, whom I wished to endow with greater powers of literary discrimination. What I hadn't counted on quite so much was the ravenous need in many such readers to be told they were wonderful. Rita Mae told lesbians, gay men, blacks, and other outcasts that they were smarter and better than their enemies, and they ate it up. I thought readers would appreciate knowing they weren't any worse than anybody else, but that just goes to show how little I know about appealing to people's basic needs.

I chalked Rita Mae's work up to the therapy phase for minorities in American literature. I didn't believe that she'd be read down the pike; in fact, she'd go into that great Trash Heap in the Sky where most pop sellers have always gone. In the meantime she lived in mansions, had affairs with international tennis stars, was interviewed everywhere, got paid handsomely for TV and movie scripts, and seemed to have a whole lot more fun than I did.

C. D. ARNOLD

Now here was a good writer, a playwright, who wasn't nearly as well known as Rita Mae Brown. Why? Because he lived and wrote in S.F. Some years after I first knew him C.D. moved to NYC, but he came back with his tail between his legs, as I knew he would when he went off with a haughty attitude about S.F. He said he was treated badly, for the most part, when he tried to get his plays put on in the Big Apple.

C.D. was a nice-looking, slender man with a very engaging manner, his looks and the manner both contributing to his S.F. success, I suspect. He knew how to make friends in the places that count, and he did it without seeming to be a conniver. He got in with Allan Estes of Theatre Rhinoceros and had any number of plays produced there as well as with Earnest Players and the One Act Theater Company.

When the One Act was selecting its eight invited playwrights for its One Act II stage, both C.D. and I were considered for the "gay" slot, a sad commentary on the Affirmative Action policies in the "art" of politically correct S.F. That is, take one black, one Asian, two women, one white man, etc. Talent by quota! Fortunately for me I was picked over C.D. I know he was incensed at the pickers, maybe at me.

But he went on with his plays poetic, delicate plays, some stronger than others. Sometimes they didn't seem quite finished, and also they required professional actors to bring the poetry to life. Unhappily for C.D. what he usually got were young men with effeminate voices and absolutely no body control. He did get some one-acts published by Terry

Helbing's JH Press in NYC and had a production there as well, but the theater world didn't exactly pursue him, the way it did Harvey Fierstein.

I used to drop by to visit C.D. when he lived a block away on Van Ness Avenue. The Victorian was all torn up because C.D.'s ex-lover and his current one, both of whom he lived with, were re-doing the entire place to make it into an inn for out-of-town visitors. (Later the owners found that there was more money in straights than in gays, and it changed its advertising and prospered.)

During these visits, I thought of myself as the slightly older, more mature artist paying his calls of respect on the up-and-coming, to impart words of wisdom. Somewhere or other C.D. said something that led me to believe he didn't know much about my work and even considered himself better than me! But then youth is usually impertinent, and we must be tolerant, mustn't we?

C.D. had worked for some years as an accountant before he started writing plays. He never struck me as well read or deeply trained in the theater. He just sort of gushed out these stage poems. He was most fortunate in having an ex-lover, of all things, who believed in him and supported him. Every time I had to grade a set of crummy English compositions from a junior college I was drenched with envy of C.D., who didn't have to work.

I met his ex-lover, of Greek extraction, named Tony, any number of times. The one I most distinctly remember is the opening party for C.D.'s *Morning Metro,* where I sat on a sofa and listened to this man brag about C.D.'s play. He was getting very thin and almost feeble, especially for someone in his thirties. It was indeed AIDS, and Tony was dying. Weren't we all? Only he died within the year. Alas, *Morning Metro* also died. Without question, it was the weakest C.D. Arnold play I'd ever seen. It was like somebody telling you his dreams for two hours, and you know how boring that is! Moreover, the set was annoying, and some of the actors had anti-charisma. Members of the audience in the front row even fell asleep and snored. And yet C.D.'s ex-lover had loved the play, or so he had said. It was a bomb with most other audience members, however, and pretty much killed C.D.'s career at Theatre Rhinoceros.

The only squabble I had with C.D. was when I put something in my *Coming Up* newspaper column, Things That Need To Be Said, that upset him. The play was *King of the Crystal Palace* and concerned love and drugs. The play certainly seemed to be condemning drug abuse, and yet a very reliable authority told me that C.D. himself had gotten high on drugs at the cast party. I thought this was worth a blind item. Of course it was obvious to anyone in the right circles that I was referring to C.D. Arnold. I shouldn't have done it, but it appealed to my sense of irony. I heard from several other very reliable sources that C.D. was furious with me. I should mention that C.D. got over it and later asked me to please plug *Morning Metro* in my column, and I did, happily, saying there was much anticipation about it. Theater folk have short memories when they need you for something else, and I include myself here.

The most recent memory of C.D. that I have is a strange, mumbly telephone message from him on my answering machine, following a review of my novel *The World Can Break Your Heart* (1984) in the *S.F. Sentinel*. It was a good review yet containing a number of swipes at me and my bleak world vision, but a money review in the sense that it probably made people want to read the book. At least it had made C.D. want to read it. He said he couldn't afford to buy it, but he'd like to trade a book of his published plays for a copy. I tried to get back to him to complete the deal, but he had to move and one thing and another, and so it didn't take place.

I have frequently praised C.D.'s work in print, because I thought in the past and still think that he is a natural talent with a great deal to give the theater world. I wonder what will happen to him. For that matter, what will happen to us all?

FELICE PICANO

The one time I heard Felice Picano speak, he was rather good. It was during his promotional tour of *The Lure*, the occasion a talk before the Gay Academic Union in a branch of the S.F. Public Library. Picano looked like a young teller in an Italian bank, the hair frizzed, the suit tight.

My clearest memory is his saying that his five earlier books, all of which had been non-gay, had received far more coverage than the new gay one, even though it was coming out from a major press with a big ad campaign behind it. Welcome to the fold, I thought.

When we spoke privately afterwards, not much of consequence took place, so it's a little amazing that Felice Picano became the person with whom I have had the most unpleasant experiences of any figure in modern gay literature.

It may have originally sprung from the fact that he didn't ask me to submit my stories to an anthology he was bringing out, while he'd accepted two from Beau Riley, my unpublished writer friend. So I wrote and asked if he was still accepting submissions. He said he was pretty full but that he would look at my things. He sent them back, saying he didn't like them well enough to throw out what he'd already accepted. I think the crux of the matter is that he obviously didn't know who the fuck I was.

I had read *The Lure* and knew it to be a total potboiler, another worthless "bestseller" piece of shit. How dare this man be in such a prominent position in Gay Letters! Some people told me Picano's poetry was better than his prose, but I couldn't bring myself to read it. He and I would turn up in short story anthologies together as the years wore on, and I always thought he was without a shred of literary value. And yet he seemed to be controlling gay literature in NYC. He was the book editor of *The New York Native* and even started his own press, Seahorse, and then became part of New York Gay Presses. Was everybody blind to Picano's hack status? Was it mere personal charm that made him effective in his publishing ambitions? I read another novel of his, *Late in the Season*, which wasn't quite as junky as *The Lure*, but still a pop book. Moreover, it contained pretentiousness up the gazoo, references to "in" artists or writers, a few foreign phrases misused, thrown about by some no-nothing literary poseur. I had a Ph.D. in literature, and could have shown off, yet I wouldn't have presumed to make shallow allusions the way Picano was doing. I thus began to think that the educational level of the NY literary world was beneath contempt in its trendiness and shallowness. I thus couldn't stop myself from reviewing the paperback of *The Lure* and saying some of these things. I also wrote a stinging satire of Picano, called "The Blur," showing him as a three-year-old girl who thinks "*Gesundheit!*" is an existentialist comment out of Heidegger.

I sent this parody around to a number of the NY publications. Again and again I got the message back: "This is hilarious, delicious, but we dare not run it." How could this Picano hack hold so much power? It was amazing to me, but then I guess I've always assumed, mistakenly no doubt, that quality ran the show from the top. The satire is included in Alyson's *Wilma Loves Betty*, if anyone cares.

Picano got his revenge for my review of his novel – although I don't know if he ever saw the parody – by reviewing my *Human Warmth and Other Stories* in *The Native* when it appeared from Grey Fox Press in 1981. He reviewed Richard Hall's collection at the same time, praising Hall, damning me. I was glad for Richard Hall's sake, because it might help sales, but at the same time who wanted to be praised by a total nincompoop who talked about Chekhov and Somerset Maugham in the same breath as if he didn't have a clue as to the status of Maugham in the book world? He could have said he liked Maugham, but only an ignoramus wouldn't try to protect himself by letting the reader know he knew Maugham to be the first of the second-rate. But then Felice Picano himself was the first of the second-rate and didn't know his ass from his elbow when it came to books. I began to see him as the Archfiend, the Anti-Christ of serious gay literature. No doubt I exaggerated his importance. He wasn't worth getting so worked up about, except that I cared about gay literature and how the rest of the world would look at it. I saw Felice Picano as giving us all a bad name. I wanted us to be great writers and have great biographies written about us, to have us taught in the universities, to be wonderful and permanent. So Felice Picano was an embarrassment to us all.

Could it be he had Mafia connections and that's how he managed to wield power? Yes, that must be it. He was the gay nephew of a Cosa Nostra don who had set him up in gay publishing, knowing that would keep him out of the world's spotlight.

I tried to make up with Picano one time, by sending him a note saying we could not like each other's work and still remain friendly. I got back a postcard with some drivel about the duchess's dinner party, or some damn thing like that, an illustration of the queenly humor that prevails in some gay literature circles. Those girls really must get over it. Liking literature does not have to mean you're a raving sissy. Does it? (Satires don't count.)

I have a confession to make. I did something I'm a little ashamed of. Nothing up till now, though.

You see, there was a very bad review of *The World Can Break Your Heart* in *The Advocate*, a review so bad that I had not yet read it. Naturally my friends couldn't wait to inform me of just how awful it was. It was written by Dennis Cooper, a minor writer whom I'm not including in these memoirs because you'll probably never hear of him outside this anecdote. Well, this Cooper had left L.A. and gone to NYC to make his way since you can't do it from the West Coast. He aligned himself with Felice Picano and Horse's Ass Press (Excuse me, I mean Seahorse Press.) The word was out that Picano was even going to publish a second book by this writer. It seemed to me that Picano and Cooper were in cahoots to badmouth my novel in print. It may have been one of Cooper's means of ingratiating himself with Picano. Maybe he just hated my novel on his own. In either case, he deserved to die as far as I was concerned.

Now I've seen writers answer bad reviews in the press, and they always sounded defensive and unconvincing, showing a lack of seriousness about their art. I'd do better than that. I decided I would have a friend in another city, unbeknownst to him, mail two letters written by a certain "Dennis." One of these letters went to Mark Thompson at *The Advocate*, saying that "Dennis" felt he was suffering from a nervous breakdown and didn't want to review any more books, so none should be sent him. The other letter went to Felice Picano and said something like: "I want to withdraw my new manuscript from your press. I don't feel it's any good at all. Please destroy it. I have also felt guilty about having you publish it because I've been downgrading you behind your back."

It seemed a wonderful idea at the time. Kill Dennis Cooper's reviews and his new novel with one fell swoop. Adequate payment for trying to destroy my baby, that is, my novel. I didn't really think either letter-receiver would fall for the prank, but if they had, I would have felt good, like Hamlet forcing poison down Claudius's gullet. I found out from somebody that I was the prime suspect. Who me? I just write my books and mind my own business.

By the way, I have written notes of thanks to various reviewers who have written nice reviews of my work. Do you want to hear about them? . . . For instance, I was nice to . . . Of course you don't want to hear such things. Case closed?

WILLIAM DICKEY

Did not think to put poet William Dickey in my original list of people to write about. He just now popped into my head. He's one of those gentlemen who have gone in and out of the closet. I met him at the MLA when I was trying to drum up subscriptions to *Gay Literature*, the literary journal I was starting. I believe Dickey bought a copy. Now that I think about it, he even contributed something, some fancy calligraphy.

He was well into middle-age then, a large, rawboned man with longish hair. (Ethan Frome comes to mind.) He was a professor, sometimes a department chairman, at San Francisco State, and a respected poet.

He invited me to visit him at his Liberty Street Victorian home one time, and I did. We sat and talked for a long while, and the sexual tension was so thick you could have cut it with a penis. I knew he wanted to go to bed even though we said nothing, but I had my doubts. I had gone to bed with my agent in London once, and it had killed a good literary relationship. I was afraid the same would happen with William Dickey. I also had a slight drip that could have been gonorrhea, although I wasn't sure.

But sex being sex, an overture was made, by one side or the other, and soon enough we were in Mr. Dickey's bed. I don't believe it was a satisfactory occasion for either party. I had a hard time getting erect, mostly because I'd been having a lot of sex in the baths. I remember a large organ on Mr. Dickey but recall little else. Afterwards, I asked directions to a vegetarian restaurant, we said our awkward good-byes, and I knew we would probably never see each other again. Mystery, the possibility of sex would have been much better than the real thing.

I sent Dickey a copy of *Something You Do in the Dark*, because that's what authors do and because I didn't want the relationship to founder on the rocks of sex. Somewhere or other I recall him saying he found my book too grim, too ugly, too painful; it would drive people away from gay life!

So a combination of bad sex and a very delicate poetic sensitivity left me out in the cold with Mr. William Dickey, and I was never even interviewed when I tried to get a creative writing job at San Francisco State. There's a lesson here, boys and girls. . . . But what is it?

JOHN GILGUN

Another person I met through my literary journal was John Gilgun, one more casualty of modern literature. John was a very talented writer who sent me a story, which I published. We began to correspond, often, and we met in person a number of times. He was a little older than me, not exactly attractive, hard of hearing, with a fish-like mouth, with the voice of some creature trapped in a deep hole in the ground. Deep voices usually turn me on. Not here.

In a sense, that hole Gilgun lived in was literal, the place where John had found himself through ill fortune and the times. He lived in St. Joseph, Missouri, god help him, and taught at a four-year college. He complained constantly in his letters of his loneliness, his sexual frustration, his hatred for the dumb clucks around him. But John wanted financial security, so he kept that job. It was more complicated than that, because he would do things that contributed to his own imprisonment.

He had a Ph.D. from Iowa's writing program. He had even had his dissertation novel accepted for publication by Lippincott. Only Lippincott never published it. How awful for John. The title was one I always loved, *America Can Break Your Heart*, and, yes, I asked John permission to name my book *The World Can Break Your Heart*, an allusion to a line in Auden, I learned later. I didn't think John ever recuperated from this first literary heartbreak.

For instance, he couldn't seem to get away for trips during the long college summers, he said, because he had sub-let his house once and the tenant had harmed some furniture or something. Another time he couldn't go because he had to buy furniture for the whole house. Why he had to fill his whole house with furniture when he said he had no company escaped me. I attributed it all to that Irish depressive temperament which I share. Brood and suffer.

For years John tried to get published, and he did succeed in getting some short stories into various publications. But buried in Missouri he didn't have many contacts. Finally I got Donald Allen of Grey Fox Press, my publisher, to agree to read *Green*, which was Gilgun's re-write of *America Can Break Your Heart*. Don liked it and wanted to publish it; however, he was pinched financially right then and asked me if Gilgun would mind paying part of the expenses himself. I said that I thought Gilgun would be hurt if asked to do that. So Don gallantly agreed to publish it anyhow.

Suffused with joy about my good deed, I wrote Gilgun to tell him the news. I got back a telephone call in which he said, "Now just who is this Donald Allen and who is this Grey Fox Press?" He persisted in this haughty tone even with Don Allen himself. Don Allen had published Ginsberg and Frank O'Hara and plenty of other important names, and, besides, Gilgun was in no position to turn up his nose at Grey Fox Press, small press though it was. He even asked Don Allen to hold off for a while, because an agent in NYC had agreed to read this manuscript! That was like saying you had bought a lottery ticket! Naturally Donald Allen withdrew his offer to publish the novel. So John Gilgun had lost out twice on the same book. You don't fuck yourself up the second time. You just don't.

The bitter letters from Missouri continued. Gilgun threw out his TV one night when Morley Safer on *Sixty Minutes* did a homophobic piece on child porn. Gilgun was terrified of anyone discovering he was gay. Gilgun had nobody to talk with. He'd go visit his old lover, Larry, in Des Moines, who also lived in dread of being discovered to be gay. This was modern life?

Then things started to improve. He met somebody in the baths in Kansas City, a counter-tenor teaching temporarily in Kansas. Sex bloomed. Good for John, I thought. Sing out, Louise! It went on for some months; then the singer died of some mysterious cancer. It was probably AIDS before we knew what to call it. More bitter, sad letters arrived, almost as sad as those from my aging mother and sister in Illinois.

John wanted us to collaborate long distance on a book, but I was wrapped up in my neo-Shakespearean play and didn't have the time. He was irked, said there were enough Shakespearean plays already. (I heard it from the grapevine.)

Then John got on the jogging bandwagon. He was running umpteen miles every day. He felt better. He went swimming. He started using Nautilus equipment. His body got hard and gorgeous; his sex life improved. He'd go to the baths and pig out. Then "AIDS" got a name, a bad one, and John had to pull back. He was lonely again. He got promoted; he took a few trips to California. A life was going on.

The biggest thing that happened to him was that a small press published his collection of beast fables in a very expensive edition with some woodcuts that won three important publishing awards for the woodcuts, not the prose as such. But

John was still the happiest I had ever known him. Yet it must have rankled a bit to know that it wasn't his writing but the illustrations that were winning the prizes.

John's melancholy abated, but did not completely go away. He came out to his aunt and uncle in California, but the openness stopped there. I was convinced he carried around a huge weight of guilt about his sexuality. Fear of the world's reaction paralyzed him in many ways. A student saw one of John's stories in a gay anthology. Did that mean Dr. Gilgun was a homosexual? John was proud of himself because he didn't deny it. That's what liberation meant to him.

He came to S.F. and called to say that he would be in touch with me on such and such a morning. So of course I waited for his call. Several days passed. John didn't even seem aware that he had kept me on tenterhooks wondering what had happened to him. I had no way of calling him. Oh, no, nothing was wrong, he said. He'd just decided to go somewhere else with some other friends. Oh? I began to think John Gilgun was like so many "sensitive" artists I've known -- not the least bit sensitive about other people's feelings.

The semi-last straw came when John wrote, asking me to please tell him how to go about self-publishing *Green*, the novel that Grey Fox Press would have published if Gilgun hadn't been so haughty, the one the NYC agent had returned of course.

So I wrote a long, long letter detailing every aspect of doing a book yourself, from printers to cover design. But John didn't do the book then. He decided to wait. Okay.

A year or so went by. Then I got another frantic plea for

information on how to self-publish his book. Hadn't he kept my letter? I had spent hours telling him once, and I wasn't about to do it again. Who knew he might decide not to do it this time either. I found it increasingly hard to feel sorry for John Gilgun.

WALTER ALLEN

Wrote to Walter Allen about 1978 or 1979 to see if he might be willing to give a blurb for the reprint of *Something You Do in the Dark*. I sent a copy along. I valued his opinion highly because he was the author of that definitive study, *The Modern Novel*. I was trying then, as I am trying now, to get major critics to include gay books of quality, preferably mine, in the mainstream. What a pleasant, marvelous surprise, then, to receive a letter back saying, yes, he was willing to let my publisher quote him about my book, which he had found "powerful and engrossing." I was thrilled.

I wrote back to thank him. His second letter was even more interesting than his first. In it he talked about his own sex life, mentioning that he was married, with grown children, but that he had a homosexual component, yet he confessed that real sex was never quite as good as fantasy sex. And what was his favorite fantasy? To be dressed up like a British housewife and abused by her working-class husband. Oh dear.

You can laugh or you can cry at this revelation. I think I did both. On the one hand, Walter Allen represented all the erudition and academic elegance of British higher education and yet he secretly longed to be an abused housewife. On the other hand, he must have lived a very restricted and unsatisfactory sex life. On yet another hand – my third – Walter Allen represented those generations of scholars and critics who were homosexual or bisexual themselves and still went out of their way to leave out, obscure, or obliterate the legitimacy of the gay presence in literature. These men and women were so terrified of the stigma they worked overtime to make it hard for us openly gay serious newcomers to get a mention edgewise. I include here such men as editor William Abrahams of *Prize Stories* and Walter Clemons of *Newsweek*, plus a whole lot more that I didn't know about at the time. Some of these came around very late in the game. Thanks a lot for your courage when it was needed most, boys!

The fact was that a great percentage of the world's literature and other art has been produced by its homosexual minority, far, far out of proportion to our actual numbers, and yet we have continually been assailed and excluded. Assholes like Christopher Lehmann-Haupt could continue to write reviews in *The New York Times* that spoke of inherently inferior gay writers, when the truth was that gay writers provided a vast treasury of art to the world.

It's only been in the past few years that certain cautious biographers have begun to spell out the private lives of Henry James, Proust, D. H. Lawrence, Virginia Woolf, and so on, and at least some of the literate world is becoming aware of the truth. I feel at times that it's a war between the Heterosexual Establishment and the gay upstarts, each side trying to claim the biggest names it can for its prestige. I don't want to claim everybody, but I feel very strongly that the public image of homosexuals would increase a hundredfold if the greatness of our clan, in all its individuality and multiplicity, was as common knowledge as the scores of baseball games.

Martin Greif, the editor of *The Gay Engagement Calendar*, deserves much credit for his series of witty and expository calendar entries about the hordes of gays in the arts and in other major fields throughout history.

Greif told me that Patricia Holt, the closeted book editor of the *San Francisco Chronicle*, told him he was wrong to unearth the sex lives of the dead. It's people like her that keep the taboo burning. There may be an ethical question about naming the names of homosexuals who do not want to be identified as such, but the other side of the issue is that there is nothing shameful about being homosexual. Indeed, it's something to be jubilant about, and the danger of the future will no doubt be, once our contributions are fully acknowledged, the swarms of people rushing to claim their gay roots. We may find, in fact, heterosexuals trying to pass as homosexuals! Maybe they'll even get shock treatments to change their orientation.

In the case of Walter Allen, I didn't understand why he was so candid with me, someone he didn't even know, unless it was the pressure to let it all out as his life neared its end. You see, actually it was his son who relayed Allen's permission to quote Allen; he wasn't able to respond himself since he'd had a heart attack. I suspect he's dead now, and I am grateful that he did at least this one brave thing before he died.

LELAND MELLOT

Leland Mellott was a poet who was totally fluent in English, French, and Spanish. He also turned out to be my second lover's former lover. (I think Leland always held that lover against me.) His fate was like something out of a Greek myth, American-style.

Bearded Mellott used to put on a knit cap, a long overcoat, roller skates, and hand out flyers on the streets. I forget if these were his actual poems or just advertisements for his readings. I should have noted that this dressing up as a sign of a personality not quite all there, if the poetry alone wasn't enough of a sign. Come on now, how many sane poets have you known?

I met Mellott when he was working for some archival group funded by federal or city money in those days of yore when such pre-Reagan joys existed. But Leland didn't keep that job for long because he was ousted by middle- and upper-class Hispanics who came to this country and took away his position; you see, they had *Spanish* surnames and he didn't. The irony was that they had wealthier, more privileged backgrounds than he did, but the funding was for Hispanic this-or-that, and so Hispanic it was. It was all part of the corrupt spoils system for so-called "minorities" (already out-numbering the "majority") that will probably lead to a rebellion.

Anyway, he agreed to "publish" my collection of stories called *The Revolt of the Perverts*; that is, he provided a name and an address and some input with printers. I provided the money and the promotion. The book has sold pretty well over the years, and I know Mellott was in fact bothered by a number of writers who wanted him to publish them, too.

Years went by, and I'd pass Mellott on the street from time to time. He was working in crummy jobs. Then he wasn't working at all. He'd have long, hard bouts of depression that I'd hear about from his ex, now also my ex. Little chapbooks of his poetry would appear from time to time, self-published, unread.

And then he was discovered by a Broadway composer who wanted to make his chapbooks into a musical, and that musical became an international hit on seven continents! (You're right. Didn't happen. Mellott dropped out of sight. He and his poetry were virtually invisible.)

Then I started receiving missives in the mail, and I wasn't the only one. My ex-lover got some as well. I'd also see letters to the editor in various newspapers from Mellott expressing some of the same ideas in the pastiches of poetry and clippings about chemical wastes that came in the mail, followed by long generic letters to us all about how Mellott had experienced a fantastic infusion of light. The letters called for a response, for sharing of this illumination. I must admit the letters frightened me. I thought Leland Mellott had gone off the deep end but good. I didn't answer any of his letters. I was afraid he'd illuminate me. There but for the grace of God, and all that.

The letters didn't stop for several years. I received a notice for a poetry reading by Mellott. I should have gone, but I couldn't make myself. I had visions of him wearing even funnier clothes than he used to and zapping the audience with laser beams.

I know it's necessary to do something to get attention for your work, but it didn't seem to be a gimmick for Mellott; it was too real. I had that feeling that you get when someone you know starts talking to himself while you're still there.

He became a symbol for me of the pathetic state of poets in contemporary times. I think they're even worse off than the prose writers. Nobody pays attention; nobody cares; you could go crazy and the world would go on watching its music videos and not even notice. Even the gays are slurping beer and watching high-gloss trash like *Dynasty* in the bars. Poor Leland.

STEPHEN SONDHEIM

Clearly it's time to talk about somebody who's a success. Surely Stephen Sondheim qualifies. I don't think he'll mind being identified as gay. I think he's said it on television in fact. And I have it on quite reliable evidence from a sex partner of his, in any case. (Just how kinky I wasn't to know until years later.)

Sondheim is one of those people I've never met in person, but we have corresponded. And Dan Turner tells me Sondheim asks about me from time to time. I once sent him a collection of my stories, but he said he didn't get much time to read. I thought that was interesting. All his energy goes into his music?

I sent him a review by Gerald Nachman of *Sweeney Todd* published in the *San Francisco Chronicle* to see what kind of a rise I'd get. I know the danger in being a bearer of bad news, but I sent the bad review anyway. I myself loved *Sweeney Todd,* and I was using the review to show the aesthetic denseness of Nachman, who was everything the middle-aged, straight, bourgeois booberie represented.

Sondheim wrote back a blast about Nachman, saying that if he had any real talent he wouldn't be a critic but a creative person. Actually I don't believe that old canard since I'm both a critic and a "real" writer. But it was nice to know that even Sondheim got incensed at negative reviews. Since this time, I've been devouring biographies of the great, and I'm comforted by the fact that even they, yes, even they, had their depressions and their despairs, their rejections, their feuds.

In my heart of hearts I'm sure I hoped that Stephen Sondheim would convert one of my books into a fabulous musical. But of course he wouldn't be Stephen Sondheim if he used gay material in his shows. That's a no-no. Not that I always write gay; it just seems the freshest material. Right this minute I feel worried and guilty because perhaps too many of my memories are gay ones. Straights do not have to worry that all their memories are straight ones. (Am I bitter? Yes, and I want to change the world.)

Take Sondheim's *Company*, for instance. All that bother about an unmarried man amidst his married friends. It's obvious that he's gay. But if gay artists were permitted to write about gay characters in the proportion that really exist in the lives of the artists themselves they would have a hell of a time getting non-gays to look at their work. Heterosexuals want to hear about themselves, and they find it difficult to project themselves into queer shoes, and I don't see this altering in any significant way for the foreseeable future the next thousand years, say. So gay artists are sort of like hired hands that aren't allowed to eat with the real folks indoors unless they play along, and even some of them get pilloried, like Albee and Tennessee, for heterosexualizing their gay characters. Damned if you don't, and unproduced if you do.

Sondheim had a Broadway flop with *Merrily We Roll Along*, and thus he had to workshop *Sunday in the Park with George* to get it produced. Luckily for him it was a success and won a Pulitzer and kept the Sondheim myth alive. Actually *George* is rather on the pale side dramatically, but I think everybody wanted to make sure that Sondheim, one of our few living treasures, didn't get dumped by the Broadway system. The man is an interesting anomaly, because he obviously doesn't give a hoot about the heterosexual love affairs he has to put into his musicals (because they're expected and required), and his real interests lie not even in other kinds of sexuality but in musical motifs, the problems of the outsider in society. It's odd that he chooses to embody his concepts in Broadway musicals, where the audience usually demands something other than what he wants to give, excluding his earlier shows like *West Side Story* and *Gypsy*, where it isn't Sondheim's soul so much as his lyrical talent that is being put to use.

Anyway, Stephen Sondheim inspires these thoughts about how much one can be "out" about your subject matter and still have widespread appeal. Dan Turner's music is not as professsionally trained and orchestrated as Sondheim's, but it's every bit as beautiful.

Turner sent Sondheim several of tapes of our various musicals, including *Cinderella II*, which was produced in S.F. in 1984. Intriguing that Sondheim's next show was a fairy tale, with Cinderella as one of the characters. Sondheim himself recognized the implication and wrote to Dan to say that he'd been thinking about such a subject for some time and didn't want us to think he'd stolen anything from us. Hmm. The Narrator from the Brothers Grimm perhaps, as it shows up in *Into the Woods*? Or having Cinderella bored with her prince? ... It's not important. But we did *Cinderella II* first! (not that the world knows this.)

I knew Dan and I should've moved to NYC if we wanted to get our musical wares seen in the place where the theatrical lights shine brightest. Maybe *Cinderella II* would have opened instead of *Into the Woods*. I'm not exaggerating when I say it was more exciting to every audience who saw it in S.F. than *George in the Park* ever was. Dan and I got compliments on it for years. Location, location, location.

Mr. Sondheim, you sure you don't want me to write the book of your next show?

As for the kinky part, after Dan Turner's death from AIDS, we discovered tons of spanking material and even a film that Dan Turner had done. He'd never said a word to me about being into spanking. Well, now I guess I know why Sondheim didn't seem worried when I told him Dan had died of AIDS.

ARTHUR BRESSAN

Artie Bressan and I got off to a bad start because the filmmaker didn't like something I did, that is, hand out flyers to call attention to the midnight show of "Beneath the Surface," a play of mine that very few people were attending (1979).

It was an Earnest Players production about a group of minorities trapped in a subway train in a tunnel, with the air evaporating, all their many bigotries and hatreds surfacing. I've never thought for one second that white people are the only ones with prejudices. For some reason that I still don't fathom, Artie Bressan objected to my leafleting the people waiting to get into his film *Gay U.S.A.* at the Castro Theater a couple of blocks away from my theater. It wasn't as though I was trying to take away his customers, because our show took place after his. He hadn't even seen the show, so it wasn't that he objected to its theme.

I had worn an eye patch to attract some attention, and maybe partly to disguise myself, so I was feeling self-conscious to begin with when Dan Turner introduced me to Artie near the box office. He was very snotty about the leaflets and told me to stop.

As I write this I am filled with anger all over again. Who the fuck did he think he was, telling me I couldn't hand out flyers to the general public! He was the most aggressive, self-promoting person I'd ever met; he wouldn't have hesitated to give out flyers for his movie at my play, if there had been any customers there!

I carried this grudge around for years. He had made me feel humiliated, since I loathe doing things like hawking my goods on street corners and in a stupid eye patch to boot and then to be assailed for it. So I avoided Artie Bressan and his movies for years. I don't much care for porn movies anyway, and that's what he seemed to be making.

I came to realize that Artie wanted to make more serious movies, and eventually he did with *Abuse* and *Buddies*. He had to do porn to make the money to finance movies he could be prouder of. Even in his hardcore work he tried to include some storyline, some humanity.

Bressan was very intelligent, very New York. He was always articulate and insightful, and he helped Dan Turner and David Lamble with several projects. He got better looking after he overcame hepatitis, cut his long hair, and lost some weight. Still, I just never felt comfortable around him. I found him too pushy, and he also liked chicken (very young men) and so we had nothing in common there.

Dan Turner showed one of our musicals to Artie, and I agreed to meet with him and Dan to hear his comments about it. I wasn't looking forward to this get-together, but it proved to be worthwhile. Artie gave us some judicious advice. I even drove him somewhere later.

We didn't become friends. Nevertheless we interacted more. But I always felt that Artie Bressan wasn't very giving. In particular I remember the morning of a Gay Freedom Day Parade, the very day Patricia Holt had called my novel *From Violent Men* amateurish. I had tried to kill myself in the garage, but then I vowed I'd "kill" Patricia Holt instead. I felt terrible, but I forced myself to go to the parade alone, desperate for some support. When I ran into Artie and told him about the harsh mention in the paper, I expected some soothing words, even insincere ones, from a fellow artist. Instead, I got a smirk and something like, "You think that's bad? I once got a terrible review in such-and-such." Now, you must believe me, even if I haven't shown much evidence in what you've read so far, that I have frequently commiserated with my fellow artists when they have had hard times. I could regale you with numerous examples, but I'm not especially trying to make myself look good here, just inform and entertain you. Am I doing a good job at that?!

I felt very sorry for myself that day, and Artie Bressan wasn't giving me even one stroke. Perhaps from his point of view I felt sorry for myself too easily. No doubt that's true. That still doesn't make me like Artie Bressan, though I respect him and some of his movies.

ROBERT CHESLEY

Somebody I liked much more was playwright Robert Chesley, whom I also met via the same "Beneath the Surface" because he came to review it for *The San Francisco Bay Guardian*. He hadn't written any plays then, or at least hadn't had any produced; he was a critic.

He introduced himself after the play, and we went out for a drink. He was a slender young man with wire glasses and a pronounced British accent. When I said that I had lived in England from 1970-72, he explained that his accent wasn't genuinely British, "just affected."

We got along quite well, and I managed even to get a quotation from his review to use in the advertising, although I think Bob was put off by the unflattering portraits of minorities, including, by the way, the Gay Man and the Lesbian, in my play. It was such differences in political attitudes that were to interfere in our friendship later on.

Bob started taking me to plays. In fact, I was going with him to see a work by Camus when John Gettys, a man I'd had sex with, called and wondered what I was doing. I invited him along with Bob and me, and, lo and behold, it was John Gettys who became my partner and still is, all these years later.

I don't know if Chesley ever entertained thoughts of having sex with me. I flirted with the idea, but I thought it would be better to have a friend rather than a fuck. Another friend pointed out to me that Chesley showed a big basket (a promise of a large penis, for any nuns reading this). I really hadn't noticed. Strange that way, I didn't know you were supposed to look for such things.

I liked Bob a lot; he was bright and droll, very interested in the arts, but he had awful body language. By that I mean he couldn't stand still for a second without twisting every which way. Too un-masculine to attract me sexually. Later on he got heavily into the S&M scene, which didn't attract me very much either. Little Bob Chesley would come into bars covered with black leather, even gauntlets and stride around with his bad body language. I remember him gloating a bit when AIDS made its appearance,. "Well, you don't get AIDS from the so-called 'impersonal' S&M sex I get criticized for all the time," he said. Right on, baby!

Bob's mother was a Communist, a handicapped Communist, a handicapped Communist with a private income. She would come up from L.A. to visit her son every now and again, especially when he started to have his plays produced. It took a great deal of trouble to get her in and out of cars because of an earlier case of polio, and with increasing age it became even more difficult, but Bob was very loving and dutiful.

His mother was generous and took tablesful of us out to dinner a number of times. Bob himself didn't seem to have to work for a living, although he did clerk at the Walt Whitman Bookshop for a time, until Charles Gilman fired him for fraternizing with the customers instead of watching them for thievery, at least as Chesley told the story. After that, Bob seemed not to work at all, while maintaining an apartment in S.F. and a room in NYC, truly a bi-coastal gentleman. I admit a mix of feelings about Chesley's very leftist socio-political sentiments and his very capitalistic private income. Give up the income, and let's see if you still have the same sentiments, I thought. The middle- and upper-class -- you've got to love their naiveté.

Bob had taught in a private school in NY for many years, had been married for many years, too, before finding his true sexual calling and following that call to S.F.

Chesley and I had many lunches, dinners, and other social engagements together. I suppose at one time we were best friends. He was good at dragging me to late-night avant-garde shows by people like Bill Talen and Winston Tong, things I would never have gone to on my own.

He also dragged me to drag shows one too many times. I've never relished men in dresses acting like fools, but drag was one of Chesley's greatest treats. One time we went to a Tenderloin bar where a pride of fat queens was putting on "Cinderella," but it was so slipshod I couldn't stand it, and left noisily. To me drag for gays was like "coon shows" for blacks. To Chesley it was liberating, a thwarting of social norms and rules, just like S&M, I suppose.

At times Bob would bring along Mark Chester, a photographer friend of his with tattoos and horrible burns on his arms. Chester held exhibitions of his photos, often of men covered with clothes pins (??) and later wrote reviews for *The Bay Area Reporter*. I guess he and Chesley were starting to have sex at this time; it developed into an affair, before it eventually developed into a fight and a refusal to speak to each other.

But at the start there I'd get these weird invitations from Mark Chester; he wanted to put clothes pins on me or something. Would I have to say "please"? This did not interest me in the slightest, especially with the burn scars on his forearms and the burgeoning beer belly the man was cultivating.

One time in the lobby of Theatre Rhinoceros my partner, John, was talking in a teasing manner with this Mark Chester, who was showing his tattoos through his open shirt. When John reached out to touch Chester's shirt and peek at the flaunted tattoos, all good naturedly, in the spirit of the occasion, Chester suddenly got all bent out of shape, simply because, when he'd reached out for John, John had intercepted his hand. "Why can you touch me, but I can't touch you!" Chester barked. It hadn't meant that at all, and I decided right then that I didn't want to have anything to do with Chester ever again. That meant avoiding Bob Chesley sometimes as well. In fact, I once hid in a storefront near a radio station rather than have to talk to Chester and Chesley. Chester didn't seem to catch on, and one time confronted me somewhere and said, "Don't you remember who I am?" I decided to let it go and say yes. I had enough enemies.

But before all this, Chesley and I would sit in my car outside his Tenderloin apartment (which I always thought an affectation, since he could afford better) and talked and talked. It was one of those times in my life when I really felt I had an intellectual buddy. True, we didn't always agree on everything, especially on what was Politically Correct. I thought Bob tended to react in a body-jerk S.F. leftist way. It wasn't that I was always conservative. I merely thought both the conservatives and the leftists had good points and bad points, especially bad points. I tried to take what I felt was good from each and discard all the rest. Why is it necessary to follow one slate or the other? That's simple-minded. It depends on the individual issue.

The main reason Chesley had moved to S.F. was that he had fallen in love with a male dancer, Christopher Beck, who had his own dance company. I never heard much from Beck himself, but Chesley would alternately bitch and grow enthusiastic about his lover, especially his dance garments, which Chesley found a turn-on. He did publicity for Beck, even helped pay some of his expenses, but he also complained about the two of them getting on each other's nerves in their tiny apartment. What I remember most is Chesley furious at the way Beck, the dancer, would lie in bed and eat candy and be depressed for days at a time. Ah, art!

Eventually Chesley turned from criticism to art himself. His first one-act play was performed at Theatre Rhinoceros. It was a raw replay of Chesley's dying love affair with Christopher Beck, and was better as therapy than as entertainment. Happily Chesley survived that play, and that relationship, and went on to write some very good plays.

He had a real facility for moving right into a power position wherever he was. I often marveled at him. I mean, how many people just show up in S.F. and become the theater critic for *The Bay Guardian* and then go to NYC and get their plays produced, and in L.A. too? His upper-class sense of entitlement worked very well. We peasants just sort of stand by and watch them.

I watched Chesley ingratiate himself with Theatre Rhinoceros. He wasn't above donating money to its fund-raisers. There was even a plaque in the lobby commemorating his contributions.

If it was genuine support of theater, it was also a wise move. I thought you got plays produced by writing good plays and submitting them; it had never crossed my mind to give money to a theater to help them to know me better. That's how dumb I was. I thought it had to do with quality and integrity. The real world is quite different, I see now.

I had to review one of Chesley's early plays, *The Stray Dog Story*, about a man who's come back as a dog, originally entitled *Heart of Dogness*, a much better title, don't you think? The play was put on with a minimum of rehearsal and a maximum of falling sets and last-minute actors, but it was funny. I sighed a sigh of relief, because I could give it a good review. It went on to be produced in NYC and apparently had a much more professional production there. I was glad for Bob's sake.

He started flying back and forth from coast to coast, arranging more productions of his plays. He was extremely prolific, turning them out almost weekly, it seemed. Finally, he decided it was time to move back to NYC. His affair with Christopher Beck was in ashes, and if you wanted attention for your plays, real attention, you had to work out of NYC. So back he went.

Then ensued a series of the most depressing letters in the history of my entire correspondence, maybe in the entire history of the world's correspondence. Chesley made the Count of Monte Cristo, locked in the Chateau D'if, seem like Pollyanna by comparison. Every single letter was filled with black, black anger and misery. He despised NYC and yet he felt he had to stay there.

In one letter he even admitted to having had sex with a gay "reverend," a self-anointed, little bloated toad of a "religious" figure. The thought of Chesley on his knees taking orders from this toad blew my mind, and caused me to doubt Chesley's common sense. Nobody's sex drive could be so virulent that he'd consent to do it with that guy. Finally he had to ask the "reverend" to move out of the guest room because he had managed to annoy the landlord somehow or other, pissing out the window or some such. If you had ever met the toad in question you'd know what I mean when I say Chesley was well rid of that character. (His name was Itkin, by the way.)

Bob finally moved back to S.F., while maintaining the room in NYC so that he'd have a place to stay on his frequent trips there. He started getting more of his plays produced. There were notable productions of *Night Sweats* in NYC, L.A., and S.F. Steven Winn of the *San Francisco Chronicle* gave *Night Sweats* a Sleeping Man review, but then he was a total jerk who shouldn't have been reviewing at all. This review and several other by Winn inspired me to write a piece analyzing the pro's and con's of the three *Chronicle* theater critics, Bernard Weiner, Gerald Nachman, and Steven Wynn, giving them, respectively, a Clapping Man, a Staring Man, and a Sleeping Man, the symbols used by their newspaper. I used a pen name on the article, to protect myself from the wrath of these reviewers should I have more plays of my own, so why I am telling you this secret? Because this is Hell and neither of us shall return to speak of what we've said here, my friend.

Night Sweats was a big hit at the box office, and yet Chesley started having trouble with Theatre Rhinoceros. We had drifted as friends by then, even though I'd picked him up at the airport when he returned to live in S.F. It was mostly my doing, because I couldn't take Bob's Political Correctness about everything anymore. (The world is finally catching up.) I'd still run into him at various functions, so that's how I would learn of his career troubles.

He said he couldn't get Kris Gannon, the artistic director of Theatre Rhinoceros, to read his two new plays, which were called *Pig Man* and *Jerker*. Next he told me that Kris had read *Pig Man* and wouldn't accept it for the theater because it showed "unsafe sex" on stage. I was distressed for Bob's sake, but I also confess I smiled inwardly a bit that the oh-so-politically-correct Bob Chesley was encountering an even more politically correct lesbian in a position to keep him from being produced.

Chesley would actually go to the theater's office and argue his case, something I'd always been extremely reluctant to do, out of a sense of immense pride, misplaced pride, no doubt. I just thought I shouldn't have to go and chat up people or "pitch" my plays; the producers should come to me.

So Chesley was out at Theatre Rhinoceros just as I was "in," "in" to the extent of being a member of the Playwrights Group and having several short pieces produced in the Studio, not exactly the big time, but better than not being produced at all.

But Chesley had found a new boyfriend to help alleviate some of his troubles, a rich boyfriend. The last time I saw him, in between his angry tales of Theatre Rhinoceros, for which he'd done so much, came tales of his travels to Europe. It seems the boyfriend had access to free airplane tickets, so naturally they had to go.

Chesley was an interesting figure in my life. There are two things for which I will always be grateful to him. One was that, when I sent out a begging letter asking for subscriptions to help publish *The Joyful Blue Book of Gracious Gay Etiquette* and received only ten or fifteen subscribers, Bob Chesley came through with $100. I think money, conventional wisdom to the contrary, is one of the sincerest forms of flattery. The other thing I'm grateful for is that one time, when an agent or a publisher rejected a manuscript of mine, and broke off the connection permanently, Chesley was there on the telephone to listen to my sobs and comfort me in my hour of need.

ROBERT PETERS

Don't have a lot to tell about Bob Peters, the poet, although I have an anecdote. I was in his house in Southern California once; he was showing me some of his many published books. Bob, I should mention, was a buffalo of a man: wide face, wide everything. I picked up a book and looked at the nice-looking, thin, young man on the back. "Who's this?" I asked, innocently, if not wisely. "It's me," the much fatter Mr. Peters answered. He looked chagrined.

As I begin to put on more weight myself, even though I don't eat any more than I ever did, I swear, and in fact have used sugar substitute and low-calorie foods for many years, I now appreciate the thoughtlessness of my question to Peters. But I truly hadn't recognized the photo as the same person.

I saw Bob snacking on carrot sticks the next time I ran into him, so maybe I helped him lose some weight. It ain't easy when middle age and your genetic makeup decide to have their day.

The moral here is: When you're young and thin, don't be stupid.

SIMON KARLINSKY

In leaner and happier days, I was friend to Simon Karlinsky, the gifted Russian scholar who has written notable books on Chekhov, Gogol, and many others. He was a professor of Slavic Studies at UC Berkeley, the only man I knew who was always on top of every literary development of our times.

I would run into Simon at all sorts of gatherings, play openings, and the like. He was a very short man, perhaps five-four, in his early fifties when I first met him, bald, bright as a bulb, with a Mongolian cast to his features. He had a lover named Peter, and they seemed quite contented with each other.

It was several years into the friendship before a rather strange episode took place. I had stayed with Simon at least once, I'm sure, when I had visited S.F. from Fresno. Nothing but nice conversations had happened.

Then about 1980 Simon invited me over for dinner. I forget if I knew in advance that it was going to be more than a tête a tête It's possible Simon told me his lover was out of town. In any case, if I spied any hints of what was upcoming, I chose to ignore them or thought I could evade any clumsy situations.

Simon and I dined. I guess I was supposed to be dessert. I'd had some wine and was light-headed but not drunk. As we cleared away the dishes, Simon and I "accidentally" brushed against each other, then fell into each other's arms and kissed. It should have ended there.

But I was invited into the bedroom, and I went, even though I wasn't attracted physically to my host. Before you could say Holy Gorky we had our clothes off and were attempting to make the beast with two backs, or some such configuration.

I'll spare you the details of this total fiasco. Suffice it to say that some sort of orgasm was reached by one, or maybe both, of the parties, followed by a very strained conversation and attempt to re-dress our bodies – if not our private grievances. A code had been broken somehow, the code that says you don't try to turn an intellectual comradeship into mere sex.

DONALD ALLEN

My life took a turn for the better when I met Don Allen in 1980. He was then sixty-eight, white-headed, portly, with a distinguished career in publishing behind him as a Grove Press editor, *Evergreen Review* editor, and especially as the editor of a famous anthology of American poets that pretty much established who was included in and who was included out.

In his senior years Don had decided to start Grey Fox Press in San Francisco to publish gay books, possibly in an attempt to make up for the ones he had skipped over during more repressive days. Whatever his motivation – maybe he even thought there was a little money in gay books – he started bringing them out. In those days I was running IGNA, the International Gay News Agency. Don sent Michael Rumaker's *A Day and a Night at the Baths* for IGNA to review. I liked it, wrote a positive review, which appeared in several publications, and one day this elderly gentleman in a suit, tie, and black overcoat showed up at the office, very cordial, offering to take me to lunch. Never one to turn down a free meal, since I was making $5 per hour then, I gladly went.

Well, that was the beginning of a series of meals with Don Allen. It is to him I attribute learning at last, in my forties, to enjoy wine with food. Before that, I couldn't understand how anybody could think that wine actually tasted good.

At these meals I'd try to get Don to tell anecdotes about Allen Ginsberg, William Burroughs, Richard Brautigan, and other writers he had had dealings with, but I must say Don was very short on anecdotes. Either he didn't have any or he thought it best not to reveal them to me. One time he offered to take me to a party Brautigan was throwing, but nothing came of this. Robert Duncan lived a few blocks from my house, Don said, but he didn't take me there either.

I found myself having to carry the conversational burden much of the time during our dinners, but I was happy to do so, since I was having my way paid. The least you can do is be chatty and charming when you don't have any money.

Don began to talk about publishing a book of mine. Naturally I was thrilled. As usual, I was between publishers, Ashley Books having turned out to be a horror story when it did two of my novels. We discussed doing a collection of short stories. Whoopee! Nobody else seemed to want to do short stories, so why not!

I gave Don the stories I'd had published in magazines since *The Revolt of the Perverts* along with some that hadn't seen print yet. We decided to call the book *Human Warmth and Other Stories* after one of the tales, even though I didn't think it one of my better stories. It was an attempt to bamboozle the poor reader into thinking he was getting less acerbic stories from yours truly. Maybe it was even true.

What I found strange is that Don didn't want to include several of the stories that I thought superior to some we did include, especially one about the Rev. Ray Broshears, a crazy "reverend." Broshears was still alive then, and Don didn't want to risk anything, even though it was fiction and the real name wasn't used in "The Reverend Rat." I've always thought it best to try to sock it to the reader. Better to be daring than bland and safe. But Don Allen was the boss, the publisher, and so I agreed with his decision.

Not a cruel editor, he concentrated on a minimum of alterations in the stories he did choose. I couldn't help feeling a little intimidated by his reputation, since he'd dealt with some of the biggest names in American literature.

He also gave me some work editing a few of his other titles, mostly proofreading, but I didn't hesitate to give my opinions too, whether solicited or not. I was grateful for the job, since I was barely making enough to live on and was not even teaching part-time at City College yet.

John Gettys, my partner, and I would sometimes go out to dinner with Don, and he paid for everything. He decided that he wanted to move from Bolinas in Marin County, where he felt isolated, to S.F., so I arranged for him to rent space with George and Kris, old friends of mine. After a few months there, Don said he wanted to get an apartment of his own, and I helped him move into the new one. He seemed to have saved a lot of money; he couldn't have afforded what he did on Social Security, that's for sure.

It became apparent to me when visiting in his new place again with John Gettys that Don drank more than was good for him. I began to drink socially for the first time in my life, although I never went beyond two or three drinks. (Still true as of 2004!)

I wondered about Don's sex life. Apparently he'd never had a lover; he wasn't very forthcoming about any of that, no doubt from a long history of being "discreet," close-mouthed, in NYC publishing circles. I know that he still had sexual interests because he read porn.

I forget the first time he held my hand, but it was one night after I had driven him to his doorstep. We just sat there in my car holding hands, saying nothing. I had no objection. People need to have their hands held now and then.

Yes, you're right. It created a tension in my soul, because I wasn't sexually excited by my publisher. But I gave him credit for not pushing his attentions on me. We didn't even kiss, just held hands. I should have known that wouldn't be enough.

Then Don asked if I'd like to go to San Diego with him, in his car; he had sold some of his literary archives to the university there and would be getting a tidy sum. It sounded like fun to me. I was so poor I didn't get to go anywhere. He would even pay my expenses, to have the company. We'd even stay overnight on the road so we wouldn't be too tired, you see.

At dinner a night or two before we left, Don said, "Oh, by the way, do you like to have sex with your traveling companions?" Now, how's that for a question for an ambitious writer with a book still not in galleys? I hesitated, then said, "Not particularly." It was the truth, and I was taking a risk, but Don just smiled, ruefully, and said no more.

We went on the trip anyway. We even stayed overnight, sharing a room, with no unseemly behavior on either party's part. Don drove every mile all the way there and all the way back, old as he was, without letting me take the wheel even briefly. We visited the archives staff and started back almost immediately.

Nothing happened on the return trip either. When we got

back to S.F., we would occasionally hold hands in my car, but I was quite open with Don that John Gettys, then twenty-seven, was becoming my lover. I appreciated Don's loneliness, but I didn't want him to get the idea that he and I would develop into a romance. I think I was underestimating the whole situation and its possible pitfalls.

Human Warmth and Other Stories came out; it looked quite nice. I did what I could to promote it. Don seemed to be very old-school, low-key when it came to hustling his titles. For some reason he got mad at me because I did something wrote to somebody about an interview or some such to get the book some attention. I thought this was strange, but it may have been a cover for other feelings that were beginning to emerge.

No doubt I talked too much about the book and my career and my goals with Don, but I thought he'd be fascinated since he was my publisher. I guess I was wrong. I'll never forget the evening when he invited me and my new partner over to his apartment for dinner. My lover was young and handsome, and we were into the hand-holding stage. I tried to curtail too many overt signs of affection between us, because I thought it would hurt Don Allen's feelings, point up too harshly his own single status. Maybe the dike had already been broken emotionally, but he took the opportunity of that dinner party to attack me for most of the evening, my egotism in particular. I won't deny this character deficiency, but I'm pretty sure his anger went deeper than that. After all, he'd spent a lifetime with writers. Everybody who's spent any five minutes with them knows they are monomaniacs, to a man! I think Don finally realized that John and I were really lovers and that meant that the hand-holding in my car was never going to turn into anything more substantial.

My heart churned for Don because I don't think anybody should be without love and sex, especially sex, but at the same time he was so unpleasant to me that night I vowed not to socialize with him anymore.

We kept up appearances, just enough to try to sell *Human Warmth*. (Quaint name, yes? The situation of the title story is a handsomer man trying to avoid the sexual overtures of an older, uglier man.) But we never recovered from that evening. I don't believe Don intended us to. Needless to say, he published no more books of mine.

He did, however, continue to send me books to review. One of his writers, whom I knew via the mails, called me once and asked if I'd mind giving a blurb for the cover of his collection of stories. To be nice, I said sure. But when the unbound copy arrived from Don Allen I was upset by how much sheer pornography the collection contained. The three people who would buy the collection because I recommended it would be mystified that I was urging them to purchase masturbation stories.

So I sent a note to Don Allen saying I couldn't give a blurb. I also told him I was disappointed in him. No doubt he had to pay his bills, and porn sold better than literature, but was this really the direction he was going in as a publisher? I thought it all rather pathetic, as life so often is, this famous editor alone and turning out jack-off stories to cap his career in literature.

JOHN EMBRY

I was introduced to the publisher of the *Drummer* magazine publishing empire by John Rowberry, his long-suffering editor.

From the beginning I was wary of the man because nobody, but nobody, had a good word to say about him. (Unflattering memoirs are still coming out!) Embry had somehow managed to capitalize on the S&M scene with coarse fantasies and liberal doses of tit-rings and big cocks and become rich. There was something sinister about this big, hulking middle-aged man that made me not want to get to know him better. Unfortunately I couldn't avoid him. Even a bout of cancer couldn't make most people shed a tear for this caricature of the ruthless entrepreneur.

Even when Embry's empire was centered in L.A. I had bad experiences with him. Jeanne Barney, a straight woman, was the editor of *Drummer* at that time, and since we were sort of friends I sent her a short play, which she intended to use until Embry read it and said his readers would find it too hard to understand.

When Alternate Publishing (the empire) moved to S.F. I began to be a regular contributor to *The Alternate*, which was John Rowberry's means of keeping his sanity in the midst of daily deluges of S&M sex, which he didn't even engage in himself. Rowberry was able to publish some quality material this way. It likewise allowed him to put up with Embry's temper tantrums, forgetfulness, and financial mismanagement.

I would go to the office often, even did some proofreading to help my spindly budget. Embry had to approve every check, and so sometimes I'd find myself having to wait until a staff member could locate him and get his signature before I could get my money. I would nod hello if I had to, but I didn't want to talk to him any more than I absolutely had to.

His publications were doing well in the late 1970s, and then Embry got too ambitious. He decided to open the Drummer Key Club, modeled after the Playboy Clubs, only for South-of-Market types. Rowberry told me his boss also spent some of the profits on a new house for himself and his lover, plus cars, the usual. The Key Club was a flop, and money became tighter. The empire moved to humbler quarters.

The staff, with few exceptions, came and went like migratory workers. Once or twice even Rowberry resigned. "What's wrong?" I asked. "That man's a liar, a cheat. I can't work for him any longer." But Rowberry would return. He was the only one who could make the empire function.

I'll have to give Embry credit for something. I did see him doing layout for *Drummer* at times, so he wasn't above dirtying his hands. As a matter of fact, he wasn't above dirtying his soul either.

Even when Alternate Publishing began to publish books I did not suddenly cotton to John Embry. But I did submit one of mine to Rowberry, *The Y*. It was accepted and we signed a contract, but then the novel lay around the office for a year or more. When I asked Rowberry why it was taking so long to get the galleys, he said he had to wait to get each book published, in some kind of complicated trade with the printer that printed the magazines. Embry wanted the prestige/sales of real books, but he wanted to do the job on the cheap. So my book lay there, changing titles almost daily, as Rowberry and I discussed calling it something else. We finally settled on *Deathsman*.

About this time poor David Lamble was hired by Embry to run his new newspaper. Lamble worked for a month gathering news stories and features, some from me, only to have Embry bail out at the last minute. He decided to buy the failing *California Voice* from Paul D. Hardman (on the cover of which my lover and I had once appeared, in some other strange publication deal). *California Voice* too disappeared almost at once. Lamble had nothing good at all to say about Embry after working with him, but he usually held his tongue.

I thought I'd been clever in avoiding having to deal with the man directly over quite a number of years, but I was too optimistic. After Rowberry had finally left for good and Steven Saylor (later a writer of gladiator porn, I believe, and formulaic Roman mysteries, in hardcover book form no less) had taken over as editor, I got a call from Steven after I queried him about the status of my novel. He said he thought I should take back the book because the publishing empire was dawdling with its book line and if the book ever did come out most likely it wouldn't receive any promotion. I sighed, but agreed to withdraw the book. Another publisher had expressed interest in it anyhow. (It never came out.)

Steven, in a postscript as I was leaving his office with my novel manuscript, said maybe I should send a clarifying note to Embry, telling him I was taking back the book. This I did.

Well, I began to have second thoughts about mentioning the affair to the unreliable Emperor Embry, and I called Steven to tell him to intercept my letter. But it just so happened that Embry was going through the mail and found my letter a few moments before Steven could snatch it to safety.

I thus got a telephone call from the Evil Emperor himself, telling me that his evil empire wanted my novel. Blah, blah, blah! He even admitted he hadn't known that his firm had accepted a book of mine! "But you signed the contract," I informed him. "I did?" he said. "Nobody around here tells me anything!" He went on and on about how his staff kept things from him.

When I mentioned in passing that I had received a $300 advance, he was very interested. Soon he was saying, "Well, if you don't want us to publish your book, you have to return the $300." Now everybody in publishing knows that authors do not have to return an advance on a book the publisher agrees to publish and then keeps beyond the deadline specified in the contract. The Emperor had already exceeded his deadline by a whole year! But he was so intimidating and I didn't have the contract in front of me, so I'm not sure if I even mentioned this to him.

I couldn't believe how belligerent and obnoxious Embry was in that telephone call. I just wanted to get him off my back, so I said possibly I could return the advance. As soon as I hung up, I said to myself, "He'll rot in chains in an S&M Hell before he sees a penny from me, after what I've been through!"

A letter from the Emperor followed, threatening me with

legal action. I got out my copy of the contact. The asshole hadn't even signed it! So legally he didn't know if I had received an advance or not. In the same letter this charming gentleman said words to this effect: "If you don't give back the $300, you'll never again be published in any of the empire's publications and there aren't that many places to publish."

Can you believe this? I couldn't. I decided not to answer the letter. Steven Saylor said I should just wait, since Embry would no doubt forget about it in a week, just as he forgot about most things.

Needless to say, the Evil Empire began to collapse. What else would you expect with a demented emperor running affairs of state? *Drummer* was sold into new hands, and as a consequence the world had to be a better place.

The only way he'll ever get that $300 is to suck it out of my ass. Then again, maybe he'd like that. But I wouldn't give him the satisfaction.

BILLIE YOUNG

Another sleazy publisher I must tell you about is Billie Young, the real name of Penelope Ashe, the pen name Billie used on a bestseller called *Naked Came the Stranger* that she instigated by having a bunch of writers write a chapter each to come up with that book. Billie served as the raven-haired "suburban housewife" front who went on all the talk shows plugging the book she had supposedly written.

She and her husband also ran Ashley Books. About 1978 my then-agent, Arnold Goodman, sold two of my books to Ashley, *Among the Carnivores* and a new edition of. *Something You Do in the Dark*. Arnold said that Ashley assured him it would do a professional, thorough job of handling the books. He knew of the company's tainted reputation.

The troubles started almost immediately. Ashley didn't want to pay for a new typesetting job for *Dark*, even though I asked to make some needed stylistic improvements. Okay, we compromised, with me taking my $500 advance for the novel, plus some more of my own money, and having my friend Jay Manning re-typeset the book. Well and good.

But then *Carnivores* didn't come out when it was scheduled for a year. Then it was edited badly by somebody at Ashley, with all the "offensive parts" removed, thus robbing it of its personality. I put in an emergency call to Billie Young, who agreed to put back most of it.

When it did come out, some discrepancies between the various editings remained, along with two scenes run together with no break. I was so upset by this latter error I went out and bought ****'s on sticky paper and went around putting them in the tiny space available between the two scenes. (It seemed more important at the time than it does now, but it was a sign of things to come.)

My favorite Ashley Books story is the time I received a call from my publisher bright and early one morning. We went over the copyediting for almost two hours. I was so grateful that they were at last being careful about details. They were so careful about details in fact, I found out later, they had the charges reversed and put on *my* phone bill.

There were innumerable humiliations and incompetencies, most of which thankfully I have suppressed; they are recorded in my letters, especially the letters I exchanged with Paul O.M. Welles, who was having a novel published by Ashley at the same time. We exchanged Ashley horror stories almost weekly. It was our mutual sense of outrage and betrayal that made us friends and also kept us sane during that period.

Just one little sample? When I visited Billie Young at her office in Port Washington, New York, she gushed over the forthcoming cover for my novel, a crescent moon with big red lips. "Isn't it great?" she asked. "Yes, but what does it have to do with my novel?" I said. "Oh, I just loved that picture when I saw it!" Billie answered, sort of.

When one night Billie Young turned up on *Sixty Minutes* in an expose, I held my breath. Interviewed authors complained bitterly about having been taken for a ride, having paid money to have their books published, having been bamboozled and mistreated in a dozen ways. It ended with

Billie chasing the reporter, Morley Safer, out of her office.

Naturally this did not make me look forward to the next year or so. But then, optimist that I am, I said, "Well, those things won't happen to me. I haven't had to pay Ashley anything. In fact, they gave me two advances." So I wrote a letter standing up for Billie Young and expressing concern for all her authors who would be sullied by the CBS report. I got a call saying my letter was going to be used on the Letters segment. But it didn't appear.

Maybe that had something to do with the fact that Billie sued *Sixty Minutes* for millions of dollars that week. (So far as I know, nothing ever came of this suit.)

All the bad things about Ashley were true, plus a few more that the show hadn't even touched on. I couldn't believe a publisher would work so hard to make its writers hate it; petty things like not sending extra author's copies unless they were pre-paid, major things like not sending accurate royalty statements.

It got so bad that my agent went out to Port Washington and demanded to see Ashley' financial records; he even got the association that investigates publishers' ethics to try to investigate Ashley, but Billie Young was a sly one, to say the least, and there was really nothing we could do. My agent remained convinced that Ashley simply lied about everything, from the number of books printed to the number sold. To this day, whenever I get a royalty statement from Ashley, usually two or more years late, it sends only half the amount due, keeping the other half in its account "against returns." If the royalties are below a certain figure, Ashley keeps it all until the next time, and on and on. Some bookstores have had such pains with Ashley they refuse to carry its books any longer. This hurts an author where he lives.

I don't understand this desire to pinch pennies, cheat authors, and make evil in the world. Eventually we wind up writing about the culprits. Don't they know that?!

JOSEPH HANSEN

Had a chance to meet mystery writer Joseph Hansen in L.A. once, but I turned up my nose. A mystery writer? Later I changed my tune, and I did spend some time with that white-goateed, heavy-set gentleman in his sixties.

The occasion was an appearance in S.F., the first time he'd been in the Bay Area in his life, I believe, or certainly for many, many years. He, David Lamble, and I walked near the ocean at Fort Funston, chatting of this and that. Hansen was showing his age, though, and couldn't walk too far. I gathered from his cryptic comments that he was a married man who was primarily homosexual.

He was a monument to perseverance in writing, since he said he'd written for almost twenty years before he got anything published. I have no real scandal about him. (See how dull that is?)

A couple of years after our first meeting Hansen and I appeared on a panel for novelists at the MLA, along with Paul Monette. What I recall vividly is Hansen saying how glad he was to be writing mysteries, because they gave him an opportunity to write what he really wanted. I'm afraid I agreed with the questioner in the audience who said, "But, Mr. Hansen, how can you feel free to write what you want if you have to follow the dictates of the mystery genre?" Hansen replied that he could sneak in gay liberation ideas, for instance, by having his hero a gay man in a hardboiled setting, thus disconcerting preconceptions about "masculine" behavior. He could also show a lot of love between his characters. To me, having to write in any genre is antithetical to doing what I wanted, as is "sneaking in" anything. I expressed the same sentiment to Elizabeth Ray, the science fiction writer, when she and I were on another panel together.

No doubt it was the success of his mysteries that allowed Hansen to publish some more serious novels. He was a very nice man, easy to talk to, but I must say I didn't want a similar career for myself. I wanted to write what I wanted to write and then for other people to like it. I have never wanted to write what they want me to write. There is a world of difference here.

PAUL MONETTE

We might as well finish off Paul Monette while we're at it. I wonder how he's doing these days. I don't hear much about him. (This is 1986) I say this because when we first met, about 1979, he was very much in the literary news. He had published *Taking Care of Mrs. Carroll* and several other books in hardback and Avon paperbacks.

I met him through Cesar Albini, a bi-cultural fan from Uruguay who had taught in a private school with Monette before both had moved to the West Coast. Cesar arranged for Paul and me to meet by having us drive halfway between L.A., where Paul lived, and S.F., where I lived. We met for lunch at a fancy-schmancy hotel resort called Ventana.

Paul turned out to be a handsome man in his thirties with a handsome lover who was a lawyer, the brother of Sheldon Andelson, a bigwig in L.A. liberal circles. At the time, Monette was doing extremely well financially, since he'd sold two screenplays plus his books. He treated me and Cesar to a luxurious lunch. He and the lover then casually spent big bucks for a blanket from the gift shop as well.

We then strolled along the ocean in a sort of secret harbor he knew about – people like Monette always know about secret harbors and smart little cafes. He smoked a lot of marijuana but seemed reasonably together. Then we all went bathing in the hotel's vast hot tub. I got the hots for Monette's lover, Roger, but I kept my feelings and my hands to myself. (I guess we can all be grateful we didn't get all the sex with all the people we wanted, considering the terrible disease that ensued.)

While waiting in Paul's hotel room to go somewhere, I listened in on his conversation with his agent, who was negotiating with no less a luminary than Chevy Chase, then a hot movie star. "What do you mean Chevy Chase wants a *million* dollars to be in our movie? Why, he's not worth more than $750,000!" Paul said.

He had his eye cocked at me as he said these immortal words. I'm pretty sure he knew how preposterous they sounded. I confess I was numb with envy, not because of Chevy Chase, but because of the sums involved in doing work that Monette didn't even respect.

It was all very enjoyable, and we said farewell, and went to our respective lives, Monette back to L.A. and screenplays, Cesar and I back to the Bay Area, via Salinas, where my car broke down and we had to sleep in the car all night because we didn't have enough money between us to get it fixed or even to stay in a motel. The next day Cesar took a bus back to S.F., while I wired to Tom Rolfsen, my boss at IGNA, to send me enough to get the car repaired. He did so, but then he demanded the money immediately when I got back. Since I didn't have it, I broke down and cried, both ashamed and unashamed because I didn't have any money, certainly not as much as Paul Monette had. Cesar Albini also abandoned me as a friend after that. It was complicated, but some of it had to do with the fact that my life was not as glamorous as he had hoped, I think. He had met me at a big book signing at Stacy's Books and no doubt thought I was more important (and richer) than I was.

Cesar showed up at that MLA panel in L.A. a few years later, to see Monette talk, not me. I found Paul's talk very interesting, because he had fallen on much harder times. His editor at Avon had more or less stopped accepting his books; the screenplays hadn't yet been turned into actual movies and you die in L.A. if that doesn't happen somewhere down the line. A considerable amount of bitterness escaped Monette's lips that afternoon.

I was apprehensive about meeting him again because I had written a scathing review of one of his novels for IGNA, using it as an example of the phony writing that the paperback companies were churning out more and more to the exclusion of better things. If you want an example, there is a scene in the book where a rich woman leaves home without any money and needs to make a phone call. She begs a dime from a woman waiting for a bus. Then, out of generosity, the rich woman, after spying the helpful woman's purse open, drops a diamond necklace inside as repayment. I couldn't believe Paul would write such hokum, but even *Taking Care of Mrs. Carroll* is hokum if you look at it the kind of fake human behavior that is the heart and soul of Hollywood films. Why do people love hokum so much? Will I ever accept this fact of life?

Paul Monette was pleasant to me. Maybe he hadn't read my bad review; maybe he even agreed with it. Maybe he was just more aristocratic than I was. Whatever, his career seemed to be going on the rocks. I think he was one of the casualties after publishers began to see that gay books did not sell in mass-market quantities and therefore their brief candle was about to be snuffed.

I don't want to sound like I'm gloating over Paul Monette's fall from grace at that time. Why does the world of literature have to be us vs. them, serious writing vs. commercial writing?

JEANNE BARNEY

Met Jeanne Barney at the same conference where I met Harvey Milk. She was an anomaly, a straight woman active in the gay rights movement. She was pretty and talented and lived in L.A. in her own little house.

I had lunch with her and John Rowberry once on a visit to Southern California, and I must say I liked her immensely. She earned her living editing and writing. Perhaps she was best known for her "Jeanne's Lamp" advice columns published in various publications.

The time I stayed with her in her little West Hollywood house I discovered that being straight isn't everything. Jeanne had a boyfriend who treated her terribly. I would lie awake in my visitor's bed and hear these awful arguments coming from another part of the house. Jeanne would plead. The boyfriend would say mean things to her. There were crashes, a brawl. It wasn't a game they were playing either. I pretended I hadn't heard a word.

Isn't it strange how people can give advice to others on how to live, how to love, even good advice, but be unable to handle their own problems? I say this more in sympathy than in irony.

BRUCE BILLINGS

Bruce Billings, the "Castro the Dog" cartoonist, is one of the most colorful people I've met, a true character. We first encountered each other at the Valencia Rose, a cabaret and conference hall in S.F.

It turned out that Bruce didn't live too far from me, and we started going out to breakfast together, usually the Patio Cafe.

In this period he wound up moving many times, living with friends and strangers until he finally settled again. Bruce was approaching fifty then, getting gray and stout. He had evidently been a looker in his youth. It was the slimmer, younger version of himself that he drew in his cartoons. He liked balloon-like peasant shirts I think because they hid his expanding waist line. His voice was high, but even though he sounded like a stereotypical gay queen, he hadn't a bitchy patch on his tongue anywhere. If anything, he was one of the most generous-spirited people I've ever known, always going out of his way to compliment people, sympathize with their problems, and tell them that something good was going to happen to them before they knew it. I finally asked him why he did this, and he said, "That's what people need to hear."

He did not like women, though, and didn't want to have anything to do with them, lesbian, straight, or in-between. I have rarely encountered this among gay men, actually.

We didn't see eye to eye on the role of violence and unpleasantness in art, I'm afraid. He said he just wanted to make people happy. He was so innocent and sweet I decided to forgive him this silliness.

To our mutual surprise Bruce had lived in Detroit at the same time I had. In fact, he had taught English at Wayne State University, although he seemed to have forgotten how to punctuate since then. He had even won a short story contest judged by Joyce Carol Oates, one I had entered, too, under a *nom de plume* but hadn't won. Small world! But he decided to take up cartooning instead of writing.

He was gifted with drawing ability, and had actually won a Draw This Car contest and received a scholarship to art school from General Motors and then had designed cars for it for many years. I'll bet most people don't believe gays can design cars, but Bruce said at least half the design department at GM was gay.

I'd learn bits and pieces about Bruce's weird upbringing on a farm, where he dressed in girl's clothes into his teens, where he was raised thinking his real father was his uncle, but it wasn't until we were asked to do interviews of each other for a magazine that I learned even more of his eccentricity.

His lover had died of alcoholism, and Bruce had found him beside the bed, a fact Bruce asked me not to include in the interview. It was from this time that Bruce dated his sexual abstinence: ten whole years. I couldn't believe he was serious, since he always had young, good-looking men staying with him, was always giving them money, but I came to believe he was telling me the truth. He liked to draw naked bodies, but he had opted out of the fast sex lane, even the slow sex lane.

He said he had tricked with Alec McCowan (now Sir Alec)

when that acting star had passed through S.F. I wrote to Sir Alec once myself, and he acknowledged knowing Bruce. Bruce also knew Charles Pierce, the male actress, and showed me letters from him. His cousin was Sinbad, or the actor who had played Sinbad and Gulliver in the movies. He and the cousin were both gay and both lived in S.F., but they didn't have much in common except blood.

Bruce and I agreed to do some cartoons together for my news agency, with captions by me and drawings by him. We did about six, but only one sold, and he seemed reluctant to do anymore. He was always trying to sell "Castro," which was about his owner's sexual exploits as surveyed by his dog.

In actuality there was a real Castro the Dog. I had the opportunity on numerous occasions to have him jump all over me when I visited Bruce. He was spoiled rotten, allowed to lounge anywhere, hand-fed home-cooked steak and chicken, indulged and babied even when he growled or snapped at Bruce. His "owner" had found him, a neglected waif in front of the Castro Theater, and had taken care of him ever since.

The truth was that Bruce Billings was in love with that dog. I don't mean that he loved his dog or that he loved dogs. I mean that he was *in love* with his dog. He liked Dora, his fat, old, slobbering other dog, but it was Castro he cared most deeply about of all his relationships, human and otherwise. I often felt like a voyeur watching them kissing each other. Forget psychoanalysis here; it was simply a given in Bruce's life that everything revolved around Castro the Dog: walking him, not leaving him alone too long, getting home to him. I said, "Bruce, what will happen to you when Castro dies?"

Well, Castro did die at the age of twelve, and Bruce almost died too. He didn't want to live, that's for sure, and mourned for a solid year. He couldn't even continue with his cartoons after the dog was gone. But then he told me that he thought Castro was trying to commune with him from beyond and wanted him to continue the cartoon strips. Bruce said it was his way of immortalizing his dog, and "how many dogs get that?"

In my state of penury I made the mistake of borrowing a hundred dollars from Bruce every now and then, always paying it back within two weeks. The last time I asked, however, Bruce said he couldn't loan it to me. I understand, but the money issue created a strain between us. I'm sorry ever to ask friends for money. So I'm writing these memoirs to make a bundle. Why should people have to wait till after I'm dead? Then I'll take Bruce Billings out to breakfast and hand-feed him steaks and chicken and try to persuade him to get another dog or another lover, whichever comes first.

ANDREA GORDON

I expect big things of director Andrea Gordon, but who knows what will become of this lady. Could be the negative aspects of her personality will cancel out the positive and she may not go as far as her considerable ambition is now leading her. On the other hand, she's not one to hide her light under a bushel.

We met when I went to review her production of a feminist play about Lizzie Borden, performed in the Mission Cultural Center in S.F., which is to say in a dreary little box with about nine people in attendance.

Because I was impressed by the production and because I noticed a call for scripts in the program, I introduced myself to Andrea after the curtain calls. She was as pretty as a model, blonde then, redheaded later, with huge dangling earrings. I wondered at first if she was a lesbian, because of the play's woman-woman theme, but then I decided that she couldn't be a lesbian and wear earrings that dangling. Okay, so it's a stereotype. (They are often true, have you noticed?)

It turns out that she was straight, man-crazy, if anything, but she had lived for a short time in a lesbian household. She moved out when her sisters kept telling her she shouldn't be having men guests over. And I thought that went out with Victoria! The nerve of some dykes telling other women how to relate to men.

Well, Andrea liked some of my scripts and we began meeting for a series of luncheons. What she really wanted was a dramaturge, unpaid of course, for her young theater company, Tour de Force, and I seemed like a good candidate. I told her upfront that my primary interest was in productions of my own plays. Andrea was excellent at promising people what they wanted. (Like most producers, I've learned.)

Then she flirted with moving to NYC because several theaters were interested in her, but she decided to stay in S.F. after all, perhaps through devotion, more likely through a collapse of the NYC deals.

Now don't get me wrong. Andrea Gordon was a charmer. As I got to know her better, I noticed her small boobs and very big hips, but her vivacity and a skill in dressing as though she were on TV every moment made one notice only her prettiness. I was surprised at myself when I took her to plays, because I saw how other men looked at her, and I understood that awful pride and possessiveness many men feel for their women: Yes, she's attractive and she's with me.

Tour de Force began having a series of playwrights' meetings, which I faithfully attended. We'd sit around and read each other's work and make comments, hoping that this purgatory would one day lead to a production by Andrea's little theater company.

We also had staged readings of plays Andrea selected, every month with an audience. This was at the Noe Valley Cultural Center, actually a church in a yuppy neighborhood. Andrea even found time to stage a reading of my musical about a transsexual, *Comeback*. She said she wanted to hold onto the script for possible future production. She told a lot of people that about their plays.

I would write up very elaborate critiques of the plays we staged-read, because after all I was the dramaturge, but Andrea didn't give copies of these to most of the people concerned; they were too negative. That, I gather, would have cost needed contacts.

Andrea's parents had died and left her an income, not oodles, but enough to get by on, enough to produce a few plays a year on a small scale. But she was getting low in funds, and I don't blame her for trying all the tricks she knew to get her theater underway in as secure a manner as possible. If you don't do it yourself, nobody else will.

So Andrea would chat up and round up umpteen members for her board, would go hither, thither, and yon, maneuvering, manipulating, being sexy, friendly, and anything else she needed to be in order to corral people who had money, prestige, and power. Off and on she would direct Neil Simon in the suburbs to keep the clothes on her back. If any paying job came along, she snatched it. She even did publicity for the One Act Theatre Company for a time, but she had so many irons in so many fires she occasionally burned herself or at least burned other people.

Her love life was quite something. She was living in a condemned house right near my lover's place with a boyfriend whom she didn't much love. Their sex life was sporadic and unsatisfying. At the same time she had the hots for a male playwright and pursued him with all the liberated woman's wiles she could muster, and she could muster quite a few. She'd moon and moan and plan and plot to get into this man's emotional good graces. She even took off to L.A. in the middle of these two affairs to sleep with Robert Woodruff, the director who'd directed Sam Shepard's prize plays. I found it a fascinating study of heterosexual behavior.

Andrea led us all by the nose for several years. Then out of the blue she'd do some play she hadn't even mentioned to any of us before, like a little-known Brecht. I hung in there, hoping my turn would come. (This is when Dean Goodman said not to trust Andrea.) But I was the dramaturge, and so I kept on. I went to the dress rehearsal of the Brecht play.

First of all, when you haven't heard of a play by a major author there's usually a good reason -- the play is no good. On top of that Andrea had cast it "color blind," that is, with Asians playing Frenchmen, blacks playing whites. You could overlook this noble-hearted effort to broaden the possibilities for hard-to-cast types except that Andrea didn't do a good job with the play and many of the actors were incompetent, whatever their ethnic background. I couldn't understand most of the dialogue at the dress rehearsal and wrote up notes for Andrea. Yet when I went to the play itself, little had been changed. It was somewhat easier to comprehend, but overall it was like a community college production with all the attendant carelessness.

I know Andrea expected me to come up afterwards and say how much I had enjoyed it, but I hadn't enjoyed it, so I didn't say anything. I didn't say I hadn't liked it. I merely left. Should I have been a hypocrite and lied? Is that what's been missing from my life so far?

Well, Andrea was pissed, no question about it. She made some announcement at our playwrights' meeting about the need for us all to pull together to support our productions, "whether we liked them or not." Pardon me, but if I wanted to be a cheerleader I'd buy pompoms.

Things drifted along for a while; then the playwrights got weary of waiting for productions that never developed. Mostly I think we all got sick of each other's faces. (The only good thing to come out of that group is that one of the writers, Alison Blake, asked me for a recommendation to Yale Drama School and was actually accepted I was the biggest name she had. I was amazed, since I doubt that *I* could get into Yale myself.)

Andrea Gordon went on and on. She's still going on. She's only about thirty now. She directed *The Marriage of Figaro* at a big festival in Golden Gate Park one summer amid a ton of pre-publicity. Her production was panned, however. She had to take some of the blame since the same actors in a companion play got raves.

But I'm sure Andrea Gordon is not one to be daunted easily, perhaps never. The last time I saw her was a perfect example of her behavior. She saw me outside the One Act Theatre Company and came sailing my way to give me a big hug and a smackeroo. "Dan! It's so good to see you!" she exclaimed. Then she spied Gerald Nachman, the critic from the *San Francisco Chronicle*, just a few steps away and leaned over and started chatting him up, even as she was still holding on to me! Before you could say, "Andrea, you're not being cool," she was off laughing gaily with Mr. Nachman, leaning close, showing him her oh-so-pretty smile, making plans.

HERBERT GOLD

Why do I harbor this lingering resentment against S.F.'s best-known straight novelist? He's never done anything to me personally. Or has he?

Actually I heard Gold speak about the Red Mouse Theory of fiction writing way back at Kent State when I was a graduate student there in 1960. Don't ask me what the Red Mouse meant, not at this late date. It's merely a coincidence that we both turned up in S.F. years later. But, no, I didn't follow him here to decipher the secret of the Red Mouse.

In case you don't know it, Gold has long been committed to living far from the madding crowd of the NYC literary scene, but he felt he suffered considerably by not being where the *there* is. As I write this, he's enjoying his best reviews in a long time for *A Girl of Forty*, which some New York-ophilic critic said was capable of taking place anywhere, not just in S.F. That's supposed to be praise. If it unequivocally took place in NYC, of course it wouldn't matter a rat's ass whether anybody else thought it was capable of taking place somewhere else. I get tired of carping about this NYC self-centeredness, but I'm not going to stop until they stop.

One time I talked with Herb Gold at a S.F. public library function in the Marina. He had just made some snotty remarks about gays in an article. Liberals like Gold sometimes try to mask their dismay about the fact that the queers aren't as invisible as they used to be; they seem to think the gays are getting all sorts of privileges, when in fact all they are getting is the right not to be put down by every other segment of society. Oh, excuse me! I forgot our privilege of no longer being beaten up on the street, the privilege of not being spat on, and the privilege of not being fired.

I don't think I called him on his article, but still Gold was rather cold as we talked. I may have made some "militant" comments, identifying myself as a gay writer, for instance. Then I saw him and a woman make some sneering joke about gays, which they covered up with a guilty look in my direction. I wouldn't ask for admiration just for being queer. I do think we can ask for an end to generic put-down jokes, at least from the liberals!

Sorry if I'm defensive. It hard *not* to be defensive when you're a queer.

PETER ROBINS

Really enjoyed writer Peter Robins when he came to the U.S. for a vacation in the early 1980s. I was happy to arrange a place for him to stay for free, to keep his expenses down. He was associated with the BBC and I imagine made a fair salary, but he was hardly filthy rich.

He had that light-haired, bony British look, with a lot of articulate and interesting things to say about the world.

He wanted to introduce me to his fellow British citizen, David Rees, who was a guest professor at San Jose State. But in conveying this invitation, Robins let out the fact that Rees had bad-mouthed a story of mine in an anthology. Who wants to meet somebody who can't read? I declined this I'm-sure-delightful person's acquaintance. (Later on a newspaper asked me to review one of Mr. Rees's books, and I am pleased to say I didn't praise it just to show how "objective" I was. I gave it what it deserved, both praise and some helpful suggestions.)

I was a little worried when I reviewed Peter Robins' first book of short stories for IGNA, because I said one of the stories wasn't as good as the others. Believe me, I know writers. What they remember is that you didn't like one of their stories, no matter how much you have abased yourself finding compliments for the ones you did like. But Peter Robins was a real gentleman about it all.

One time I taught this same story collection as a guest teacher in a Gay Literature course. I've done better teaching in my life, that's for sure. I also recall that the students' response to Robins' stories showed me emphatically that they didn't read for literary values, most of them. They read simply to be assured that they were valuable people. I thought that was a pretty sad commentary on where they thought they stood in society. I am beginning to think the real reasons that people read have nothing to do with literature.

TIM WOLFRED

Tim Wolfred was a member of the College Board of City College, an elected office; he also was head of the AIDS Foundation. He's one of the few publicly-elected gay officials in the entire universe, as of 1986. Since the College Board is generally looked upon as a stepping stone to higher office, I wonder how high Wolfred will go.

A tall, sartorially splendid man, Wolfred is noted for his abilities as a negotiator and a subtle wheeler-dealer. I've always liked him, from the first time I saw him, which was when I interviewed him for my novel *From Violent Men*. At the time Wolfred was an aide to Supervisor Harry Britt, but he was just about to run for the College Board, so I thought his insights into the mind of the politician might be very helpful to the authenticity of my book. They were.

He thought politicians did a lot of bad things because they always tell themselves they're going to do good things down the road when they're in higher office. Often they keep on telling themselves this forever. I didn't really use Wolfred as such in the novel, but he thought he noticed himself in the portrait of the aide to the gay Supervisor. Actually he is in the book more in the psychology of certain characters.

I had dealings with Wolfred because he attended meetings of the Gay and Lesbian Educational Support Coalition (G.L.E.S.C.), especially as we made our nefarious plans to get gays on the Affirmative Action list. It seemed to be the only way to get a job in an era of intense minority-mongering. Blacks, women, Asians, Hispanics, Eskimos were all on the list. Gays were still fighting exclusion from faculty positions and deanships, never mind *favored* treatment in getting such plums. It seemed obvious to me that the only way I was ever going to overcome my poverty was to help engineer slots for gays; we certainly weren't making it just as whites with advanced degrees, numerous publications, and lots of talent and experience. Affirmative Action had turned from a good idea in 1965 to a system whereby people with chosen skin colors and ethnic heritages were more automatically equal than others. It was supposed to be a choice between complete equals, but instead race became almost everything. As of this writing, nothing has come of these attempts to out-Balkanize the Balkans.

I've been in Wolfred's home, seen him exercising in a gym, had him wink at me during a demonstration against the very Board he was on. (October 21, 1986). We demonstrated because we were sick and tired of not having full-time teaching jobs. But it's hard not to like somebody who winks at you. Wolfred is even a Good Guy, trying his best to placate all sides in a heavily competitive city.

A smoothie, no question. I envy him that. I don' t envy his having to sit through Board meetings where the members discuss "Authorizing contract with Effie Poy Yew Chow, Ph.D., to obtain two series of workshops for staff stress management through East West Bio-physical Energy Systems."

Wolfred could easily wind up being S.F.'s first gay mayor. We shall see.

TERRENCE DAVIES

Happened to be attending a press screening for filmmaker Terrence Davies' *Trilogy*, the three short movies he had made with some British grants, three moving portraits of growing up not only gay and Catholic but in ugly, ugly Liverpool. Talk about the deck being stacked against you! Afterwards, this plain, skinny man with a too-quiet voice proceeded to answer questions from the audience. Several times people had to ask Davies to speak up. I was to learn later that his quietness masked other feelings.

I had no intention of getting to know him better, but I stopped in the lobby when I saw my critic friend Penni Kimmel talking with Davies. It turned out that he was poor and looking for a place to stay for a few days while his films were being shown in the S.F. Film Festival. So Penni and I agreed to take turns putting him up.

I'm afraid Davies felt his educational and cultural deprivations severely. He had been raised in a large, dumb Irish family in England and had worked in a boring job for many years before a modicum of freedom came his way through winning some awards. One of the first things he asked for in my house was a copy of T.S. Eliot's "Four Quartets." He wanted something to read, you see. Sure.

What I noticed most, despite the very quiet voice, was the immense rage inside the man. He had been humiliated by a BBC executive when he'd tried to get a job there. He considered himself homely and undesirable and thus didn't try to have sex. Actually some young film fan made a pass at

Davies in my presence, but he chose to ignore it.

We had a number of days and evenings together, and what came through was this very polite, very gentle man who hated just about everything in the whole world.

He had read some of my short stories in a collection from Faber & Faber, *Mae West Is Dead*, and said he enjoyed them the most in the book. He said he hadn't really known they were mine because the names of the authors were listed only in the back. Amidst so much general animosity, I felt blessed to be found worthy. But of course Davies was staying in my house!

After he left, I discovered that he was angry at me as well, although he hadn't told me that. He had fought with Penni Kimmel, his other host, before he had left for home, then had called her to make up. That's when he said I had helped humiliate him in a restaurant because he hadn't left enough of a tip and the waitress had banged his saucer, or some damn thing. Since I wasn't paying attention to how much he was tipping, only to our conversation, I didn't feel responsible for yet more shame that he carried away with him.

I received a copy of his novel as dark and as guilt-ridden as his films but very well done. I gave it a mention in my column. But I didn't really much want to visit Terrence Davies in his tiny bed-sitter in London if I ever went there again, a talented, little, soft-spoken wound of a man seeing slights everywhere. (I really MUST learn something here.)

Christmas Leubrie

She may not be known to a wide circle, but Christmas Leubrie played an important part in my life, so I'd like to tell you about her.

She was my student in a class at City College of San Francisco the summer of 1982. One of her papers was about how she served as midwife to lesbian couples who wanted children. Well, I've always wanted to have a child or two, no doubt because of cravings for immortality, to say nothing of the Catholic programming that demands that sex result in "procreation." At the bottom of Christmas's paper I wrote: "How does one get involved?"

Thus began a series of negotiations and meetings between the midwife and me as well as with a lesbian couple, whose names I didn't know and whom I did not meet in person. Anonymity was the game, since the idea was for the women to keep the baby, if it should come to be. While I would have no financial responsibilities or other duties except as donor, there was a strong possibility of contact down the road.

Christmas did a family background check on me for hereditary diseases, insanity, and other dangers, then a medical test of my sperm for fertility and motility and whatever other "tillities" were important for making a woman pregnant. Naturally the mother-to-be wanted to know some things about the father-to-be besides his sperm count. Christmas was able to supply this since she'd known me as a teacher and became aware of me as a writer as well.

On my side, I had certain concerns too. I wanted my child to have as many genetic advantages as possible since he was going to have to live with being the offspring of two queers, so I was happy to learn that the mother was attractive, of European stock, and intelligent. She and her lover had been together for three years in what looked like a permanent, financially secure, loving relationship, Christmas said. The lover had tried once but hadn't gotten pregnant, so now the other one was going to try, with me. If that proved successful, then the other woman would use me as a donor later. That way the two kids would be related by blood.

I was most concerned that the child be wanted. God knows there are too many kids brought into this world by people who didn't want them and don't take good care of them. I reasoned that if two lesbians were going to all this trouble surely they must want a child; it wasn't going to be something that popped out nine months after some forgotten episode in the mother and father's life.

We signed a contract about our mutual expectations and limitations, with Christmas keeping copies signed by both parties. I've learned since then that such contracts legally aren't worth the paper they're written on. A natural father always takes precedence over the mother's lover or her parents, should something remove the natural mother from care of the child. But I've never wanted to raise children. In fact, I am amazed by people who don't mind wiping mouths, noses, and butts from morn to midnight, plus feeding, dressing, correcting, teaching, and fretting about their kids. Then the kids turn fourteen, go all hormonal, and accuse you of being an asshole because you won't let them wear a ring in their nose. Who needs it? My books are my children. Managing them is hard enough!

As I say, we did agree that if and when the child started asking about his daddy, probably when he/she went to school and noticed that other kids had daddies and he/she had two mommies, then I would put in a strategic appearance so that he/she wouldn't spend the rest of his/her life searching for the lost father. A woman editor told me she thought this was a good idea, for she had never known her own father and had spent much of her life wondering about, even searching for him. Secretly I thought there were plenty of worse things a child could have happen in his life. As a matter of fact, I think being a little peculiar, like not knowing who your father is, is just as likely to make you creative as it is to make you a basket case. I've never understood why people crave a "normal" child anyway. "Normal" people don't do much that's interesting, it seems to me. Give me a talented, mildly neurotic person any day.

We cemented our plans. Ovulation for her, garlic pills for me. Two days in a row, October 19 and 20, 1982, I was to deposit my sperm in glass artichoke jars provided by Christmas, who promptly at five P.M. would be waiting in her van in my driveway to receive the precious fluid, now wrapped in a towel, to whisk it away to the waiting mother-to-be. It came to pass, and Christmas then proceeded to deposit the sperm where it would do the most good. I don't know whether the insemination took place in the house or in the van. I like the van idea.

During the first "donation," my partner, John, came over and we had sex. It would be 'our" child, you see. *Aww*. We even flirted with the idea of mixing our sperm together in the jar, but we didn't do it. Besides violating the agreement I had made, that would have meant it might not be my child. I am hardly alone in this desperate wish to continue in some form after I'm gone: "And Curzon begat So-and-So, and So-and-So begat more So-and-So's."

Christmas told me that it was the second donation, not the first, that took. But she also told me it would be a girl, so our knowledge of biology is still iffy apparently. Because it was a boy! I don't know if he bounced, but he was healthy and normal in every way. Thus Zachary came into the world on July 17, 1983. Actually I didn't know about it for almost a week. In recompense for stud service, the two moms sent me, via the midwife, a box of candy. No, I didn't give out cigars.

Yet I was surprised at my traditional "sexist" reaction, that proprietary, macho feeling: "I produced a baby and, by God, a boy at that!" I began to see why people stare fondly at their offspring; it's themselves they're looking at their second chance.

I was grateful that the moms sent me a photograph of the baby almost as soon as they got him home. To date I've received a picture every six months or year or so. I don't carry baby pictures in my wallet, but I'm thrilled when people look at the ones in my house and say, "My, he looks just like you!" or "He's a doll!" He does indeed look like me when I was small: little nose, big mouth, blondish hair. In the notes about him that I've received from the moms, he is always described as Mr. Energy, an enthusiastic and happy child. Wherever did he get that from?

I sent one of the pictures to my mother and father, telling them it was their grandson. I was vague about the details. I wanted my dad to know he had a grandchild at last. They seemed reasonably pleased and didn't ask any questions. Really. Heavens, let's not discuss that!

Not everybody was supportive of this venture into modern biology and ethics. A woman librarian friend of my partner scowled at me and said I was "immoral" for bringing a child into the world in this way. Nonsense. It isn't necessary to have one male and one female to raise a child well; it's the quality of the child care, not the sex of the parents, that counts.

It's mostly the genetic makeup of the person that counts; that's what I really believe, unfashionable though that may be. You can't make a silk purse out of a sow's ear. Nor can you make a sow's ear out of piece of shit. How you turn out is a balance between what you're endowed with and the particular configurations and pressures of your environment. It's all a crapshoot, anyhow.

I wrote a play, *Future Meetings with My Unknown Son*, based on my worries about my possible son. In it I explore some of the types he might grow up to be, from a father-hating murderer to an okay, nothing-special kind of guy. I couched the worries in different theatrical styles, from Greek tragedy to comedy of manners to Sam Shepard, to make it interesting to people other than myself. My agent's reader said it was a "'gay ghetto play.'" For God's sake, if anything is supposed to be of partner's interest to heterosexuals, it's having a baby! Why shouldn't they be overjoyed to see a play with a twist? My agent sent it out anyway.

Sometimes I wonder what I would do if it turned out that my child needed somebody to take care of him. Blood is pretty thick, I see now. I'm sure I would find some way to take care of him. Maybe I'd even keep him home from the American school system and save him from all the horror that entails, by educating him myself.

I also wonder what will happen when he's old enough to want to get to know me. What if I don't like him? What if he doesn't like me?

Well, it won't be the first time dislike has occurred in a family. At least we won't have to pretend and remain chained together. But what if he thinks I owe him something for bringing him into this vale of tears? What if he becomes a leach, a creep? How about a great human being? (That would be nice too.)

It is questions like these that led me to want to have a second child, with the other mom, as we had planned. Isn't that why many people have more than one child? You increase the odds at least one of them will turn out all right. Unhappily, however, a second child of mine was not to be. Although immensely pleased with the product, little Zachary, the moms, after thinking hard about it, decided that, because of AIDS and because I admitted that I wasn't monogamous with my lover, they had better use a straight man as the donor the second time. My feelings were hurt. After all, I could have lied about my lack of monogamy. Besides, as we now know, straight men aren't necessarily safe from AIDS. But the deed was done without me, and now Zachary has a baby sister that isn't really his sister.

What will happen to us all? The world will probably little note nor long remember what we did here. But it does show something about modern times, don't you think? And how creative human beings are in propagating the species, despite the odds.

THE ANGELS OF LIGHT

The Angels of Light began as an offshoot of the old Cockettes, an early gender-fuck, outrageous performing company, most of whom have now died or disappeared. The Cockettes would make a lively memoir in themselves, but I wasn't around in their heyday. (Note: A film about the Cockettes was finally made years later.)

I came to the Angels of Light after seeing several of their shows, notably *Holy Cow*, *Hotel of Follies*, and *True Tales of Hollywood Horror*. *Cow* had been a city-wide hit. *Hotel* had been a gigantic bomb, and *Horror* had been so-so. I thought I could write them a better show; it was time they added a professional script to their wild costumes, great dancing, and general low-budget extravagance, so I wrote to Rodney Price and Beaver Bauer, the current artistic directors of the group, and offered my services. Earlier Rodney had asked me at a party if I might be interested in writing a script around him, based on his ideas. I wasn't ready then. Now I had an idea of my own.

Rodney replied, and we got together for a pow-wow. He was thirty-four, black-haired, primarily a tap dancer, but he also did authentic Indian dancing; he was handsome but also had bad acne on his back. He survived on some kind of public assistance.

He seemed interested in doing a show even though he hadn't seen any of my plays or read any of my books. My idea was to do a sequel to the story of Cinderella and call it *Cinderella II*. I hadn't worked out the plot completely, but I knew that would be the easy part. What if Cinderella decided to leave Prince Charming because he was too perfect? The possibilities were delightful. I wanted to use Dan Turner for the music.

Rodney was worried about Adrian Brooks, a quite talented but egregious queen of monomaniacal self-importance, who had written himself into the lead of earlier shows. There was talk of a revival of their *Holy Cow* show, only Rodney didn't want to work with Adrian again, for Adrian had a way of taking over any project. Ultimately Rodney said he would do my show, especially when the funding for the revival fell through.

Soon after, I met blonde Beaver Bauer, who did the wild costumes, and also played featured parts in the Angels' productions. The group had won umpteen Critics Circle awards for costumes and sets, even one for best musical, for *Holy Cow*. I realized that writing for the Angels meant writing to please Rodney and Beaver by providing good parts for them to play. I envisioned Rodney as Prince Charming and Beaver as Cinderella. He liked the idea, wanting to prove to the world that he could act and sing as well as tap dance. But we decided early on that Beaver would play the Fairy Godmother, not Cinderella, because Cindy had to sing a lot, and Beaver had a voice like a frog with a girl in its throat.

I submitted a draft of the script to the two artistic leaders; they made some suggestions; for instance, they wanted a male villain to balance the evil stepsisters, and hence Tickle the jester was born. Rodney, in private, also asked me to beef up the part of the Fairy Godmother for Beaver's sake. I had no trouble accommodating myself to the demands of writing for a specific company. If anything, it was sort of fun.

Rodney had his heart set on casting certain people in certain parts, chiefly Fran Sholley in the title role. After she auditioned, I was reluctant because she hadn't read very well, although her singing had been okay. But bi Rodney was having half an affair with her and had been in acting classes with her, so he was sure she was more talented than she seemed. (She was.) He also wanted me to write a tap dance competition into the plot for him and his friend Wayne Doba, which I did, but when I heard Doba read I insisted that he not be cast as the evil jester; he just wasn't strong enough in the part. Rodney reluctantly agreed, and we settled on Tommy James, who turned out to be fine in the role but a major temperamental fly in our ointment as time went by. Wayne Doba, a couple of years later, began to garner rave reviews for his acting talents. (So we all make mistakes. Auditions are not the most reliable means of getting a cast together, nor apparently is casting people you think you already know.)

I remember a read-through of the script with various actors, some of whom, I found out later, weren't all that crazy about my script and didn't want to do the show. (Just goes to show that actors can be as blind as writers.) We held it in a gym-like, smelly dance space full of echoes. Dan Turner and I sang the songs without accompaniment whenever they showed up in the script. I'm no singer, and I hated having to perform, but, by Jesus, I sang for all I was worth, since I wanted to convince the doubting Thomases that the show was good, as I knew it would be on the stage.

When Rodney said that Janice Sukaitis wanted to play the part of one of the stepsisters, I began to have my first tiny ulcer in what was to become a whole hospital full of ailments. Janice Sukaitis, you must understand, was a very talented, off-the-wall performer who seemed likely to be fabulous as an obnoxious, strutting, aggressive stepsister, but she also had been the person who had written the lumbering, incoherent books for the preceding two Angels shows. Obviously she knew that she had been bypassed in putting together the new show. I feared a Fifth Column, an enemy within our ranks, beset with jealousy and anger. I underestimated the woman; she was a positive fiend of dissension and destruction.

I asked to hear her audition, and such mugging and showing off you wouldn't believe, unless you're in the theater. I thought she might be a teeny bit intimidated by the man who had replaced her, but she was a veritable Mouseketeer made of brass as she strutted her stuff there in Dan Turner's living room.

Then she said she didn't want to do the show, and I breathed a sigh of relief. Then she said she did want to do it. She was cast, and so was the die. For every evil stepsisterly deed she did onstage, she doubled it off.

For musical director we got Scrumbly Koldewyn, who had been the musical director of previous Angels' shows as well as an actual Cockette; he had also written the music for those other shows. So again we were inviting trouble. Later Koldewyn expressed dissatisfaction with my book, but eventually he came around, once the show was in rehearsal, and behaved like a gentleman, and said it was the best Angels show ever. He also drove a hard bargain for his services and was the highest paid person in the company.

Where the money for this wonderful upcoming production was coming from was always rather vague. I expected the Angels of Light to produce it, but when I saw the run-down house the Angels lived in, complete with part of the roof fallen into the bathtub, I wondered if they had any money at all. Rodney said they had borrowed money from an "angel" fan of theirs and from Rodney's father to finance the previous show; they hadn't quite balanced the books yet. But he never worried about the financing too much, he said. If you did, you never put on any shows. The Angels' way was to close their eyes, put on their tap shoes, and let it all come together somehow.

I thus became not only the writer and lyricist but the producer. I had no money in the bank whatsoever, but we managed to get a starter loan from the "angel," after begging. Some other fans coughed up some here, some there. Our big hope was to have a fund-raising, ticket-selling evening of highlights from the new show, thus filling our coffers with enough money to put on the show for real. Crowds would flock to the performances, money would roll in, and we'd all live happily ever after, just like in the fairy tale, or a Judy Garland-Mickey Rooney musical.

We checked out scads of theaters, all of them too expensive, inaccessible, or unavailable. We finally selected Theatre Artaud, a huge barn of a place. *Hotel of Follies* had been a disaster there, without adequate microphones, among other things, and so we all approached this space with trepidation. But we signed the contract in my name, of course, and set off on our merry way. Theatre Artaud was having financial obligations of its own and demanded half of the rent for the entire run even before we opened, plus the rest before we even used the space and could bring in any money. Two days before opening, three staff members cornered me and said we couldn't open until we gave them another $800. It made me sick with worry, but somehow I got it. It came out of the advance my publisher sent me for *The World Can Break Your Heart*. To this day I hate the guts of those Theatre Artaud people and hope they die.

But I'm getting ahead of myself. Let's go back to the fundraising performance, or the Preview Party, as we began to call it. I had been on David Lamble's radio program on KGO with former Olympian Tom Waddell, both of us discussing how we had fathered children within a month of each other. Waddell had this fabulous house with a stage in the front room, a converted hall, and he mentioned that I could use it sometime if I wanted. Well, I took him up on his offer, and we arranged to have the Preview Party in June, 1984 at his place. Invitations went out, rehearsals continued, in earnest now. We were working in the basement of the Angels' house, complete with a hole in the floor, but the show was beginning to come together, at least the five numbers we were planning to do. The director was great, adding lots of clever blocking and business to the script; Rodney was choreographing the numbers. Beaver got out some of the costumes from older shows for us to use and was likewise busy designing splendid-looking ones for *Cinderella II*. We would have her exciting drawings on display at the Preview Party.

The night was to be free, and Janice Sukaitis even catered the party, hoping to elicit bigger contributions and ticket sales for opening night that way. I was flabbergasted when one hundred and seventy people packed Tom Waddell's house that night. I think Waddell was flabbergasted too, and more than a little worried about his wonderful wooden floors and nice furniture. The collectibles had been locked away in the glass cases along the walls for safety. Probably smart.

Dan Turner and I did a little pre-show bit, sitting on the edge of the stage, and then the show began. The lighting wasn't too good, but the crowd was eager for a good time, and the cast came through with flying colors. The songs were great, if I must say so myself, and I didn't have to. It was a total success, and everybody was buzzing with enthusiasm about the show and what it promised to be. People bought opening night tickets right then and there and made donations, but when we totaled it all up, it was only a little more than $1000, not really all that much. Apparently the after-show pitch hadn't been clear enough.

I stayed behind to clean up the few spilled drinks and crushed grapes that the crowd had left behind; they actually had been very well-behaved, and I could see Tom Waddell breathe a sign of relief as he followed my vacuum cleaner around. He had watched the show from his balcony above the huge living room, like Lorenzo the Magnificent.

With the odor of even the little bit of money we'd made in the air, mouths began to salivate, appetites began to increase. The cast had worked hard, and they wanted to be paid something. So I gave the participants $100 each out of the production's account. In the tentative budget we had drawn up, vastly inflated figures for actors and musicians had been mentioned, not by me. But the level of expectation rose in all directions.

Out of the Preview Party we got an offer from a very talented designer, Ric Tringali, to do our sets. He came up with terrific ones: huge painted cycloramas, you name it, all to be flown on pulleys above the stage. The budget flew up, too.

Beaver Bauer needed more money for the fabulous costumes, even though she was a genius at getting materials at discount houses. But what are you going to do when you have ten dancing Question Marks for the closing number of Act I? The budget went up.

Then the director quit. He said he needed to make more money doing industrial shows. We had an emergency meeting at his apartment. Nothing was resolved, and we had to find a new director, with the opening a month away, the theater rent already paid, and bills mounting daily. I asked my friend Ed Decker to take over as director; he wanted to, but his children's theater board wouldn't let him divide his energies. Ed recommended a director friend of his, whom I knew nothing about. We offered him $1000 to take over, sight unseen.

I appreciated his dilemma, stepping in with a complete cast in place, except for a couple of parts, and so I did my best to go along with his suggestions. I made the few alterations in the script he wanted, improvements actually. But he wasn't about to rush into blocking the play and spent many precious days discussing "beats" with the actors. Opening night was looming, and we weren't anywhere close to being ready.

Rodney Price continued with dance rehearsals, including changes of dancers, squabbles with Tommy James (the evil jester), who was to choreograph some of the numbers, and even a third choreographer involved! Rodney thought it would be nice to have four ballet dancers as well. One of them insisted on being paid for rehearsals. We paid him for weeks, and then he dropped out when we finally got to the performances. Another ballet dancer was a single mother and had to bring her baby to rehearsals, had to check on it constantly. I held this baby while she danced. It was a heavy! But anything for my art.

Our sets were going up in Theatre Artaud. But the sound equipment wasn't adequate. We had to have proper sound for a musical! Somebody knew somebody who could get us mikes for such and such. The budget went up some more, and then some more.

Then we realized that Theatre Artaud's lighting wasn't adequate, despite the huge rent. Some of the equipment didn't even work. We had to scamper around and rent more lights from an outside company, in my name, natch. Then of course we had to have a lighting designer to special this, special that.

I was writing checks every day, putting my own unemployment money into the show's account. I called my sickly eighty-four-year-old mother, who lived on Social Security, and begged her for $5000, promising to pay her back with the show's profits within the next six months. She consented. The show could go on.

I was the publicist as well now, writing up press releases, calling reviewers, arranging interviews in newspapers, doing the program. I was exhausted, since I attended every rehearsal as well. I made some adjustments in the script when Cinderella felt that she didn't have enough to do in the second act. Actually this led to one of the funniest scenes in the show, but at the time it was exceedingly annoying. We wrote a new song; we dropped two.

Then my father died. There was a call on my answering machine from a relative in Farmersville, Illinois, giving the brief, unsentimental word. He had died in his sleep from a stroke. He didn't look good when I got there for the wake, so just before the crowd came in, I asked the funeral director if he could possibly add more rouge to my father's cheeks and lips because he looked brown. The funeral director agreed, saying, as he dabbed at my father's face, "Are you single out there in San Francisco? I'm single here too." So I was cruised by a man painting my dead father's face.

I stayed with my frail mother for ten days in Farmersville, trying to decide what to do with a woman almost eighty-five and too weak to fly out to S.F. to live with me. She decided she'd stay in her little house as long as she could. She had a woman to come in once a week from the county and buy her groceries and do her laundry and sometimes cook her some food.

But my mother wouldn't eat it most of the time. She ate Gerber's baby food, and then only the sweets. She weighed ninety pounds and was clearly undernourished, walking around with a cigarette dangling from her lower lip, threatening to set the house and herself on fire at any minute. But she wouldn't budge from her home. Her greatest fear in her old age had always been that she'd wind up in a nursing home. Then a representative came from the county and told us my mother, because of federal budget cuts, couldn't have the woman helper come out anymore. We worked something out, despite the bastards.

I had to get back to *Cinderella II*. The opening was approaching rapidly, and we had lots of tasks to do, from hiring a house manager to getting the third-class bulk mailings out in time to reach potential customers. We were almost sold out for opening night, but we had six weeks to fill after that.

John McGehee was a twenty-four-year-old, plump, spoiled man of independent means who was our stage manager. He tended to be hysterical at times, but he was also faithful. Besides, he'd put $3000 of his own money into the show. But we got into some dispute about something or other. Neither one of us would apologize, so we didn't speak, and haven't spoken to this day. At the time he had a crush on Dan Turner, which I was glad about since it kept him working hard and putting more money into the show. If I'd been smarter, I would've apologized to him at the time and run him over with a truck after the show closed.

Every day now I would go to Theatre Artaud to get the ticket reservations, sometimes as many as a hundred and fifty. I played back each call, sometimes several times when it was garbled, and called the customers to confirm their reservations. I did this to encourage people to send their money in immediately to be assured of tickets. The budget had gotten so out of hand that I had to snatch literally every dollar I could get. I would even agree to come back to the theatre anytime anyone wanted if they were willing to bring money for their tickets. I would rush to the bank afterwards to deposit the cash, usually just in time to avoid bouncing a check.

I got calls from companies wanting to supply us with cut-rate audiences or with T-shirts, calls from minor actors needing BART fare, from actors with drug problems, from everybody you can think of, and several you can't, including Dan Turner wanting to get co-lyricist billing in the program even though I had written 98% of the lyrics. I was too tired to argue about any of it. Yes, yes, yes! Let's just get this show open and hope it's a big hit.

The show still wasn't completely blocked, and the new director was doing what he had done in a pedestrian way. Rodney and Beaver complained to me about that and also about the fact that the director wouldn't listen to their acting suggestions; they didn't feel comfortable in their roles yet. How do you handle all this? You pray your script and songs will carry the day.

We pressed on. Janice Sukaitis, I learned afterwards, began to plant her greatest seeds of dissension now, predicting the show would be a flop even as she gave me big smiles at every rehearsal. She tried to get me to change what happens to the stepsisters at the end. I had them coming back as nuns with their own school, ready to paddle all those bad little bottoms out there. Janice wanted them to come back at labor leaders! If that doesn't show why her previous two shows had been bombs, nothing will. She had either boring ideas like that or else wanted to have a scene where she'd insert a tampon on stage. I resisted her last-minute alterations. Even though she couldn't write worth shit, I had to admit she was hilarious as Odia, a stepsister. The other stepsister was being played by a man, Martin Xero, who was good too.

Suddenly we had to have some last-minute auditions for the role of the Father. Then, out of anger and frustration, I added a nasty prologue, which would have alienated any audience; it was dropped. We cast one of the actors, not good enough for the Father, as the Narrator, that is, an unseen voice trying to tell the Brothers Grimm version of the story while my characters are trying to tell the new story. The Narrator was terrible. I wanted the director to fire him, but we didn't have anybody else, and the time was growing short. Maybe he would get better with rehearsal. (Later he took me to Small Claims Court for $300 he said I owed him for playing the part. He lost. I should have sued him for his acting.)

Ever optimistic, we ordered champagne for opening night. Another bill. (Still not paid.) We were sewing in shifts at the Angels' house, trying to finish the costumes on time. The pumpkin that Cinderella and Prince Moe had to wear, given out to somebody to make, came back looking more like a banana. Beaver had to make another one.

The management of the Farm, where we were holding some of the rehearsals, said we couldn't tap dance on their downstairs floor. They wondered about the rehearsal rent, too. We made excuses.

Rodney went to the homes of some friends of his and begged for some money. We got some. We could go on.

I was eating fast food and milk shakes every day, my rewards to myself for all the stress I was under, making myself fat for my art.

Finally opening night arrived. We were sold out and turned some callers away, only to discover that some people who had purchased tickets didn't show up; there were thus some empty seats. Three long-time Angels' aficionados came in staggering drunk and fell in the aisle leading to the ramped seats as the overture began. We had had five previews, the only times we had run the entire show, including all the songs and dances in sequence. Rodney had wanted more previews, but I had pushed for opening so that we could take in some money to pay the huge bills, including the one to my poor mother. The director hadn't rehearsed the set changes with the crew, and so the waits between scenes were horrendous; one of them last forty minutes! Oh, my god, could we really open the show?

Since Rodney was a dancer, we had incorporated, not one but two ballets, into the show. I knew these were running too long, but how do you tell your balletic artistic director that? You hope it will all iron itself out somehow.

We opened about three previews too soon. The show was very good, everybody said, but it was too long, especially the first act. Bernard Weiner of the *Chronicle* had said he couldn't come at first, because he'd be out of town; then he said he could make it after all. He would be coming on the third night of the show. His review was unquestionably the most important because it would be read by the most people and then summarized with a Little Man recommendation (or not) every Sunday until we closed.

We opted to make some cuts to shorten the show, not in the ballets, the real source of the problem, but in the script, maybe a song. But whose lines, whose song? The director had not lost his cool up until then, but now he panicked and walked out. He came back. We discussed; we went over the script; we trimmed and trimmed until there wasn't a piece of flab left. I recall a horrible picnic between the opening weekend and upcoming Thursday performance when the

Chronicle was to be there, horrible because we argued about whether to cut Beaver's song about how it's not easy to be a fairy. How do you say we're going to shorten the show by cutting your song because you can't sing? You don't say it, that's how. "What about *his* song? *He's* not so hot!" somebody would say. What an afternoon of potato salad and savagery!

Beaver's song stayed; we cut some more verses out of the other songs. Nobody touched "'The Nightmare Ballet," which had grown more elephantine with each rehearsal. After all, we had to use those four fucking ballet dancers we'd hired! I thought the show was as lean as it could be script-wise. Reviewers always blame the book for inadequacies, have you noticed, and yet the first things to go when there's trouble are character, nuance, and motivation. One of the reasons I had picked a fairy tale to begin with was I thought nobody could jump all over me for writing a "thin" story, the way critics usually do for musicals. Believe me, there's no room to cram in a story with all the other things you're worrying about.

Weiner's review was favorable, overall, but he gave us a Staring Man instead of a Clapping Man even though the summary was very positive. He also said my script was "ordinary," and I was crushed. Most people noticed only the positive things he said; it was certainly a money review in the sense that business resulted from it, but my witty, wonderful script that had audiences rollicking with laughter was "ordinary"? I felt like throwing in the towel. Other people were saying it was Broadway caliber. Actress Jane Dornacker sent roses backstage and said she loved it and that it was a definite step-up for the Angels. Somebody called to say he wanted to produce it somewhere else, maybe in NYC.

(Nothing ever came of this, although much, much later Liza Minnelli's agent said he thought it would be a good movie for Liza. Nothing has come of this so far either.)

As the show played, it got tighter. That's all it had really needed in the first place, besides fewer ballets! The word of mouth on the show was excellent. We started getting audiences from all over, even though some people would call and say they didn't want to come to that crummy part of town out of fear. We discovered that kids loved the show, even though it was meant for adults. The children of residents in Project Artaud would come back again and again to see it, sitting on the floor down in front. We had a free performance for fellow artists in the area and rocked the place, with a joyous, wildly appreciative full house. In other words, we had a hit.

We were playing four nights a week, Thursday through Sunday, with the biggest houses on Fridays and Saturdays; it looked like we might pay off our bills after all. I was up to my ears in debt, having borrowed to make the show happen. I was running the box office every night, to get the cash into my hot little hands so that I could deposit it the next morning. There were continuing bills to pay, and I promised myself that I would get myself out of debt with the in-coming proceeds. By the end of the run I should be solvent again, though I wouldn't make one penny from the show.

However, certain people in the company began to make big trouble. Miss Janice Sukaitis, evil stepsister and rejected playwright, began to circulate rumors that I was pocketing the "vast" profits from our enterprise, in effect, stomping on the faces of the poor working actors. It is true nobody had been paid since the original $100, but then I as the writer, lyricist, producer, box office person, and general flunky hadn't received even that hundred dollars. In my desire to keep the performers from having to worry their pretty little heads about finances while they were trying to learn lines, songs, and dances, I had carefully concealed from them how much debt we were in, debts in my name.

But evil stepsisters will be evil stepsisters, and our last-minute Father and certain other individuals began to clamor for full pay. We had an emergency meeting with an actors' representative. A strike was the alternative. I couldn't believe my ears. I was being accused of exploiting the actors when the truth was . . . But they had seen the four musicians getting paid, the lighting bill getting paid, and so why didn't they get paid? Because there were nineteen of them, that's why, and to pay them the salaries they wanted would have closed the show and left me in debt for years. But they didn't care, or enough of them didn't, and so we had to agree to pay them out of the box office proceeds. That meant that each would get about $30 for four performances for each remaining week. No, that's not good pay, but the money was coming directly out of my hide. I had not received one penny of compensation for all the work I had done, and now just when I thought I was going to get back the $7500 I had borrowed to put into the show, I was confronted by belligerents who thought I was taking advantage of them! I began to see why nobody would want to put on a show. The Angels of Light had put on free shows until just before I got involved with them, and now money was everything. The paltry amount each actor would receive would not compensate them much for their work, but it would keep me from recouping my losses. Somehow I had become a Boss, and I was too proud to go on my knees and beg for mercy. I was relieved of my box office duties so that I wouldn't be able to get the money.

So Janice Sukaitis got her revenge for not being allowed to write another Angels' show, bringing Beaver and Rodney to tears backstage by telling them it had been her idea to have the strike. When Rodney told me this outside, I dropped him wherever he was in a hurry to go and then drove back to the theater, at fifteen miles per hours, not faster because my car needed a new carburetor, determined to have some revenge of my own.

Some of the actors were still around, removing their costumes and makeup. There was a little birthday party for somebody. When I saw the birthday cake, I saw Janice Sukaitis's face in it, even though she had left already, and I screamed and attacked it with the cake knife, tossing it into the air and breaking into tears, sobbing, "You would've been paid, goddamn you! You would've been paid when the debts were paid off, goddamn you all!" Actors bespattered with cake looked at me with amazement, trying to calm me down, but I wasn't to be calmed. I threw some other things and stormed from the theater. I was having a nervous breakdown and I knew it.

Then I got word that my mother was dying. I had better come to Illinois. A nurse called from the hospital, wanting to know if I wanted to keep the support systems going if that certain time came. . . . I said no.

When I got to the airport, my countrified brother-in-law was waiting for me. "'How is she?'" I asked. "She passed away last night, Dan," he said. I wept as we drove to his house and he told me how she had resisted going to the hospital even after she'd developed pneumonia, knowing that she would probably die there, but then she had consented, had even hugged all the family as she sat in the hospital bed covered with tubes and IV's and all the other indignities of modern death.

I attended her wake in the very same funeral home and looked at her body in the very same spot where my father had lain four months before. I didn't want to see my feisty, vibrant mother dead, but when her three sisters, down from Detroit, said the funeral director had done a fine job on her, my sisters and I agreed to have an open casket. I even went up and looked down at her thin, little face. "Thanks for the $5000 loan, ma," I whispered to her.

It was only my mother's death that enabled me to withstand the debts engendered by *Cinderella II*. The $7500 came out of my share of her estate, about $11,000. (Minus $5000 of that I.O.U. to my mother.) Somehow my parents had managed to save $41,000, including the house, during the sixteen years they had lived in retirement in a flat little farming town in the middle of nowhere with nothing to do. "Remember the plays I used to put on in the garage?" I had said to my mother during those ten days I had spent with her after my father died. "You see, it was good for me," I added, alluding to *Cinderella II*. "I'm putting on real shows now."

I have still not recovered financially from that show, two full years later as I write this, peanuts of course to most people but all I had in the world. And I didn't even tell you the really bad parts: the theft of the light dimmer, probably by one of our crew, the . . . But enough is enough, right?

People, when they find out I wrote it, still compliment me on how terrific that show was. Lots of people even saw it more than once. Still, the praise doesn't convince me it was all worth it, not even with a blowjob from the Holy Ghost thrown in.

JAMES BROUGHTON

What a breath of sweet, fresh air James Broughton was. Then in his mid-seventies with white hair and white beard, he seemed to be that rarest of creatures, a poet who had it together. Once married to critic Pauline Kael, when I met him he had a male lover half his age. They appear to be very happily in love.

I have not seen any of the films he's made, but I did hear him read some of his poetry. The first time was under circumstances dear to the heart of S.F. Broughton was dressed in a nun's habit, his beard still much in evidence, as he appeared on stage with the Sisters of Perpetual Indulgence in a combination entertainment/pagan religious ceremony before the Gay Atheists League of America, of which I was a founding member. Sister Sermonetta read *Graffiti for the Johns of Heaven*: perfect little gems favoring sex, the body, emotional openness, all those things that would seem to be what all heavenly people would support, only they don't. I'm sure there are some who don't think there are any johns in Heaven and they certainly don't have graffiti.

Another time I saw Broughton was at a talk I gave at the Walt Whitman Bookshop in 1984 or '85. He and his lover honored me by attending, and I even got a hug at the end. I realize I'm in danger of losing my credibility as a curmudgeon, an image so carefully worked on. But I felt all gooey inside because such a good poet, such a nice man too, had bothered to come to see me. Later I heard him on the radio explaining why he and his lover, after traveling all over the world to find a place to settle down, decided to return to S.F. That's where they felt most at home. I feel the same way.

Broughton may have a nasty underside, grasping, killerish, and cruel. But I doubt it. And if it's true, I don't want to know about it. Even I have to maintain some illusions.

GEORGE BIRIMISA

Another older writer who's a sweetheart is George Birimisa, known for such plays as *Pogey Bait*. We met at a time when our writing concerns were veering in opposite directions, he toward prose fiction, me toward plays. Unfortunately George had a hard time placing his newly written books, and I sympathized with the arduous labors he went through, not only writing them but submitting them to publishers. I gave him some leads, leads which didn't pan out.

He kept himself in good shape well into his sixties, but he had severe eye trouble. He was almost blind in one eye, as a matter of fact, and had one or more painful operations, then a cornea transplant. In TV movies, the semi-blind always get better. In real life, George did not. (There was something rather unsavory about the actual cause of the eye injury, best left unspecified.)

He devoted much of his energy to a writing project for senior citizens, and somehow hung in there even when the going got tough and stayed that way.

Somewhere in here he even participated in a body-building contest for men over sixty!

MISS AMERICA

In 1985 I was asked, as a part-time teacher in the English Department, by Don Cate of the Drama Department of City College of S.F. if I would like to write the script for the college's Fiftieth Anniversary Celebration to be held at the huge Davies Symphony Hall. It paid only $300, but I needed the money. I had no idea I'd get to meet Lee Meriwether, former Miss America, TV and stage actress, plus some other people less charming than she.

The script job, it turned out, involved several preliminary planning sessions with some college officials. The first time we met was in the home of the school's publicist, who greeted us in her robe. The next time, two weeks later, we met in her bedroom sitting in chairs at the foot of her bed as she writhed and tried to remain coherent. She died two days later, of cancer. It's the closest I've ever been to a dying person. No one had told me she was sick.

The plan we worked out, as this woman lay dying in front of us, was for representatives of the college from all the decades (1935-1985) to be on stage to give a short speech each, as if at a birthday party, with a big cake wheeled in at the end. Not David Wolper, but not bad.

Lee Ann Meriwether, who had attended City College, would be M. C. It was my idea that the speakers should tell colorful anecdotes. So it became my responsibility to call ex-presidents of the school, politicians, police chiefs, even some literary celebrities, you name it, then pick their brains, and write up their words in a coherent, clever manner, to prevent them from either freezing up or running off at the mouth during the actual Celebration.

Naturally some people were better than others at summoning up anecdotes. A blind man who was a runner was particularly good. I looked into some City College history and made up anecdotes for the verbally underprivileged.

Jade Snow Wong, author of *Fifth Chinese Daughter*, was a major pain. When I told her what I was calling for, she got all huffy and said, "I am a writer! I will write my own words to speak. I will be very good." She didn't know that I was a writer too, I guess. I didn't want to usurp her role. I was just irked that she didn't know who I was and wouldn't surrender herself into my capable authorial hand. Because her husband had just died, I decided to be accommodating and benign with her. We agreed that she could write whatever she wanted as long as she kept it under three minutes. When I found out a little later that she had complained about me to the program coordinator, I felt doubly irritated. That's what I had gotten for letting her have her way! When she finally spoke on stage the night of the Celebration she was adequate, on the dull side, though she did manage to get a plug for her book in.

Lee Meriwether, on the other hand, was fun to work with. Yes, she picked and chose through the speech I wrote for her, but she actually used some of my words. I was amazed. I didn't mean for her to be a slave to the script. Don Cate and I were just concerned that the performance part of the evening come off smoothly. After all, it was intended to be a public relations triumph for a college that was at the same time fighting bad PR about administrators misusing their powers and basketball players accused of sex crimes.

We held one rehearsal for the performance, with Susan Jackson-Woodruff acting as director. She and I had worked out a plan to have typical dances of the various decades, culminating with break dancing, which I was sure would be a crowd pleaser. (It was.) It was also a way of being sure we had some black representatives on the program. Indeed, there was much concern that ethnic, racial and female categories get visibly displayed during the program. I included gays as one of these groups. But the gay representative, Sal Roselli, chose not to show up. So the speech I had written for him was hastily given to another minority member to read. He chose to *omit* gays from the list, deliberately. One of the white females on stage had also, I learned later, objected even to mentioning gays; she wanted them to be included in something like "and all are other friends." Fuck her and fuck all the minorities that are prejudiced against my minority!

The person I think of most when I replay that rehearsal and the performance itself is a former California State Assemblyman who showed up with several official proclamations for the college: from the Board of Supervisors, from this self-promoting politician, you name it. He said he was trying to get one from the governor, and even President Reagan might be sending one. Nobody seemed to have the nerve to stop this self-serving blowhard in his tracks, although I did tell him nicely that we wanted to keep the show moving along at a fast clip. Niceness is wasted on such people. Despite his assurances, I knew he would take too much time, and so I wrote up some funny lines for M.C. Lee Meriwether to say in-between all those boring proclamations we were threatened with.

Sure enough, the night of the show this fat blunderbuss

came out with not one, not two, not even three proclamations, but seven of them, all of which he proceeded to read in their entirety. Lee Meriwether had looked over the jokes I'd written for her and said she didn't dare use them. Why not? All I wrote was: "We seem to be blessed with an embarrassment of riches, don't we?"

After the one from the governor, who was notorious for having cut funds for junior colleges, including City College, she was supposed to say: "We seem to have more proclamations than state funding!" I suppose you don't get to be Miss America by saying satirical things, but I felt sorry for poor Lee Meriwether having to stand there for twenty minutes, smiling, looking pretty in her evening gown, saying nothing, as this total jerk scored points for himself, he thought, with various politicians. He didn't appear to have a clue that he had stopped the show, and I mean stopped.

The first speaker from the various decades, the same woman who had objected to mentioning gays as being part of the City College family, also departed giddily from her script, triggering a series of ad libs that made the ad libbers look gushy, inarticulate, and long-winded. Luckily some of the people stuck to their scripts and were much better. It wasn't even that they were saying my words. They were saying their own words, telling their own stories, in words I had fashioned to make them more lively and interesting than they tended to be without outside help. The evening was a success despite the goof-ups.

I ran into the president of City College at the Bay Area Theatre Critics Circle awards ceremony soon after this. My musical *Cinderella II* had been nominated for some awards.

But the people who had played Cinderella and Prince Charming were now having a major fight; life was imitating art, and so instead of using a song from our show, as promised in the program, Rodney Price came out and did a tap number to a song by Irving Berlin or somebody! I tried to explain to the president of City College during the intermission that I hadn't plagiarized this famous song for my musical. Sitting next to him was this beautiful, beautiful woman with her hair upswept, dressed like a Greek goddess. She was so gorgeous in fact I barely nodded when he introduced her to me. The noise level was so high I didn't catch the name. I discovered later the beautiful, beautiful lady was none other than Lee Meriwether. You so rarely see stunning people up close, and it's intimidating when you do. I don't know what she'd done except put her hair up and changed her gown, but she seemed even more attractive than the woman I had written lines for a few short weeks before.

Doug Holsclaw & Leland Moss

When *The AIDS Show* was being put together, I admit I was preoccupied with *Cinderella II* and didn't think *Artists Involved with Death and Survival*, as it originally was called, would go very far. After all, it was meant to run for just four performances. When it turned out to be a big success that ran for almost two years and even wound up in a video version on PBS, I was amazed.

Of course I wanted to have a skit even in a little show and wrote one about a fundamentalist minister being icky-sweet in his basically un-Christian Christianity to a group of Bible school children. It was well performed in the first read-through by Chuck Hilbert, with no rehearsal at all, and it was voted into the show by those present. I didn't even attend any rehearsals because I was so busy with my musical. Leland Moss was the director and shaper of the various skits, and he did a splendid job. He was a good writer and actor as well, and so nobody objected that he included four of his monologues among the twenty-one pieces.

I thought it was a terrific show when I finally got around to seeing it. And so did a lot of other people. It got excellent reviews and even went on tour to Fresno, San Diego, Boston, and other cities. A bigger tour was planned, but somehow it never got underway.

Some of the cast changed during the long run of the show, but my skit remained, the leading part now played by a woman as the minister. I would hear rumors from time to time that my skit gave offense to some, like the religious mother of one of the actresses. Good, I thought. I'm hitting home. This was even before the real-life head of the Southern Baptists issued a public statement like the one I had my so-called parody of a minister say --that AIDS is a punishment from God for sexual sins. Such nonsense needs to be pilloried every chance you get, and why should I feel guilty for revealing religious fools for what they are?

I liked Leland Moss, bespectacled, transplanted New Yorker, former script reader for Joseph Papp. I was glad to have such a talent in charge of everything. And Doug Holsclaw was good to have around since his two skits in *The AIDS Show* were first-rate. He himself seemed a cold queen, rather Scandinavian and boney, but there was no denying his theatrical abilities, both as writer and performer.

The trouble began when money started to appear from the success of *The AIDS Show*. During the run, I received maybe $150 in royalties for my five-minute skit, and I was overjoyed. Then bigger bucks began to rear their heads. There was going to be a second edition, *The New AIDS Show*, with growing possibilities of TV airings and such. Who wouldn't want to be a part of all this? An Emmy perchance?

So I began devoting my Sunday afternoons, for months, to the gatherings that Leland Moss arranged, wherein we could present our new skits, meant to be combined with the old skits. We writers and actors would read, listen to each other's critiques, and then re-write, have them read again, maybe several times. Leland said it was all going to be decided in a democratic way, with the participants of the first show having priority, yes, but all to be worked out fairly. My ass!

Somewhere in here Doug Holsclaw was made co-director, and he was added to the staff at Theatre Rhinoceros as well, thus cementing his place in the power structure that was being created along with the new skits. That was all fine. He was a talent to be reckoned with. Perhaps his greatest talent was being adept at getting more than his own when it came to divvying up the pie. Leland must have taught him everything he knew.

I remember sitting through six hours of new skits, six full hours, with all of us writers watching, benumbed, along with the woman artistic director of the theater. As usual, there was pressure to include work by women, whether or not it was as good as that by men. Guess what? Jeannine Strobel, a performer who had not attended a single workshop for the new show, had a piece accepted! How terrific for her. Guess what else got into the new show? That's right, two more pieces by Leland Moss and another new one by Doug Holsclaw! Okay, I thought, they're in charge. If I were in charge, I'd probably pick my own stuff too.

What I hadn't quite counted on was that my skit from the first show would be dropped. Not only did I not have any new skits included, I was out in the cold altogether. I was too angry and too proud to run screaming into their presence and tell them the world needed my skit. I bit my tongue and didn't say anything. I don't know all the machinations that went into what wound up in the final version of *The New AIDS Show*. I just knew that I had been aced out.

When it was this *second* show, and not the first, that got videoed late in the day by Ron Epstein, a winner of an Academy Award, no less, and by Peter Adair, film maker of

Word Is Out, I was pissed as hell. All the writers of the second show got to be interviewed, their skits captured for a large audience to see, and paid handsomely besides. Those people whose skits were dropped, the actors who were dropped, that is, some of us people who had created the very show that originally got all the attention and drew in the audiences and the johnny-come-lately video-makers, were outraged, and rightly so. Cut us out just when the good stuff starts to come in? Fuck that.

If Leland Moss and Doug Holsclaw were to give a graduate course in how to alienate as many co-artists as possible, especially under a "democratic" system, they could not have been more thorough than the way in which they handled this. I've said many times since that if the video-makers had wanted some real drama in the backstage pictures they shot for their documentary, they should have interviewed those of us who had labored long and hard in those workshops, only to be bypassed for material that Moss and Holsclaw wanted in, that is, their own stuff.

I had the opportunity after this to chat with the man who wound up editing the TV version of *The AIDS Show*, once the two original fellows threw up their hands in despair. He said his major task as editor had been getting some variety into the program. It was all: "Oh, we're all dying! Isn't that awful." Or "We can't have sex anymore. Isn't that awful!" No doubt this was a result of a few select people cramming in as much of their own narrow material plus politically correct material from politically correct sources as they possibly could cram. This editor said a skit about a Bible-thumping minister would have been welcome for its different angle on the subject of AIDS.

Those of us who had been in the first show had been promised to be mentioned "in perpetuity" in all future credits for the show. Yet we didn't get to share in the windfall when it finally came and we weren't listed in the credits either. I guess perpetuity isn't what it used to be. I have contented myself – not very much, as you can tell – with the fact that the first *AIDS Show* was the one that got published in *West Coast Plays*. (Big deal.) You try to control your fate and your place in history, and still you can't!

SEAN PENN

Went down to Hollywood in August, 1985 because I had an appointment with the creative executive of Orion Pictures, who had read *The World Can Break Your Heart* and told my agent (nearly senile Bertha Klausner) that it was the best thing the agent had sent her. I was not about to lose this contact with the glories of moviedom.

I borrowed money to go, rented a car once I got there. That in itself is a tale since I didn't have a credit card of my own, and four different car companies turned me down when I tried to use the one my colleague Isabel Gilbert had loaned me. But I managed somehow, got a hotel in West Hollywood, devoured William Goldman's *Adventures in the Screen Trade* so that I'd know what to expect, and waited breathlessly for my appointment the next morning at Orion Studios in a huge high-rise in Century City.

Yes, I was there in plenty of time, sitting in the waiting room clutching my precious screenplays and screenplay ideas to my chest. Who should be sharing the waiting room with me but two movie producers. We did not speak, but I didn't have to try to overhear their conversation. It was as if they were putting on a display of how stereotypical Hollywood producers can be. One of them was waiting on the results of the first weekend of his movie, anxiously, since the first weekend is a good indicator of how the movie is going to do for all eternity. I later found out the name of the film was *The Return of the Living Dead* and it did all right, as schlock often does. All these two producers talked about was money and more money. One of them was about to have a new telephone system put into his house, with a zillion special features, no doubt so that he could make even more money.

Just then Frances Doel, the creative executive, came in, an elegant, slender British woman, a mistress of decorum and warmth. She spoke to the producers; she spoke to me, assuring me she'd be with me shortly. When she disappeared, one of the producers even spoke highly of Frances behind her back. Then the producers were called into the inner sanctum.

A second later a short, thin young man in sunglasses came into the waiting area and began to pace within inches of me. I had seen him in several motion pictures, so I was pretty sure who it was, Sean Penn, the bad boy of Hollywood. Everywhere I had driven since I'd been there I'd heard on the radio about the upcoming marriage of Madonna and Sean Penn, and here he was right next to me the day before the wedding. He seemed very restless; he also had a reputation for beating people up if they took photographs of him or his bride, so I decided not to ask him if he wanted to make a movie out of any of my scripts. He didn't speak to me either. In a movie of course, he would have spotted a couple of words in a script I just happened to be looking through and he would have said, "Is there a part in *that* for me?" and the rest would have been Hollywood history.

What actually happened is that he went up to the receptionist's desk and identified himself quietly and said he had an appointment and, in effect, why the hell were they keeping him waiting. She said she'd check. As he waited, he paced by me again. Finally, after a minute or so, the receptionist called to him: "What did you say your name was again?" Mr. Penn glared at her and managed to say, "Sean Penn!" If he had been a bigger star at the time, or if his latest movie had been a hit, he probably would've had her fired for not knowing who he was. I thought it was delicious.

When I went in to see Frances Doel, I asked if Sean Penn and Madonna were planning to make a movie together. She said, "They're threatening to." Well, it so happened that the movie they made right after this was a complete and utter bomb. You see, Sean Penn should have asked for a script of mine after all!

TERRENCE MCNALLY

I attended a panel discussion at the Magic Theatre in S.F. in 1985 where several noted playwrights talked about modern theater. Mary Rodgers, Wendy Wasserstein, Ted Talley, and Terrence McNally vied with John Lion of the Magic Theatre and a large live tortoise which was part of the desert set the panelists were sitting on. The tortoise seemed to scare the wits out of some of the playwrights, who kept lifting their legs and looking around as though they expected to be eaten alive, losing their train of thought and making themselves look like characters in a Three Stooges movie. I thought the winner for public personality and charm by a long shot was Terrence McNally. So he is the one I chatted up at the cocktail party that followed.

For some reason I was in a self-effacing mood that day -- hard to believe, I know. So I wouldn't give him my name when he asked, although I mentioned that I was a writer. The truth is I was afraid that if I said it and he and the others listening had never heard of it, I would've been crushed. Not saying my name did make me seem mysterious and more interesting, I'm positive. People want what they can't have.

Since McNally was the Vice President of the Dramatists Guild besides being a playwright (not yet very famous) and a rumored protégé of Edward Albee, this in the past, I decided a week or so later to send him a copy of my novel *The World Can Break Your Heart* and tell him I was the man he'd conversed with in S.F.

I didn't hear anything for months, and so I assumed he

hadn't liked the novel. Then I got a postcard apologizing for the delay, saying he'd been busy with two or three new plays of his own and he'd just gotten around to reading my book. It was a dream come true, for he wrote: "I've just finished it and I think it's very powerful. Congratulations on a difficult job wonderfully done."

I wrote back to thank him and to ask about Liza Minnelli, since he'd worked with her on *The Rink*. Her agent had expressed interest in my *Cinderella II* as a movie for her. I wanted to know if I could expect star turns from Liza. So far I'm still waiting to learn the answer to my question. Believe me, I'm willing to put up with a few star turns to have Liza Minnelli in my movie. I've gotten this close to Hollywood riches. Whether it goes any further I will learn.

(Well, now we all know what happened to Liza Minnelli's movie career!)

SUZY BRIGHT

Suzy Bright was pure San Francisco: a feminine, leftist lesbian who edited a magazine called *On Our Backs*, about how to have better sex and thus a better life.

I met her when she became a regular on David Lamble's "Traffic Jam" on KPFA radio in 1986. She was a tall, sound-limbed woman who wore very large glasses and was the most sensual woman I have ever met in my life. She was very aromatic, in the best sense. You felt that she might burst into orgasm at any minute. The last time I saw her, for instance, as we waited in the public room outside the studio, she wondered if I'd mind if she changed her pantyhose, whereupon she ventured to remove her old pantyhose and put on her new ones, managing to continue our conversation without getting more than a very short distance away from me. I have never known anyone, male or female, more at home in her body. She made me feel like an old prude.

I gave her a lift from Berkeley back to S.F. one time. She was in a hurry because she was going to an all-woman orgy. Seven friends of hers would meet periodically for dinner and then have group sex. So some of the lesbians were getting hot just when the gay men were now almost monks out of fear of AIDS. Afterwards, when I asked her how the orgy had gone, she said she hadn't felt much like sex once she got there, so instead she'd offered to shave any woman who wanted to be shaved. I take it she meant legs, although she didn't say that. She said that three women agreed, and she had used up twelve razor blades.

Suzy wrote articles for *Forum* magazine and was always having to withstand the onslaughts of the more sex-negative members of the world, but she didn't seem to care one whit. She was truly a missionary in the realm of sexuality, even if that wasn't her position most of the time.

She's the only woman I've ever known who said she enjoyed pornography. She wanted the whole world to enjoy their bodies. What strange ideas she had! A true subversive in today's neo-Puritanism.

ROMANOVSKY AND PHILLIPS

Romanovsky and Phillips were a gay comedy/singing duet that made a considerable splash in the 1980s because they knew how to entertain but also because they were a male couple whose loves and fights were a part of their act. Singing groups of any type usually fade, so these two, still very much a team as I write, may not last forever either. If they survive the pressures they put on their relationship, they will amaze everybody.

They not only lived together, they performed together, wrote music together, and traveled long distances in their car to their gigs all over the country together. I doubt anybody can withstand so much togetherness. When and if they get on each other's nerves, the act will disappear, since so much of the act depends on the proper chemistry between the two.

They're only in their late twenties/early thirties as I write this. Maybe they will still be performing together in their sixties, appearing on their own TV show. At the moment, however, gay male lovers are not allowed to perform in most venues. R&P have been told to take the gay part out and they could play many more places on the strength of their talent alone, but they want to do what they want to do, because that is what is special about them.

I reviewed Romanovsky and Phillips when they were getting started, at the Valencia Rose, a gay venue in S.F. I liked them, although I did think Paul Phillips tended to go on a bit during the talking part of the act. He likewise was partial to earrings and fem attire that did little for me. Ron

Romanovsky seemed more controlled, darker, deeper, and, yes, more talented.

David Lamble used to promote them shamelessly on his radio show, and one time we all went out to dinner after an interview meant to plug their first show at the San Francisco Music Hall, at a time when gay performers just did not have such venues. They were anxious that the show attract at least five hundred people to prove to the management that they were a draw. The show did very well actually.

I was surprised to find that in person my reactions to Romanovksy and Phillips were different from what I had expected. Paul seemed less sexy offstage than on. (I must stop this 'sexiness' evaluation, I suppose, since I'm losing my own. I always used to assume I could have just about anybody I wanted, but I am beginning to see that that isn't true any longer, if it ever was.) In any case, Ron seemed moody and difficult, whereas Paul, the butterfly, seemed nicer, warmer, more generous overall. My reaction may be colored by the fact that Paul had read one of my novels and liked it and wanted to trade two of their albums for my latest book. Talk about a Pavlovian response! I even thought his singing had improved!

My reaction was confirmed by an ensuing episode in which David Lamble and editor Ed Dundas tried to make a documentary of Romanovsky and Phillips on tour. Paul was all for it, but Ron was more standoffish. Since performers generally disappear faster than spermatozoa, I thought it foolish for Ron to put up resistance to what could only enhance his career and probably prolong it after he and Phillips went their separate ways. Maybe this documentary will come to be, maybe not.

I wish the two of them well, but show biz, like love, is fickle, and when, as in this case, the love *is* the show biz, can disaster be far behind?

FRANCES FITZGERALD

When I read the "Castro" section of a new book called *Cities on a Hill* in *The New Yorker* in late 1986, I sent the author, Frances FitzGerald, a note thanking her for her scholarship and for helping to elevate a worthy but neglected group (gays) into the august presence of the powers-that-be. I also sent her a cartoon I'd done with Joe Kirby showing three fat, balding business men in identical suits looking at two passing gay men and saying, "What I really hate about gays is the way they all look alike." FitzGerald likewise had the first name of John Molinari, possibly the next mayor of S.F., inaccurate. She was grateful for the correction; she liked the cartoon, too, and she wanted to meet during the S.F. part of her book tour. I would be delighted.

I should mention that I had also complained to her that it was certain people who always got quoted in books and articles about S.F. gay life, and I wasn't one of them. Armistead Maupin and Randy Shilts and Ken Maley had much better media connections than I did. But I was determined to get some of the action.

I asked Frances FitzGerald if she'd like to be on KPFA with David Lamble and me to discuss her book, which was not only about the Castro, but about the Rajneeshpuram in Oregon, old folks in Florida, and Jerry Falwell's Liberty Baptist Church in Virginia, all visionary communities according to the thesis of the book.

Now, to tell the truth, I had never heard of Frances FitzGerald. I didn't know she had won a Pulitzer Prize for her book about the war in Vietnam, *Fire in the Lake*. I just wanted to help somebody who had been objective about my world. There was also a rumor that she was married to William Friedkin, who had faced angry demonstrations over his anti-gay movie *Cruising*. How could such a woman be married to such a man? Well, it turned out she wasn't married to him; she wasn't married to anybody, although, at forty-six, she *was* engaged.

She said I should arrange with Ken Maley to be sure I was invited to the party he was throwing for her a couple of days after she would arrive. I promptly called Ken and got his answering service and left the message that I would like to receive an invitation. Well, the invitation never came, but I went to the party anyway. David Lamble had received the invitation, even though it was I who had arranged for the author to appear on the show. But I had made up my mind I wasn't going to stay home and sulk. I was going to attend if it killed me. Even if Maley came up to me and said, "Can't you take a hint?" I was going to that party. I'd been aced out of too many things by this time in my life.

It was held on Telegraph Hill, right behind Coit Tower, with a splendid view of the Bay Bridge and sailboats, lush vegetation, and other ritzy houses near the one where the party was being held. Overly clean, handsome young men offered you golden champagne in fragile glasses. Patés and other delicacies stood on a table awaiting your mouth. Caviar doesn't even taste that good to me; it's the idea of caviar that counts. Everybody was pleasant or witty or talented or rich. I loved every minute of it, even if I hadn't been invited.

Let me clarify something. I'd lived for the past nine years in the Mission District of S.F., which, to put it mildly, was a run-down section full of winos, street people, immigrants, and others who, whatever their gifts, were not what you could call "A" types. Rather than patés and sailboats what I see day after day is the Twenty-Five Hour Donut Shop full of burned-out, doped-up, pathetic, creepy individuals. I need to get out of this world into the elegant one more than I do, if I am to keep my sanity.

Frances FitzGerald almost didn't matter. She was surrounded by admirers, so we didn't get to speak intimately for very long. And when we finally did, not much of import occurred although I was surprised by her reply to my question about how many copies of her book her publisher would consider a good sale. Frances, a tall woman, pushed aside her page-boy hair and said, "Oh, I let my publisher worry about things like that." Well, yes, it must be nice not to worry about grubby things like money, and Fitzgerald didn't, because she had a private income. I wanted a private income, too, so I could stop caring about whether my books sold or not, including this one.

Yes, I wanted to go to fancy parties and mingle as I did that day and have my name recognized and people pleased to meet me. "Oh, so you're Daniel Curzon!" several did say to me that day, and I felt vindicated for all the effort I have put into my writing. It didn't even matter whether they liked my work or not, just that they had heard of it.

"That's Valerie Williams over there," somebody said, not pointing of course. "Who?" I said. "Robin Williams' wife. They're estranged. And see that woman talking with her? She owns Esprit clothes. She's worth three hundred million dollars." But is she a nice person? I wondered.

Then there was Jessica Mitford, all seventy-odd years of her, looking terribly British, speaking in a veddy, veddy top-drawer accent, especially for a Commie. I was introduced to her, but couldn't quite deduce the full meaning of what she was saying, except that it was something like: "My sistah's not rally a Nazi, you know. She talks like a Nazi and acts like a Nazi, but she's not rally a Nazi deep down inside."

I had a wonderful time up there in that rarefied air. How can I go back to Grub Street?

HAROLD NORSE

The poet Harold Norse lives a few blocks from me, but I've only gotten to know him in the last year or so. I heard him read years ago and I reviewed a book of his once, but our paths didn't cross on a personal level. I knew him as one of the Beats, of course, but I didn't know he was such fun.

One night he was at someone's house watching a film about young men playing basketball, a subject that didn't interest me in the slightest; he was sitting at a table in the same room. But nobody introduced us, and so that opportunity was lost.

Another time I saw him rushing about with copies of reviews at an ABA party, terribly worried about promoting his books. I thought, "Am I going to be doing that when I'm seventy?"

That was the night I learned that Norse was writing his memoirs. I reached up and pinched him gently, saying, "That's so I'll be in your memoirs." Then it dawned on me that perhaps I should write my own, and before I got too forgetful or died. After I started, I asked Harold if he would meet and talk about writing memoirs since he had just sold his to William Morrow.

He said yes, and we had a great luncheon and afternoon together. Harold is a little man who won't reveal his age, but he's no spring chicken. He's been everywhere and known everybody of consequence from Auden to Arnold Schwarzenegger, and still he's desperately poor and thinks continually about how to make ends meet. He's been mugged and has heart trouble. He lives in a tiny house that he won't let me see the inside of because it's too messy. His life makes me angry at my culture, because it does not support its writers. If anything, it penalizes them for daring to observe and immortalize it in art. The only justification for this that I can see is that writers outside the system aren't reluctant to point out its faults.

Harold tells me that his editor crossed out certain remarks in the memoirs. "Just what can you say about the living?" I wanted to know. "I'm finding out," Harold said. "My editor says I can fight to have things put back in." "Isn't truth an absolute defense against slander?" I asked, ingenuously, thinking of my own memoirs, which are the truth and nothing but, along with some personal judgments. You can make subjective judgments about public figures, I'm told.

Not long ago I went to Harold's book signing at City Lights Bookshop. He had called me and asked me to come. I went because I like Harold. I even bought a book. I can't afford $9.95 for a paperback, but I bought it to help out a friend, to help support literature. I sincerely hope Harold lives long enough to complete his memories for the rest of us to savor. He told me delightful stories of James Baldwin, Tennessee Williams, and other glamorous names. Why do we always savor writers so little while they're alive and so much after they're dead?

SISTER BOOM BOOM

Why have I waited so long to get to Sister Boom Boom, who no doubt is one of the best-known people I know? I must be resisting him. I didn't even put him in my working list of names.

The reason may be that I've never felt all that comfortable around Sister Boom Boom, or Jack Fertig, his real name. Maybe it's because I had nuns in Catholic school and there's a lingering fear. Maybe it's because we haven't had any real drama in our relations. It's hard for anyone to write without drama. Well, to tell the truth, there was a little tension between us.

Long before he was Sister Boom Boom I encountered Jack in my lover's bedroom, or I should say that I wanted Jim to be my lover. We had tricked, become roommates, and now I was developing a bad case of romance. So when I saw red-headed, white-skinned Jack Fertig peeping out of the other bedroom in my apartment, after a night of casual sex with the man I loved, naturally I was furious and didn't want to meet this creature, even though he wanted to meet me and Jim tried to introduce us. I went into my bedroom and slammed the door. After Jack left, Jim came to see why I had acted so strangely, and that's when my declaration of love came out, and soon Jim and I were referring to each other as lovers. Since that turned out to be the worst "love" affair I've had in my entire life, the source of much grief, I wish Boom Boom had stolen Jim away from me right then and there!

I knew that Boom Boom had read *Something You Do in the*

Dark and had wanted to meet its author. For me to turn down an interview with a fan must mean I had the lovesick blues indeed.

Boom Boom was in his early twenties at that time and not yet the media personality he was to become. But he started making appearances in drag even before the Sisters of Perpetual Indulgence discovered they had habits they couldn't control. I have a distinct vision in my head of Jack Fertig and another man wearing kooky gowns and wandering around the rotunda of S.F. City Hall during the mayor's wedding celebration. He said hello to me, and I was rather mealy-mouthed, I'm sure. Drag always made me feel uncomfortable. It seemed like showing off, doing anything to get attention. "Oh, I see what you gays want – the right to wear lipstick and dresses!"

Come to think of, some of my feelings about Sister Boom Boom in general have to do with how one gets attention from the larger world. I want it, I admit it. All artists do, yet I certainly haven't gotten as much as Boom Boom has gotten over the years. But then I was never willing to wear nun's clothing, fishnet stockings, high heels, clown-white face makeup, or chant to various goddesses while waving a dildo in the air.

Instead, I was hung up on being "normal," "masculine," and writing what I considered quality literature with gayness as my starting point for the human condition. Every time there was an interview with Boom Boom on TV or a spread in a newspaper, my heart squeezed a bit with envy. But then if I was so envious, why didn't I do something about it and become a male nun too? Because for all the immense publicity

Boom Boom got, he, I thought, lost credibility as anything the least bit serious. A freak show is all that most people saw, however much he and the Sisters might have a genuine agenda about venereal disease or pagan worship or what have you.

One year Boom Boom M.C.ed the Castro Street Dog Show, along with Jane Dornacker (now deceased; she died in a helicopter accident while working as a comic traffic reporter for a NYC radio station.) I think that Dog Show was the same day that actress Shirley Maclaine appeared on stage and got a big kiss from a mannish older lesbian, a picture that later appeared in a national scandal rag, but which didn't seem to hurt Shirley Maclaine's career since she went on to win her Oscar a couple of years later. At the Dog Show I remember thinking that Boom Boom was funny, but you could see the gears clicking in his mind as he searched for jokes. I noticed that up close too. There was this quality of calculation about the humor that somehow made me uneasy. That Dog Show, with owners and animals dressed alike doing tricks, with semi-naked bodies on display, and all the rest of it, crowds in the blocked-off streets, the intense cruising, was probably one of the last unadulterated, extravagant Good Times that the Castro had before AIDS took a lot of the joy out of the air.

I'd run into Boom Boom when he was out of nun's drag, too. Once he was in vampire drag for Halloween, and I recall a ride back on BART from a radio show in Berkeley with Boom Boom and Jon Sugar that had to be a highlight of my life for sheer laughs per minute and also constant worry about the wary citizens who kept staring at us. The trouble with funny times is that it's hard to capture the exact lines that seemed so great at the time, whereas what was said in a quarrel comes readily to mind. And I don't think I'm alone in such remembrances.

Boom Boom always had the hots for my third lover, John Gettys, made no bones about it, and often cruised him in my presence. Happily, that lover wasn't tempted to have sex with Boom Boom, the way the first one had been. (There was a Frenchman squeezed in there somewhere as well.)

Just when you thought Sister Boom Boom was dead as a media star, he'd manage to come up with a new gimmick to get attention. The most recent was his announcement of his upcoming marriage to a woman! That was milked for every drop it contained, and several it didn't, and then the bride up and went. What a genius for publicity Boom Boom had! I sincerely doubt that we've heard the last of him.

Indeed I just met with him and Dan Turner to plan a fake fag-bashing during Mass at St. Mary's Cathedral in S.F., but we were warned by Arthur Evans that interrupting a religious service might be a felony. In addition, Archbishop Quinn of our Catholic diocese, no friend in the past, has been quietly supportive of gays lately, at least as far as AIDS hospice care goes, and so we were advised by another knowledgeable source that forcing the Archbishop to make a public statement on the Pope's recent anti-homosexual pronouncements would be bad politics. I think I learned more about politics that afternoon than ever before in my life.

So we'll just have to wait until the Pope shows up in person next year and make noise then. We're planning a big vat full of cum: A Vat for the Vatican, plus our "The Pope Is Coming, So Should You" campaign.

Of course all the attention he knew how to get didn't convert into money for Sister Boom Boom. He continues to be a towel boy in the Jewish Community Center and does horoscopes to earn a living; he lives in a seedy South of Market apartment and tries to make do along with the rest of us. The whole Sisters of Perpetual thing should have converted itself into a show business act or a chain of fast-food restaurants, you would think, wouldn't you, if it had followed the typical American success syndrome. The Sisters play Vegas! The fact that this didn't happen attests to the basic integrity of Boom Boom and the Sisters; they were into changing consciousness about maleness, about stereotypes, about orthodoxy. It really was basically more political than self-aggrandizing. They didn't make a buck from it, but they did make waves.

ROBERT FERRO

When *The Family of Max Desir* was published, the publisher sent a review copy to Eric Bauersfeld of KPFA radio, who didn't know anything of the author, Robert Ferro, and wanted to know if I might care to read the book and interview the writer on the air. Always in the market for a free book, I agreed, though not with any great eagerness. For the name Robert Ferro didn't strike any chords with me either. He's published at least one other book since then, *Blue Star*, so he's better known now.

I was able to talk quite a bit with him off the air when I drove him around and learned that Ferro had been part of the short-lived Lavender Quill writers group in NYC, along with Edmund White, Andrew Holleran, and Felice Picano. Since Ferro was the last one to receive national attention, I asked him if he hadn't been somewhat jealous of the others. He proved to me a master of charm and discretion, but I ferreted out some of his less public opinions, one of these a distaste for Felice Picano, who had imperiously criticized Ferro's writing over a luncheon one time. "What is it about Picano that keeps that hack in power?" I wondered, surprising Ferro, because he didn't seem to realize that some of us on the West Coast take literature as seriously as some do in NYC, complete with rages, turf wars, and assassinations, at least of character. Ferro explained that Picano had a certain in-person charisma that insured his career. I trotted out my Ph.D. and said I thought there was a conspiracy of narrowness and preciousness in the NYC gay lit crowd. Apparently this didn't sink in because *Blue Star* is a mix of two stories, a terrific one about Italy and a boring-as-hell one about an underground temple in Central Park. New Yorkers must think everybody else cares about Central Park as much as they do.

Ferro didn't seem to know my work, for which I forgave him. You have to be tolerant of Eastern provinciality. Those people don't get out much, you see.

Ferro was still in his thirties: nice-looking, with a rich-Italian ambiance. He was quite pleased to be on a national book tour; the paperback rights to his novel had even been sold, the one and only offer a substantial one. He and his lover of many years were planning to live on the money for a year in Italy.

We attended a party together at the home of Larry Lee, a biographer of Jack Kerouac and others, likewise a TV producer. Larry Lee seemed to have the NYC contacts that I envied; he was also a good conversationalist and a good host. Successful people often are quite nice.

Some reporters (including Randy Shilts) and others on the literary fringe were at the party, snorting a white substance. I felt square, but I was not attracted to drugs myself since I knew too many people who were trying to be drug-free. Why go through all that to get where I already was? I believe some of these people have opted for Squaresville since that time.

Ferro said he wanted to read a book of mine, so I sent him one. But I guess he's been too busy with his own writing to read it.

JOSEPH TORCHICA

Another writer I met through an interview was Joseph Torchia, the author of *The Kryptonite Kid*. But it wasn't about that book that I spoke with him but about his second novel, *As If After Sex*, which I had received as a review copy.

When I read it, although I liked it, I knew that Torchia was going to need some help promoting it. My prediction turned out to be all too true. It got some good reviews, but it also got some of the harshest reviews I've ever seen, particularly from certain gay reviewers who protested its dark vision. Writers aren't allowed to display gay guilt anymore; it's bad modeling for our gay youth, you see, even if reveals the truth. Maybe especially if it reveals the truth.

It turned out Torchia was living in S.F. at the time, and I called him up. He was a very short young man with a beard, working on his third novel already, about snails, of all things. He said he was gay but was currently involved in a sexual relationship with a black woman, not so much out of bisexual desire as out of fear of AIDS. I'm always fascinated when people can pledge their allegiance to different flags like that. (Snails are bisexual/hermaphroditic; maybe Torchia was just doing research?)

He was happy to be working with editor William Abrahams, for whom this was a first gay novel. Torchia said that *The Kryptonite Kid* is gay too, even has a sex scene in the hospital, but it's done so subtly that nobody had noticed. The book had sold 25,000 in hardback and was even being taught in some high schools. Moreover, he'd received only one bad review out of some four hundred. I knew in my heart that he was going to have a far harder time with his second novel, but I didn't do more than hint at this prediction. I'm sure I felt solicitous because of my own experiences as a "negative" writer.

Torchia threw a party to celebrate his new book, and I attended, but I was in one of my reclusive moods and didn't mix well. Besides, Patricia Holt, the Dragon Lady Feminist of the *S.F. Chronicle*, was there, splendid in her pants suit and short hair, and all I could bring myself to do was glare at her and leave.

But that was not the end of my contact with Torchia. He solicited my aid when he sent out a reply to the cruel reviews when they finally came out. Paul Lorch of *The Bay Area Reporter* had read just a few pages before dismantling the book in print. Steven Saylor pummeled it in another publication. I asked Dan Turner if he could review it for *The Advocate*, knowing Dan would probably like it.

To facilitate this review I arranged for Torchia and Turner and me to meet at the Cafe Flore, a reasonable facsimile of a trendy hangout for upscale punk-look-alikes and literati. As we snacked, Turner mentioned that Jack Larsen, a closeted friend of his in Hollywood, who had played Jimmy Olsen on the old *Superman* TV show, had read *The Kryptonite Kid*. Then Turner proceeded to tell a long anecdote about Larsen and how his career had developed from playing Jimmy Olsen to writing libretti for operas. When the long anecdote about Larsen was over, Torchia said, "Yes, but what did he think of my book?"

JUDY GRAHN

Poet Judy Grahn has received a great deal of attention, for a poet. I had never met her even though we had back-to-back sessions in the same room at an MLA meeting. As a recall, Grahn and her fellow poetesses decamped just as the men came in to make their appearance.

So I was looking forward to meeting her and sharing authors' tales of mistreatment and misunderstanding, as we are wont to do, when Steve Abbott, another writer, pointed Grahn out to me at a party he was throwing at his place. She was not unpleasant-looking, perhaps on the chunky side, in her forties.

I was chatting with Ronald Chase, a painter, who was very good at making people feel good about themselves. He seemed to know all my books and spoke of my career with flattering thoroughness. "Let's say hello to Judy Grahn," I said, not wanting Chase's praise and attention to go too much to my head.

As we engaged Ms. Grahn in conversation, I said, "Hello, I'm Dan Curzon."

She said, "Oh, and what do you do? . . . Are you a poet?"

My face fell, I'm sure, in several directions at once. You aren't famous if you have to spell out how famous you are!

QUENTIN CRISP

Even though he managed to annoy segments of the gay community by his persistent internalized homophobia, Quentin Crisp also attracted a great deal of love and affection because he seemed in some perverse way to be a sexual pioneer, at least as portrayed in the film version of his life, *The Naked Civil Servant*. Happy indeed the man who has the brilliant John Hurt to play him flitting about!

I had seen Quentin Crisp twice on the stage after he began to make a career for himself in his seventies as a sort of stand-up Oscar Wilde, in velvet clothes, with broad-brimmed hat, ascot, and full face makeup, though by the time I got to meet him in the flesh he had calmed down the blue mascara a bit.

Even though he had answered several of my written questions in his live performance in S.F. one year, I hankered for a more personal get-together, and thus I wrote Mr. Crisp when another writer sent me a xerox of Crisp's reply to him. The reply said something about there being too much sex around.

Since I thought people didn't get nearly enough sex in their lives, eight hours of grueling daily work, rewarded, if they were lucky, by eight seconds of orgasm every few days, I wasn't sure that Quentin Crisp and I would get on, but I thought a cheery letter to him might be a nice gesture.

Well, it so happened that he was planning a book tour for *Manners from Heaven* and would be in S.F. very soon. He would call me. I let it go at that, not expecting him to follow through. But, lo and behold, one night I came home to discover a cryptic message on my answering machine. "Oh, it's only Quentin! I shall call again." I cussed a bit, for missing him, since I'm home most of the time, day in, day out. I was sure he would be too busy to call again, and he hadn't left a number where he could be reached.

Yet he did call again, and I was home that time. We agreed to meet at the home of a board member of Theatre Rhinoceros, where he was being put up, possibly put up with.

I was all a-twitter with expectation when the big day came, and I must say Quentin Crisp carried off his act, his persona, what you, will with consummate skill. He seemed a bit shopworn sitting there among the motes of dust and sunlight, some lint here and there, but he also showed ramrod posture and the air of an old prince sixty-fourth in line to the throne, certain he'll never make it, but not throwing in the royal towel altogether quite yet.

I took Mr. Crisp to a nice Mexican restaurant in the Castro. As we chatted on our walk to our destination, a number of passersby stared at us, mostly at him. A few called out in greeting to this living legend of militant effeminacy; a few rushed up and gushed in his face. It was sort of neat to be out with my seventy-four-year-old date.

I don't know if Mr. Crisp lets down when he goes to bed, a positive puddle in the bedclothes, but in person he maintained his Crispness from first to last. By that I mean, he was continuously charming, witty, and anecdotal, unnaturally so. He did respond to particular questions I put to him; still, a good many of his responses showed the polish of performance.

In fact, I had previously heard some of them from the stage.

He was mystified that he ever upset anybody. "All I want to do is please," he said, with that air of hit-me-fuck-me surrender that irritated certain people. It irritated me a little. He didn't think gays should fight for their rights; they should accept whatever the straights deigned to give them.

I wondered about his book sales, and he wasn't the least bit reluctant to discuss his poverty. He said he lived in a shabby one-room apartment full of dust near the Bowery in NYC because "I want to conquer the world." His books didn't sell all that many copies, he said, and he'd only just sold out the first edition of *The Naked Civil Servant*, years after its publication and despite the famous movie. He did public performances and book tours, but he barely made ends meet. I believed him. It's often true that famous writers do not make much money. (I don't believe the world knows this.)

It became apparent that Quentin Crisp hadn't a clue as to my work as a writer. His swift acceptance of my invitation I thus found odd. Did he just hope to get a free meal from a fan? His graciousness about what I bought him at the restaurant, his delight in being treated was as saddening as it was satisfying to me. The old man was the patron saint of the passive. He said as much when he said, "I don't go anywhere unless I am taken."

I believed him as well when he said he didn't have sex anymore. I don't know if the desire had drained away or if had just become too much of a pain in the ass, so to speak, as the years had galloped off. In some ways I spied what I call the St. Augustine Syndrome in Crisp, that is, fuck till you drop when you're young, then carp against the young having sex when you're old. But a second thought led me to wonder if he'd ever had that much sex. He had probably always waited for it to come to him, and, if it didn't come, I suppose he didn't either.

I walked him back to his abode and decided to leave him so that he could rest for the performance he was to give that night. I was amazed at how much he had "given" at lunch, and now he was going to give once again to a larger audience. For some reason I decided not to attend the performance this time around.

I did send him a copy of the piece I wrote about him in my column in the newspaper *Coming Up*. He wrote back that he was pleased with my generous treatment of him. Then I sent him a copy of an interview with me that George Heymont had done in *Stallion* magazine. In it I was quoted as saying some raw, candid things, such as my envy of other writers, and some other ugly truths. I don't know why I was surprised when I got a note back saying that my interview had quite "frightened" Mr. Crisp. I think my naked aggression about truly wanting the world to make a fuss over me went right to the core of his way of dealing with the world. I was the Other.

Don't know how long Lady Quentin Crisp will live; it can't be that much longer. I don't know what I feel about him, actually.

How can one tell the prancer from the prance?

JON SUGAR

Had been aware of Jon Sugar's considerable presence in the S.F. entertainment scene long before I met him. It was Halloween when our paths finally crossed, an appropriate occasion since Sugar (born Jonas Zuckerman) was truly one of the most bizarre characters I've ever run across.

He was a large, ever-expanding man in his mid-thirties, his hair going gray, at least until he noticed and dyed it a pronounced black. He was illegitimate, fat, Jewish, neurotic, and funny as hell.

I made the mistake of laughing uproariously at his antics on a BART ride back from Berkeley with Sister Boom Boom. Both had appeared on "Fruit Punch" on KPFA. When I included Sugar in a column on Underrated Things in S.F., thereafter there was no avoiding him.

At first I welcomed his friendship. Jon Sugar certainly made every occasion special. If I felt blue or bored, all I had to do was go out with him and we'd have an adventure of some kind.

He had just founded G.A.W.K. (Gay Artists and Writers Kollective) in order to provide opportunities for like-minded people to socialize. It also provided Sugar a chance to pick up any number of cuties in his official capacity as G.A.W.K. greeter. For such a chubby man, Sugar certainly did well in the bedroom. But then he said he wasn't fussy and liked them all, just as long as they were breathing. (There were doubts along this line about several of his tricks.) He'd find men getting off the bus at the Greyhound terminal; he even attracted a surprisingly large number of devotees who had heard him on the radio. He told of one longer affair with a nice-looking chap who wasn't really all that turned on by Jon's body, but somehow he stayed. "Foreplay consisted of two hours of me begging," Sugar said.

He lived in an apartment in the Haight District that reminded me of certain parts of Calcutta. In two small rooms were crowded four roommates, one of whom was a certified schizophrenic on medication, another a "masseur," whose clients paid to worship his body. Mattresses were spread on the floor for beds, the toilet leaked, and mold-covered casseroles dwelt in the refrigerator. One time the schizophrenic relieved his bowels in the bathtub, leaving smears on the shower curtain. When Sugar queried him, he said, "I didn't think you'd notice."

I would have died in such an environment, but Jon seemed to thrive. He was adamant about being an "artist" and not being "an office worker," the lowest of the low to him, even if it meant that he never had any money and was always facing eviction. Needless to say, one of his closest friends was "an office worker," the man who took Jon in once when he was evicted.

Among the younger men Jon attracted was one who became the lover, Jerry, or Little Jerry, to distinguish him from Big Jerry, another (non-stop-talking) friend of Jon's. Little Jerry was twenty years old and possessed of a squeaky voice and a large penis, the latter displayed to advantage in a porn magazine at least once. In between bouts of loving Jon, he went off to be the kept companion of a gentleman in NY

State, returned, only to go off again to perform similar chores in Seattle. He and Jon always said they loved each other very much; there was some evidence for this; they fought a lot. They were like an openly gay Laurel and Hardy.

I attended a party at Jon Sugar's apartment in 1985 to celebrate Dan White's suicide. Dan White was the man who had killed Harvey Milk. He shook off this mortal coil by gassing himself in his garage. Although it was in bad taste no, because it was in bad taste, Sugar decided we would serve Twinkies with candles on them. It was my addition to the frivolities to suggest that we all tell stories of where we'd been during the White Night Riot. We toasted Dan White's death. He would have done the same for us.

One evening Jon arranged for himself, Patrick Mulcahey, and me to meet at his place and talk for several hours. We all were craving a good, long conversation. Out of that came Mulcahey's generous recommendation of me to the producers of the soap opera he wrote for, *Santa Barbara*, for whom I did a sample script, which they paid me for and said they liked. But they wound up hiring another writer who had been given the same script to write. I was competing and didn't even know it. (That writer was fired five scripts later.) I wanted the $70, 000 per year the job would have paid, but I'm not sorry I didn't get it since it wouldn't have left me time to do work I respected more. It did get my financial hopes up, however.

Jon Sugar had a positive genius for making trouble, delighting in offending people with his remarks. He would not draw the line at anybody. Once while performing at a lesbian coffee house, a woman dropped a tray in the kitchen. "Let's hear it for women power!" Jon told the audience of mostly women. Yet for some reason he was always rather gentle with me, saying he respected me and my talent. He didn't read much of course, which probably made my talent seem even more wondrous because of distance.

We were sitting in a pizzeria one time when a drunk came in and sat at the counter opposite us. Fat Jon caught his eye, inspiring the drunk to say, "You sure don't need any more pizza." "Yeah, I need more alcohol, so I can be a drunk like you," Jon answered.

Another time we went to see *The Two-Character Play*, one of Tennessee Williams' later plays, not one of his better ones, here in a very weak production. Not content with disliking the play intensely himself, Sugar had to walk around and solicit comments from other audience members as we were leaving. I'd never dream of asking strangers what they thought of anything. But Jon spotted this thin foreign gentleman in a stiff sports jacket riding down in the elevator with us. "What did you think of the play?" Jon said. The man had enjoyed it. "So you enjoyed that, huh? Jon went on. "Do you work here? Are you the janitor?" He kept up a steady barrage of put-downs, some more oblique than others. I cringed but couldn't escape because we were in an elevator.

Even after we got out on the sidewalk, Jon couldn't resist going back to ask this same man what time it was. By now, the man had figured out, even with his limited English, that he was being twitted and said, "I don't give the time to assholes!" Jon came back with more smart mouth, and the man got more and more irate, and finally said, dukes up, "You want to fight? You want to fight?" "Is this a multiple choice test?" Sugar said. But the man pressed him, and Sugar backed down, infuriating me since I wasn't about to let a friend of mine look bad. "I'll take you on!" I said, and the foreign gentleman and I proceeded to engage in fisticuffs. Or at least I shoved him. When he stumbled, I realized that not only was he small and thin but he was physically handicapped too! His wife attended to him and escorted him away. I felt like such a fool. How could Jon Sugar have gotten me into such a low-life, embarrassing situation! Beating up the handicapped! Then on top of it all we couldn't find my car and wandered up and down many streets, with me yelling at Jon for being such a troublemaker.

Naturally the next time I heard Jon telling the story, it was about how he had out-witted this dumb cluck at a play.

Sugar later got into a power struggle with members of the "Fruit Punch" collective, of which he was a member. The sides became drawn, and David Lamble, as executive producer, had to act as mediator, deciding for the other side, even though he liked Sugar, because the other side knew how to run the control board and Jon didn't. I think the others may have picked a quarrel in order to get Jon out of their hair, because he tended to dominate any project he was a part of.

Jon was gifted as a singer and harmonica player as well as a comedian, but he couldn't quite get his act together. He always managed to do something excessive just when he should have been making a big name for himself and thus get banned from a performance space or the radio or whatever.

A director of a staged reading of a play of mine decided it would be a good idea to cast Jon in the part of a tattooed, heavy-breathing bisexual who has just come out of the hospital to keep a sex date. As you might guess, Sugar showed up for the reading in his Jockey shorts and a dinky robe. He said all his lines with utter insincerity and got spooked by a telephone sound cue and forgot to throw open his robe and flash the other cast members, his idea in the first place. I knew we shouldn't have cast him; he needed to say his own lines to be really funny.

He had done a rap record before I knew him and had tried to market it every which way he could. At last he succeeded in selling it to a record company and the contract was to come special delivery in a few days. It was six months if it was a day before anything arrived, and then a lawyer told Jon the contract was so lopsided in the record company's favor he shouldn't sign it. In the meantime Jon had done a wacky interview with me in *The Bay Area Reporter*, and I returned the favor by doing an even wackier one with him for the same publication. (Sample question: "Is it true the Pope wanted to write a blurb for your record, but you turned him down?" Answer: "Yeah, that dizzy queen gets her skirts up over her head so much you can't trust her.")

A year went by and the revised record contract still didn't arrive. Jon was counting on that one song to lift him out of poverty into the national spotlight. I warned him about putting too much hope into one project.

Maybe one of the strangest trips in my whole life was the time I drove with Jon Sugar and Little Jerry in my car to look for Humphrey the Whale, who, as you remember, was a humpbacked whale that somehow got misdirected in S.F. Bay and went up the Sacramento River. We joined the throngs at a bridge near Rio Vista, waiting for Humphrey to surface.

Sugar's size led us to imagine that we were searching for his lost brother.

Jon Sugar had immense talent and he shouldn't have squandered it, appearing with deafening Heavy Metal groups in dives, or burying himself in White Trash Debutantes when it fronted for Divine and such, making pennies. If he could have marshaled his abilities, he could have knocked the socks off most comedians. But he didn't want to compromise on his outrageousness, his gayness, or even his spontaneity, so Jon Sugar never got a commercial act together, not so far, and I doubt he ever will.

He would also write articles for various publications; they were at times semi-literate until manicured by a good editor, but they had pizzazz in spades. He hated nicey-nicey articles and wanted to blow everything and everybody out of the water. He loved to go into red-neck areas around S.F. and interview people on their prejudices and then taunt them to their faces, writing the whole thing up in a militant camp, don't-bottle-anything-up way.

He said some people came up to him on the street and told him he was a disgrace to the gay community. He'd ask them if they wanted to go home with him.

Jon had grown up in Miami, a white, fat, Jewish kid who learned to survive by being funny. "How original," I teased him. He said his schoolmates used to accuse him of sucking off his dog, but he won their hearts by saying, "I only jacked him off." Jon wanted to be liked so much, at times it was painful to watch him. And yet he'd dig at people until he got their goat.

His Jewish mother lived nearby, and he spoke with her on the telephone often. She didn't quite know what to make of the creature she had spawned. He said the first thing she said to everybody was, "Yes, I'm Jewish."

Jon had back trouble, and finally he had to have an operation. Before that he'd been forced to crawl around his apartment on all fours, naked and immense, a piece of toilet paper hanging from his behind because he couldn't reach it. "You look *marvelous!*" his friend Bill Bent told him, looking through the door.

Jon finally got on my nerves when we spent a New Year's Day together at David Lamble's. He spoiled every word game we played in one way or another and absolutely demanded that he be the center of attention for the entire day. My enthusiasm for being in his presence began to cool considerably.

You got the feeling, often, that he wasn't talking to you personally. Rather, you were an audience which existed to react to Jon's jokes and antics. He would call you and tell the same joke three times in one day, as if he didn't even attempt to remember whom he told what to. He'd complain of loneliness as he talked to you, only to have his Call Waiting Service interrupt every phone call with anywhere from five to ten calls from others.

I began to seek ways of extricating myself from quite so many Sugar attacks. I stopped returning his calls, but he didn't seem to notice. He was overwhelming, like sex with a sperm whale. You can have too much of a good thing.

The last straw came when he asked for a ride to Berkeley

and then showed up with another rider besides himself. He hadn't bothered to ask how crowded my car was. Since I had some other people, I didn't have enough room. Actually, it wasn't the ride itself that made me angry.

It literally was the last "straw" that overbalanced my mounting resentment against him. I flew into a rage, asking him why he thought people didn't return his phone calls, why so many people despised him, why he couldn't keep his friends, or his lovers, pointing out how he had no consideration for other people, how his egotism exceeded that permissible to human beings, even to Jewish comedians!

"Are you just teasing?" he said. At least he didn't say, "Let's have sex!"

I wouldn't see him after that. Once in a while I'd run into him on the street. I'd stay for a minute or two. He was always hilarious, but I just couldn't take more than a small dose of the man. But he wouldn't take no for an answer. He started calling me again and we'd talk, for limited amounts of time. He didn't offer me his new phone number, and I didn't ask for it. He was living with a friend in Pacific Heights ("Specific Whites," he called it), the poshest part of S.F. after being evicted from the Haight. He said he would be sure to call me again, to regale me with more jokes and "dish," and I'm sure he would. And he has.

Daniel Curzon

I've met myself in writing these memoirs, and I'm not completely happy with the person I see here. I've literally had hundreds of thoughts about what to say to conclude this book. I could justify myself for some of the things I've done, but I guess I'll have to let them stand or fall on their own in your eyes.

I don't believe I've been a rotter in my dealings with people, but I have spotted an unseemly amount of vindictiveness, envy, pettiness, and egotism. I don't think I'm alone in these faults, but I'm rather ashamed to see that I'm so base in my emotions. I'd like to believe that I'm more complicated than what comes through here; my career as a writer is just about everything; sex is next, followed by lack of money. Scratch me and not only do I bleed, I scratch you back. Compliment me and I'm your slave. I want people to like and admire me, yet I insult them and tell them off. You have to like me the way I want to be liked. I think I'm pretty smart, but what comes through are the actions of a stupid man, at least not a wise one. Too needy, too idealistic underneath all the curmudgeonly bravado. I'm trying to learn from this look at my relationships with people in my past. For one, I hope I can be less easily hurt by slights, real or imagined. I've got to learn to give more, not always to want, want, want. Me, me, me. It will be difficult. I don't know if it comes from a profound inferiority or a vast superiority complex. Maybe it's a mix.

Part of the problem, a major part, is that I don't have

enough money to live on, and this is not a result of my personal inadequacies. It comes from the exploitation of part-time college teachers. I am taking part in demonstrations against the College Board so that they'll change the policy and hire more of us with a salary higher than $9000 per year. I can't be a nice person on a salary that keeps me bitter and resentful about my poverty. I don't have the financial ease to rise above things. I can't even afford to publish my own books if I choose to.

For ten years now I've lived marginally. I was never what you could call a sweetie pie, but I'm in danger of going over the edge into maniacal, self-destructive rage. I desperately need some happiness! Surprisingly, these memoirs have made me happy. They have made me realize that I've had some pretty interesting episodes in my life. I've also kissed very little ass along the way.

My next project is to write a blockbuster novel, not because I think the world needs yet more trash, but because if I write such a creature, being very careful not to condescend to the form, I may get rich and thus have the wherewithal to continue writing what I really want to write, no matter who else likes it or doesn't. I thought that if I became a college teacher I'd have job security and the income to be able to rise above having to write junk or hold crummy jobs that rob you of the time and energy you need to write seriously. But I am being squeezed out of my ivory tower by economics over which I cannot maintain sufficient control, for all my dedication and anger. I worry about old age coming, with nothing but Social Security to live on, with my books probably out of print because it's not advantageous for publishers to keep them in print, about having no more books accepted.

I have devoted most of my waking hours for the past twenty-five years to being what I consider a serious writer. Often I feel that I have succeeded in writing precisely what I want and that I've been very brave. Other times I feel only a handful of people know or care what I've done.

Whatever happens, I hope I can benefit from putting aspects of my life down on these pages. I haven't put everything, nor included everybody I could have. Some of the things were just too nice and dull to be very interesting; some were simply too unkind.

Some of the people I've been hard on in this book have crossed my path since I began it. I made myself talk to Armistead Maupin at the Frances FitzGerald party, and he was downright charming. I was downright charming right back. It's a skill, Dan, that has to be cultivated. I'm sure you can do it if you practice. Even Randy Shilts seemed nice, with his new boyfriend and a new regimen without alcohol. I even hugged Arthur Evans at a Thanksgiving party!

Dan, your problem is maintaining what you see as your honesty while at the same time not doing yourself in because you alienate and annoy people so much they don't want to have anything to do with you. You must work this dilemma out, how to be yourself and how to live in the world, too, how to win at the game of life.

It is my hope that these memoirs have proved to be lively and informative. They do capture, I hope, some of the first flush of the gay rights movement and life at the end of the second millennium and some of the players in it, an age that surely cannot come again.

UPDATE – 1989

As of today, June 14, some things have changed since I wrote the above. Please let me bring you up to date.

LILY TOMLIN has done quite well, though more on the stage than on the screen. I don't know her any better than I ever did.

I still have not found my letter from JOHN STEINBECK.

JOYCE CAROL OATES is almost forgiven. She has written at least a dozen books, no doubt, while I've pondered what to say about her.

HARRY BRITT has just brought about a domestic partners bill in San Francisco, legitimizing same-sex relationships more than ever dreamed possible a few years ago. He's also the president of the Board of Supervisors.

Good old ROBERT PATRICK gave a good review to *Curzon in Love*, my newest novel, in *The New York Native*.

N.A. DIAMAN, the writer whom I sort of badmouthed in these memoirs, showed up for my reading from this same novel at the main branch of the San Francisco Public Library. So did my ex-lover, who is the basis of the villain in the book. I panicked a bit, but luckily the selections I had chosen for that reading weren't too damning, and so the ex didn't attack me. In fact, he came up afterwards and asked if I'd see to it that his ashes are spread on San Francisco Bay when he dies. Weird.

CURT MCDOWELL, the filmmaker, died of AIDS.

GEORGE KUCHAR, at the funeral, told me to go and look at Curt's body in the casket because it looked very good. Ordinarily I don't want to see anybody in a casket, but I went to look. He looked absolutely terrible.

MARION EATON, the actress, is taking care of a ninety-year-old man, but she's also made two films for Vestron. Horror films, but what the hell, it's show biz.

ARTHUR BELL died of something besides AIDS, thank god. That is, thank god for the difference, not for his death. We are losing so many already. (Edward Guthmann was a movie reviewer for the *S.F. Chronicle* for many years He and I never clicked.)

ARTHUR EVANS, whom I avoided for years because of his political correctness, wanted a ride with a friend of his to a Thanksgiving dinner party I was attending. I wouldn't take him, but he came anyway. There finally we talked. He turned out to be quite nice, much more easy-going in person than in print. (That's true of me, too, by the way.)

VITO RUSSO has AIDS. He was on TV recently at a conference in Montreal saying he expects to live, if the cure people are talking about comes to fruition soon.

RANDY SHILTS had an AIDS book published. He got interviewed on *Sixty Minutes*, "NBC Nightly News," and everywhere else you can think of it, in his endless quest for best-sellerdom. He knows how to sensationalize, that's for sure. Has a mini-series based on the book coming up.

LESTER COLE died of old age.

DEAN GOODMAN has done exceedingly well. He's been

getting important acting jobs. For instance, he was the villainous corporate president in the Coppola movie *Tucker* and is doing other movie and TV roles. He brought out *Prme Time*, a *roman a clef* novel in which I appear as a character, Lester Hoffman, a very sympathetic portrait. The book is basically Dean's *thank you's* and *fuck you's* to people in the theater world. But so self-serving. (But this memoir hasn't been, at least not too much. Right?)

JOHN GILGUN, whom I had written off in 1986, is now my summer housemate. He's in the next room right now. When I bought this condominium a year ago, he went in with me for 10%. How did such a change come about? Well, it just so happened that he was on sabbatical last year and wrote me when I happened to need a roommate to help share expenses. When he came from Missouri to stay with me in San Francisco, I discovered that what I had interpreted as insensitivity was in reality a result of John's poor hearing.

He's almost deaf, causing him not to hear many things or misinterpret them. Of course he is a poet and thus spacey too, but I've discovered that he is a warm, generous guy. He's also learned his lesson about not turning down offers from publishers. The novel that he first wrote in 1957 and that he revised in 1981 has been accepted by Amethyst Press and will appear in 1990, at last. It's a good book, which he has revised for the final time, and I will provide a blurb if the publisher wants one. John also has had a book of poems, *The Dooley Poems*, accepted by an imprint of the University of Southern California for a limited edition. All this is great news, and John is soaring. Nobody deserves it more. He's somewhat worried how his gay novel will be received back in Missouri, where he still teaches, but he'll cross that bridge when he comes to it. I'm sure he's together now and the anti-gay bigots won't win.

As of now, I can see us being part-time housemates for years to come.

Last year STEPHEN SONDHEIM wrote that he wanted to attend my play when it opened in New York off-Broadway in October, 1988. He sent me his telephone number to call him. I did call to get his advice on the previews of my play, which had been very erratic. As I was talking to Stephen about a weak performance I'd just seen the night before, I was informed that I was speaking to Sondheim's assistant, a *different* Stephen. Well.

DAN TURNER told me Sondheim tried to get back to me twice, but I was never in. I was at rehearsals and previews. Turner has become famous as one of the longest surviving AIDS patients. He's even been interviewed by "Larry King Live" and appeared onstage with Pearl Bailey in Geneva, Switzerland.

ARTHUR BRESSAN committed suicide when his AIDS diagnosis took a turn for the worse.

ROBERT CHESLEY has AIDS now too, when last seen had had noticeable KS lesions on his body. His play *Jerker* turned into a major censorship case when it was broadcast on KPFK in Los Angeles. A fundamentalist father riding in his car with his son heard the show and complained to the FCC, which clamped down. The repercussions are still being felt around the country, including at KPFA radio, where I am now Critic at Large on "Fruit Punch."

DANIEL CURZON's new agent, George Ziegler, is trying to secure the rights to two of his novels from Ashley Books (Billie Young) by proving that the books are not really in print any longer. Knights Press has agreed to reprint *Among the Carnivores*, *Something You Do in the Dark* as well as his *Gay Etiquette Book*. Hope he gets the rights back.

He also got tenure and full time status at City College of San Francisco. It took a threatened lawsuit on behalf of twenty-two teachers in the English Department, but it has been a *major* transformation. He has some money now. Onward!

PAUL MONETTE had a big success with *Borrowed Time*, a memoir of Roger, his lover who died of AIDS. He won a Lambda literary prize, I believe. He also met my friend Robert Prager at a signing and invited Robert to Washington, D.C. for the ceremony.

(Later Monette went on to win a National Book Award for *Becoming a Man*. Good for him. He got more serious as a writer, but it took AIDS to transform him.)

JEANNE BARNEY and I still exchange Christmas cards. In her last one she said she was in AA and doing well. (Some years later she got pissed at what I wrote about her in these memoirs. And I was nice to her!)

BRUCE BILLINGS, the cartoonist, and I have drifted apart after I tried to borrow money one too many times.

Reviewed HERBERT GOLD's novel *Dreaming* for the *Los Angeles Times* rather coolly but positively. He didn't contact me about it. I now review frequently for this newspaper.

Saw PETER ROBINS in London in 1988, had a great conversation. He's started a press with David Rees. I could have met Martin Sherman, the author of *Bent*, if my lover and I had stayed for the party Peter was giving. But we were off to Cambridge to meet Milo Keynes, the nephew of John Maynard Keynes, who turned out to be a heavy-drinking, closeted, old-fashioned British eccentric who resented his uncle's greater fame and kept forcing drinks on us.

TIM WOLFRED became head of the San Francisco AIDS Foundation and is now retiring from that post, overworked, ready for a life of mere politics.

TERRENCE DAVIES had another film, this one about British life in World War II, apparently a harder, less sentimental view than some of the other works about this period that have been coming out. Davies even won acclaim for the film on the BBC. I didn't look him up in London, though.

SISTER BOOM BOOM has died . . . of sobriety. No booze, no drugs, no Boom Boom? A shame, in a way. He's now a cleric with an Episcopal church in San Francisco, not much in the news anymore. Does this mean that all this time Boom Boom simply hungered for orthodox drag?

ROBERT FERRO died of AIDS or killed himself because he had been diagnosed and his lover had already died of the disease.

QUENTIN CRISP wrote me an odd letter, offering to review *Curzon in Love* any way I liked if my publisher would send him a review copy. What a strange offer.

Don't see JON SUGAR anymore. He reminds me too

much of what I don't want to be marginal, poor, and overweight. I did make a video of him in the hospital, over the top as usual, flashing the camera in his hospital gown. Somebody else finished the video and now Sugar flashes it all over town. (In fact, ten years or so later Jon Sugar and I renewed our friendship, only to have it explode *again* after two years. Yikes!)

CHRISTMAS LEUBRIE, the midwife, came to my reading at A Different Light Bookshop with her lover. My son, Zachary, is growing fast. I have yet to see him in person. She told me she and her lover have pretty much decided not to have a child since they babysat for a long weekend with my son and his "sister." Mmmm. This will keep me from becoming sentimental about the joys of raising my "my own child."

By the way, my play, with the title altered to *My Unknown Son*, was produced in New York City on 42nd Street at the Kaufman Theater. This happened because it was first produced in a workshop production at the Circle Rep Lab and was seen by actress GERALDINE FITZGERALD, who liked it so much she called producer MARTIN KAUFMAN, who put it on off-Broadway a year later. It was a look at my fears about how my son might turn out: angry, stupid, snotty, or homophobic. It played for two weeks and got a rave from a critic who saw it on a good night. The bulk of the critics came to the last preview, which, alas, was an off-performance. Opening night itself was wonderful. Friends of mine flew in from Chicago, Vancouver, Missouri and San Francisco. I wish it had played longer, but I couldn't control the performance of the lead, who was great one evening and off the next. It's all in the breaks. I felt terrible, but I didn't feel bad, if you know what I mean. How many people in this world get a play produced off-Broadway even for two weeks? Besides, I have other plays and will have other productions. Want to bet?

RODNEY PRICE of the Angels of Light died of AIDS. Two weeks before he died someone made a video of him dancing and singing in his wheelchair. Macabre. Touching. I could have gone to see Rodney perform this last bit live in a theater, but I couldn't stand the thought of him shrunken and skeletal. I don't want to see the video either.

LELAND MOSS has AIDS. It is an epidemic.

SEAN PENN and MADONNA are divorced, or all but.

TERRENCE MCNALLY had a nice big hit with *Frankie and Johnny at the Claire de Lune*, a valentine for heterosexuals.

SUZY BRIGHT reviews porn for *Penthouse* magazine and appears on National Public Radio and is quite the rising star, a leader of the lesbian sex explosion. They'd better watch those excesses. The men have.

ROMANOVSKY AND PHILLIPS broke up as lovers, but they continue as an act. DAVID LAMBLE found out that his article on them in the *Bay Area Reporter* was rejected because Bob Ross, the owner, said to his editor, "I don't like stories about divorce, do you?" Bob Ross is a censor and a jerk, another gay plantation owner.

DANIEL CURZON has been partners with JOHN GETTYS for nine years now. They even still have sex! He also has a full teaching job at last, even if it's at a community college. He gets to teach creative writing and other classes. It's not Stanford, but he does help a lot of immigrants learn English. And the creative writing students, even the ones released from mental institutions (seriously) are certainly more interesting than the rich, normal ones he'd get at Stanford. (Later Note: A friend of mine, Wilfrid Kaponen, who teaches there, said even Stanford isn't Stanford anymore. So there.) Curzon has some money now, and that makes all the difference in his attitude. It is amazing how mere money can help one bear up under those vicissitudes.

Life is mixed, of course, but he seems to have arrived. He just gave a reading in Vancouver at the Gay Games and people showed up with handfuls of his past books for him to sign. He gets some fan letters and fan phone calls. He seems pretty well known, although fame skips. (He still meets people who have never heard of Joyce Carol Oates either.) He feels strangely fulfilled and happy these days. He's off to England next month with his lover to meet Eric Glass, a literary agent who has requested about five of his scripts for a producer. One of these is based on the Salman Rushdie case. (It all sounds good to him. Real good.)

(In 1989 this agent presented my play *The Blasphemer* to three producers in London. They said we would be bombed if they put it on. So they didn't.)

UPDATE – 1992

Here it is November 8. This memoir is as close to an autobiography as I'll ever write, I guess, it and my letters and some poems and a few journal entries here and there.

Well, let's see what's happened:

Saw old PHYLLIS LYON and DEL MARTIN not long ago at a hearing of the San Francisco Public Library's Library Commission. The Christian Coalition and a few other homophobes were protesting the display of the rainbow flag (that is, the gay flag) at the Harvey Milk Branch, where it so happens my lover John Gettys – we're in our thirteenth year now – works as a library technician. It was somehow heartening to see those old gals still out there fighting. What a world when people feel threatened because a flag the color of the rainbow is taken to be an affront to others. I'm happy to say that the Library Commission vote to retain the flag. Are we gays on our way to Sacred Cow status?

A Lutheran pastor spoke against the flag and cited the Bible. I found out later that it was the same minister that my lover had when he went to Lutheran school. I wish I'd known that at the meeting, so that I could have spoken to the minister and said, "Do you remember John Gettys? Well, he was one of your prize pupils. He's my partner, and he's the person you're protesting against." When will it finally sink in that gays are stunning overachievers if they're anything!

JOYCE CAROL OATES sails on and on, more famous by the minute. I was contacted by Greg Johnson, who is writing the official biography of Ms. Oates for Dutton. He asked for and got my Oates letters, some fifty-two, but I think I'll find more, as well as her dedications to me handwritten in her books, plus sections on her in these memoirs. I also *found* my STEINBECK letter while filing all my old correspondence! Great! My mother hadn't lost it after all.

GREG JOHNSON himself seems to be turning out to be a person to note. He's had two collections of short stories published, one by Oates's press, making me wary of the treatment I'll get in this biography (as DAN BROWN, my legal name) since he owes her. I reviewed his book of stories from Johns Hopkins on the radio recently. He has a novel called *Pagan Babies* coming out too. He's only thirty-nine. We probably will meet when he comes from Atlanta to S.F. in February or March to promote his novel. He'll interview me then about Oates as well. Is it not strange that he's has a gay novel coming out now and he can be Oates' friend and even biographer when gayness was the main problem that destroyed our friendship all those years ago? Well, at L.P. Hartley so wisely said: The past is a foreign country; they do things differently there.

HARRY BRITT has retired from the Board of Supervisors, as of last week. The gay man who ran to replace him, CLEVE JONES, did not win. But there are two lesbians on the board now. The rumors are strong that one of them, ROBERTA ACHTENBERG, will get a post in the new BILL CLINTON administration. I didn't write up Achtenberg for this memoir, but I could have. I call her ACHTUNGBERG because she's another poor-me-victim kind of lesbian. I was on a panel with her where she called a man who paid for sex with teenage female prostitutes a "baby-fucker." She's another fascist of the Left.

ROBERT PATRICK is living with his sister's family in Atwater, California, having lost his NYC living/theater space. But I heard from LARRY MYERS, who himself deserves a chapter in this book, that Bob just sold a screenplay. I sure hope so. LARRY MYERS is a New York theater teacher/playwright with a squeaky voice and questionable ethics; he promised me a good review even before seeing my play (*My Unknown Son*, NYC, 1988) when he was interviewing me for *Stages* magazine. It turned out he didn't care for the production; he blamed the direction and the interview didn't appear either. But I wrote MYERS a letter of reference for his tenure at St. John's University a month or so ago. He promised to use a play of mine when/if he does an anthology. We'll see. The beat goes on.

N.A. DIAMAN still shows up everywhere, skinny as a pole.

MARION EATON has completely dropped out of sight, my sight at least.

BEAVER BAUER of the ANGELS of LIGHT was at a screening of MARC HUESTIS' movie *Sex Is* recently. She looked a bit tired around the eyes. We said hello but didn't get to talk much. MARC HUESTIS was sitting on the floor next to her, talking away. I must have given him a bad review or mention once upon a time. He's always been distant. Maybe it's me. John Gettys and I ran into him at C.D. Arnold's memorial and he barely acknowledged my presence, so I vowed not to speak to him anymore. But lately I've run into him a few times and he was grudgingly forthcoming. I liked his film, but didn't like the whining Asian in it. This "poor-me-I'm-an ethnic minority" bullshit has got to go! Somebody said to a friend of this Asian that he had a big cock, for an Asian. Yes, what a terrible, terrible thing to say to somebody!

ARTHUR EVANS has been diagnosed with AIDS or HIV.

DAVID LAMBLE said EVANS was complaining about the decline in street life in the Haight, where he lives. If the Ultra-Liberals are complaining, you know it's bad.

VITO RUSSO died of AIDS. DANNY MANGIN has taken over with the gay film retrospective, but his presentation isn't as good as VITO'S, though he's a nice guy.

RICHARD HALL just died of AIDS at age sixty-five. He didn't come to see *My Unknown Son*, begged off via BETTIE GERSHMAN, owner of Knights Press. He did come to see my two pieces in *Homosexual Acts* off-Broadway in 1991, but didn't stay for the second half of the evening. We'd had dinner earlier, with Bettie Gershman and some friends of friends. He said nothing about having AIDS. Maybe that's why he went back to NYC from San Francisco? Maybe that's why he didn't give me his new address? I didn't ask for it. Did a memorial piece on him for the *James White Review*.

C.D. ARNOLD, the playwright, also recently died of AIDS. I didn't know he had it. I went to his memorial service at the big former home of TOM WADDELL.

J.D. FREEMAN, the actor, was there, reading a poem for C. D. since he started his acting career in one of C.D.'s plays. It was a good poem. He's a fine actor. He said maybe C.D., of all the people there, would be the most remembered for his work. (?)

Others did scenes from C.D.'s plays. It was all touching, but, boy, how many funeral services can I go to! The last thing that night was talking to C.D.'s lover, who said C.D. prepared a volume of his plays for the proposed archives at the S.F. Public Library. He wants to be included very much. Of course he does. All of us writers do. I'm happy that I mentioned the archives to C.D. the last time I saw him in a Thai restaurant on Market Street. He hadn't known about them until then.

RANDY SHILTS is trying to get RICHARD GERE to appear in his screen version of *And the Band Played On.* Apparently WHOOPI GOLDBERG has signed on to play a part. Whoopee . . . (It went on to win an Emmy. And Randy has become the Establishment's token gay saint. Go figure.)

DEAN GOODMAN is now elderly. He's been interviewed for a documentary on his former mother-in-law, MARLENE DIETRICH, who died about a year ago. Dean has also acted in his own piece about his life in the theater and in several one-acts he wrote. He seemed a little less than pleased with me because I didn't rave about the one-man memoir piece when I wrote it up for *The Bay Times.* For actors it's never enough.

JOHN GILGUN has had several books of poems published of late. But he got screwed on the royalties for his novel by Amethyst Press, which was taken over by the usual crooks and is now defunct, I believe. The more things change, the more they remain the same.

John wrote me several brutal letters from Missouri a year and a half ago and said he wasn't going to stay in our condo anymore. He accused me of all kinds of sins; the one that hurt the most was "racism." All it means is that I refuse to accept the goddamn liberal guilt-trip game any longer. I call bad behavior as I see it. Enough of this cry-babyism! Any criticism is "racism" instead of the truth. Besides, anti-white racism has become the norm now. John expected me to argue back, argue it out, but I took the high road and didn't answer, except for business matters with the condo. (Is the high road the road that you are most likely to fall off?)

Then John, after more than a year, wrote and asked for a reconciliation. It was mature of him, my lover said, and so I agreed and signed my response "your friend." We even met, with DAVID LAMBLE and my John, for a dinner here in S.F. last month. It was a bit strained, but generally good. We correspond now, but I'll be buying his share of the condominium.

(Then he got angry again at me when I bought him out, unable to deal with basic arithmetic. Good-bye to all that neurosis. And good riddance!)

DAVID LAMBLE is unemployed and making my life difficult because I co-signed so that he could get a credit card to cut down on the loans he was asking for and not repaying. He built a $2000 limit up to more than $3500, but the worst part was his missing some payments and putting a blot on my credit record. I am trying to refinance and raised some personal credit card limits, and I have to explain that it wasn't me who missed the payments. I was turned down for one credit increase as a direct result of David.

David has more annoying habits than he used to. I guess some he learned from me. He goes on and on about his FILMS and who is showing them and what's happening to his

CAREER. Artists can be so egotistical it's unbearable sometimes. (I guess we all need to forgive each other.) My lover is secretly furious with David for abusing the money, for not working, for thinking he doesn't have to work because he's an ARTIST. But I understand where David is coming from.

ROBERT CHESLEY died of AIDS. I didn't go to the funeral. I saw very little of Bob after he returned from NYC. He, I felt, was too P.C. for my taste.

TERRENCE DAVIES and I had lunch in London when I was on sabbatical in 1990. He was trying to raise money for his new film, and apparently he got it, because last summer someone told me, in London, that he'd seen it and that it was good.

Also had lunch with ADAM MARS-JONES, who used two of my stories in *Mae West Is Dead* (Faber and Faber). He's very upper-drawer and said DAVID HOCKNEY complained that he couldn't understand Adam's accent. Hockney is from Bradford, which is working class or was. Now it's Muslim. MARS-JONES and I talked about his possibly having a child, as I have done, and the false accusations of child molestation against his married brother. I am putting such a theme into the book I'm writing, *Only the Good Parts*. I am happy to report that I paid for both ADAM MARS-JONES' and TERRENCE DAVIES' lunches. (My mother was right. Money matters.)

Also took PETER ROBINS to dinner in London in the summer of 1992. Peter is always a charmer, though he doesn't answer letters. He was doing mocking imitations of the Grand Dame Camille that he said DAVID REES has become since being diagnosed with you know what. Since David Rees apparently criticized a fine story of mine somewhere, I don't mind seeing him mocked.

TIM WOLFRED just won re-election to the Community College Board of City College, with the most votes, but his political career seems stalled.

CHRISTMAS LEUBRIE is forty-two and hearing her biological clock ticking very loudly. She wants to have a baby after all, but wants a co-parent. I don't know if she was interested in me or not, but I don't want to co-parent. I've seen enough of the hardships of child rearing with ZACK, my son that Christmas helped create. Yes, we finally met when he was seven. He cried for a long time when he saw the picture I sent before I went up to Oregon, his mother told me. Now what do you suppose that meant?

Zack's mother broke up with her long-term lover and now lives with a woman named Cindy. Zack is nine and we see each other about every four months or so. I also call on the phone, but it's a strain talking to a kid, I must say. I finished a novel based on this siring experience, with many liberties for drama's sake. Most of it was written before I even met the real-life people. Just finished what I hope will be the final version, following a letter from my agent in London (Jeffrey Simmons), who said he and his reader were fascinated by the first half but though it went on too long after that. I've trimmed 68 pages out of the 540. Will that be enough? I no long kill off the baby with SIDS or having the mother shoot the Bulgarian nanny. It's interesting how you can leave out such things and still make the story work I hope. I feel good about it.

MADONNA, without Sean Penn, is the talk of every town. Her book *Sex* just came out.

SUZY BRIGHT was listed in the *Chronicle* as one of S.F's "cultural elite." Been on TV, does interviews and even gave a show or two at the Castro Theater. Gays are moving into the mainstream at last!

LEE BRADY is a good, good friend. She reads my work and praises it. She is a playwright and critic too, won the best musical award for *Southern Lights* from the Critics Circle last year. She and I attempted to put on a bill of one-acts by the two of us, but when we had the reading at her house her play was a bomb. I felt horrible about that evening, but we seem to have transcended it. Lee doesn't take theater failures as much to heart as I do.

CAMILLE PAGLIA sent me a postcard after I sent her a review of her book *Sex, Art, and American Culture*. Here's what she wrote on 12/11/92: "Dear Mr. Curzon, thank you very much for your splendid radio review. I loved the idea of it infiltrating and annoying quite a few trendy Berkeley academics! I just attacked Princeton last weekend with Cindy Crawford. I was in butch blue jeans mode. High noise level, let me tell you. I called Princeton a 'mausoleum' as is the mind of all the politically correct. Thank you for your support. Best Camille Paglia."

I love what this woman is doing, but attacking Princeton *with* Cindy Crawford may be going too far. Did she hold Cindy by the leg or the neck?

DANIEL CURZON is fifty-four years old and not happy that he weighs about 235, but he feels he's been very creative of late with several novels rewritten several times, plus eight short stories written in a two-week period in the fall of 1992. His lover is grumpy today and even threw something across his living room. John is bored, about to get this B.A. at age forty but resentful of homework, his job. Whatever! I comfort him. Our sex life is sporadic nowadays; maybe it'll revive. We eat out a lot. I'm not as sexual as I used to be, but I don't want to give it up entirely. I never thought I'd say sex is not crucial to a lover relationship, but it isn't. Dining out, talking are. I think I've fallen in love with John, and he with me, at last. It's only taken twelve years.

UPDATE – 1994

Today is August 27, and I thought you might be interested to learn that JOYCE CAROL OATES hasn't forgotten me. *Playboy* interviewed her last November (1993), and she mentioned this male "writer" who had threatened her life after all she'd done for him, etc., etc. And here all this time I thought she was repenting over the way she had treated me! I guess it just goes to show it all depends on whose perspective it is. She has of course distorted the facts. I care primarily because she's probably going to win the Nobel Prize, and so everything about her life will become scrutinized. I'm part of that life, just as she was a big part of mine, and I want the facts told truthfully. I wrote a letter to *Playboy*, trying not to be too much of a crank, but, really, the gall of Ms. Oates talking about "homoerotic" themes without a blush yeah, now that it's safe to do so!

God bless her, her memory just isn't very good. Not nearly as good as mine! (Time will tell, I do believe.)

I dare say I haven't exactly bent over backward to make myself seem either admirable or successful in this memoir, but things aren't going too badly for me. Dialogus Play Service is publishing ten of my plays. *The Kenyon Review*, no less, is bringing out a story of mine in the Winter 1995 issue. (Perhaps I should mention that I had my first gay sex right after I had two of my stories rejected, one by *The Kenyon Review*, and Oates, naturally, my best friend then, had two accepted at the same time, one by *The Kenyon Review*.). But now it's my turn. Three other magazines have accepted stories as well.

I've also been included in a bio-bibliographical book called *Contemporary Gay American Novelists* and, last but not last, I hope, I'm in the Gale Research Company's *Gay and Lesbian Literature* volume, one of only two hundred such writers of the twentieth century. With all the politics that goes into literary reputation these days, that's not too shabby. And I didn't even know somebody on the Advisory Board! I'm getting there! I feel it in my bones. I'm getting there at last.

UPDATE – 1999

DANIEL CURZON got a lot of grief (and attention) because of a lawsuit he brought against a website purporting to give student (and *only* student) reviews of teachers at City College of San Francisco, starting in fall, 1997, and continuing on for three years. I will spare you the infinite minutiae that a lawsuit can engender and try to avoid the Lenny Bruce Syndrome that beset him at the end of his life because of his legal problems.

Anyone should be able to relate to having filthy things said about you that aren't true and aren't even by the people they say they are. Take these real ones from the website, for instance:

"Hi, I'm Curzon-Brown and hot for some dick riggt [sic] now, . . . I'll even let you fuck my boyfriend, steve, he likes it when I shove big cilindrical [sic] objects all the way up his ass until he starts crying, the, i hope he `does the same for me."

"That's to teach you a lesson Curzon-Brown, you fucking piece of shit fag ass hole, maricon, puto, miefdero, ass lick, donkey fucker, you really do pick up boys on broad st. you cuntfaced fairy, queer. Ohhh yesss, please harder harder, moooooo, quack quack, oink oink, bark bark. Farm animal fucker!!!!"

"[Curzon-Brown's #1 student was probably a hot-looking stud who refused to get rammed up the ass by Brown. . . . His ass is probably brown from all the black faggots that have shoved their big ass dicks up his asshole. . . . I wish you kill yourself, there's no need for faggots in this world, they are an abomination."

"I took his butt-fucking class, and he raped me in front of the whole class, it was embarrassing. . . . But he did rape my friend's 3 year old brother and almost turneg [sic] hs rectum inside out."

"I do not understand what he thought he was doing when he killed that student last year for not handing in his assignment. He routinely keeps the pretty girls after class for 'extra credit' assignments, and they come out screaming a few minutes later."

Curzon-Brown is a Fucking Faggot, he should get a life and be straight, faggots are a major threat to humanity and nature, they disgust everybody, especially if they're teachers."

"[Curzon-Brown] whipped out his cock and tried to shove it down my throat in the middle of class! I sit in the very front and he always was making passes at me, that faggot. Several times he invited me to the bathroom because he wanted to suck my dick but I told him to get the fuck away and he grabbed onto my balls so tight they almost exploded. Then his grip gave out and I decked that boy-fuckig [sic] queer."

"I got failed and he told me he was gonna kill me if I told anyone here [tried] to rape me. He was always making fun of us girls and he was always trying to grope me!"

"I seen [Brown] tooling for anus on Polk Street."

"Instead of questioning the student I know where Curzon lives."

"Fortunately, this creep will probably die of AIDS."

"Why don't you burn in hell now, you evil piece of garbage? The planet has too many haters as it is. Die now."

"He ain't no man, he's a bitch!! Oh shit, man just let us put down this queer. We all know he's an asshole."

BRAVE NEW WORLD

Unfortunately the ACLU legally defended this hate site and such "reviews" as protected speech and "merely 'flames' typical of the brave new world of Internet discourse . . . ."

Thus the American Civil Liberties Union used its members' money to defend vicious, homophobic hate speech. This showed (and still shows) the sick state of American law and an utter cultural contempt for teachers. Lie and spew hatred all you want to about teachers; after all, they're only educators, and you don't even have to be their students! Cyber thugs, take heart because you are protected by the law even when you falsely accuse teachers of rape and murder and anything else you damn well please.

The Teacher Review website let anyone post on it, anonymously, without a shred of proof of who they said they were and no one had a legal right to stop these people from providing lies to whoever wanted to read them. So what happened? Teachers praised themselves under fake IDs. Enemies got back at others for real or imagined gripes. It was insane, and yet it was the law of the U.S. (It still is. Title 47, Article 230 allows the Internet to have "Special Privilege" and a lack of accountability not permitted to any *other* form of publication or media.)

I can see that voices might be raised that I here in *Dropping Names* have said some unkind things about certain people. But I haven't said them anonymously. Nor have I written about people I didn't interact with, and whatever I have said is TRUE! Many of the "reviews" of me on the website were sent in by people who saw me on television and weren't ever students of mine. Moreover, the website seemed official, connected to and supported by the college. It wasn't, but that was the definite impression.

A Double Standard

In the lawsuit the webmaster of Teacher Review was given "discovery" about the Plaintiffs (me and DAVE WALL) by his Internet Service Provider, but the court (Judge David A. Garcia of S.F. Superior Court) indicated its unwillingness to give the same kind of information about the webmaster to us and our lawyer (Paul Kleven, a great guy). Thus cyber thugs spewing their homophobic hate speech and other blatant defamation against any number of fellow teachers (not just us) were enabled. But libel and false light are not protected by the First Amendment and never have been.

The Defendant webmaster argued through the ACLU that the legal Complaint was "meritless." It would be interesting to see what the ACLU considers to be of "merit" if false and scabrous accusations of murder and multiple rape by teachers and other "reviews" accusing them of outrageous sexual conduct and crimes are "meritless." Such reviews continued to come in to the Teacher Review website for years.

If even one "review" of a student had appeared on a *student* review website and was purported to be written by a teacher but in actuality was not written by that teacher, there would have been no end of outrage over such unfairness. The very idea of daring to criticize poor students! Not just grades sent privately – the whole truth: "Ms Creep earned a C in the class even though she was twenty minutes late every single Saturday and has a vocabulary smaller than Koko the gorilla's, because American educational standards are in the toilet." "Mr. Recent Immigrant writes and speaks terrible broken English, but he worked harder than any of the lazy native speakers and thus earned an A for language skills we used to call sub-standard." Oh no, you can't speak of the great American myth that Everybody Should and Must Go to College (even though it's not really college work).

The webmaster, Ryan Lathouwers (no caps for him!), in setting up and running the website so that there were not even the most basic of guarantees that it provide the information it said it provided, that is, that these were real student reviews of teachers they had actually taken classes from, as would be assumed by any visitor to this so-called online "resource," has demonstrated both bad faith and malice against teachers in general and the Plaintiffs in particular, to say nothing of abysmal current educational standards of accuracy and fairness. He indulged himself in the power he had obtained over teachers and acted in a reprehensible manner. And then he boasted in the book *Web: Studies* of his plans to bring similar sites to over 6000 colleges in over 200 countries.

Teacher Review was said by its defenders to be "a welcome addition to the City College community." Even more teachers would no doubt have spoken out against it if they had not been terrorized into silence by the very real threat of people sending in nasty "reviews" of them to keep them intimidated. Sorry, the website was "welcome" primarily because it allowed people to say disgusting things they could never say in person, in magazines, on the air, only through the anonymity of the Internet, where libel, false light, and intimidation have been allowed to thrive under a Kafkaesque interpretation of a so-called 1996 Decency Act. The irony of course is that these "reviews" were examples of the very Indecency that the "Decency Act" was trying to curtail.

I continue to urge all teachers and their supporters to cancel their memberships in the ACLU and to write letters and make telephone calls of protest to the ACLU for misusing members' money on such a despicable legal posture.

The ACLU also libeled "Daniel Curzon-Brown" on its webpage and in its newsletter by claiming that I brought this lawsuit because I wanted to stop my students from reviewing me. I could live with my actual students reviewing me if they had just one review each and if reviewed by all of my students, not just some of them, the angry ones. What I couldn't live with was *non-students of mine* reviewing me! This happened a lot since I dared to speak out publicly about the many offenses of Teacher Review. The same few people sent in numerous false reviews under different disguises, and every time anyone complained about the website, it was assumed, falsely, that it was coming from me, under different names, and I would be libeled some more. What fun it must have been!

DAVE WALL and I lost the case because the judge (David A. Garcia) threw it out, and we had to pay the ACLU $10,000 because people had said the filthy things quoted above! The webmaster did let me off the hook for $2500 when I had to declare bankruptcy. Sweet guy.

Since Then

Only now are the courts at last beginning to address the enormous wrongs being committed in cyberspace. For example, a Commonwealth of Massachusetts appeals court ruled on July 18, 2000, that a student's website that attacked and threatened his teacher was not protected free speech. Commonwealth Judge Jess S. Jiuliante said that "speech that is lewd, profane, libelous and insulting is not constitutionally protected."

Many of the attacks on me and Wall on Teacher Review clearly fall within the same framework since they were lewd, profane, libelous, and insulting in the extreme, as you can have seen for yourselves.

It was one of the most stressful periods in my life, and I tried to commit suicide, but I just couldn't manage to get the right pills. And yes, it was also exciting as hell.

SENATOR DIANNE FEINSTEIN did respond personally to my plea for help: "I strongly believe in our First Amendment right of free speech, but I also believe it is important we reconcile First Amendment freedoms with other concerns. While the Internet is a valuable and important source of information, it is not above the law. There are laws that make it illegal to defame a person, whether verbally or in print. Clearly, as your case illustrates, there is more to be done."

We're still waiting.

DAVE WALL retired early. He'd had his Physics labs cancelled for lack of enrollment once he took on the hate site. He hadn't had filthy reviews, like mine, before he spoke out against the Internet Inquisition.

Trust me, you don't want this to happen to you in your job, if you have any hope of maintaining your integrity.

UPDATE – 2001

The whirligig of time! How much we change. How much we don't. One thing I have noticed is how much faster each year goes, the older one gets.

What has happened to the players in this book?

JOYCE CAROL OATES still hasn't won the Nobel Prize, but she has been short-listed apparently. You know what? I hope she wins it. Everybody should have a Nobel Prize. (It can't hurt the value of the fifty-two or so letters I have from her, either.) I myself have had two offers to purchase my correspondence and manuscripts, one from the Labadie Collection of the University of Michigan and the other from the James C. Hormel Collection of the San Francisco Public Library. No doubt the Oates letters make these archives worth quite a bit more. Grrr. I gave twenty-six boxes to the Hormel about five years ago for a minimal tax write-off. This time they say they will pay. I am employing ROGER WICKER of the Turtle Island Bookshop in Berkeley, on the Hormel's recommendation, to archive the materials. He has done several carloads so far. I bring them across the Bay Bridge to his shop and he charges me seventy-five dollars per hour to examine and catalogue. I have asked him if they are worth more than I'm paying him, God willing. He allows as how they certainly are. I have some debts I need to pay off, so I hope I'm not too disappointed here. What is the bubble reputation worth?

Unfortunately I had to sell the nine first-edition, personally inscribed books that Oates gave me back when we were friends. I got $2000 for them from a dealer, who no doubt doubled his money. I asked him to do the archiving as well, but he declined, pissed, I do believe, because I wouldn't sell the Oates letters to him.

I needed the money for my lawsuit against the hate website against teachers.

Ms. Oates was the subject of a biography written by Greg Johnson and published by Dutton in 1998, called *Invisible Writer*. I figure in it as Dan Brown. Johnson said he had more pages on me, but the editors cut the book back. What's there captures the true sadness of our break-up, which apparently was the low point in Joyce's life, as it probably was mine. (Who knows. Mine's not over yet.) She has convinced herself over the years that I sent her a screaming letter, but she never opened it! So she doesn't know. It was actually an apology. It's in the archives somewhere, still unopened. Another thing that comes through in the biography, over and above her anorexia and panic attacks (now given names) is a rather whitewashed presentation of her sexual psyche, no doubt because her husband is still alive and so is she. The book also pays too much attention to How She Suffered as a Woman, all that poor-me-feminist claptrap. Joyce Carol Oates never suffered one second from being a woman or a woman writer. In fact, she has always benefited, been sought out, coddled, promoted, indulged, and lionized in a way that any man can only envy.

I still believe she was stingy and homophobic in the way she treated me, also short-sighted about the value of literary liaisons. I don't obsess about her, the way I once did. Time's wingéd chariot is hurrying near. She looks old in pictures now. Sigh. (I promise to forgive her completely if I get a pretty penny for her letters!)

Not to sound too mercenary, but I did manage to sell my JOHN STEINBECK letter about three years ago. "How could you sell it?" people have asked me. Because I needed the money, that's why. And I wasn't exactly reading the letter every day. Besides, I do have copies of it. I sold it through a dealer, who had to make just two telephone calls to cement the deal. I don't know who bought it, some private collector.

I learned something about how letters are given value by those who sell them. Are you curious how much I got? Well, the main thing, of course, is the reputation of the letter writer. Steinbeck's fame has risen steadily since the cooling-off period right after his death. (For god's sake, he's even a bed and breakfast in the Salinas/Monterey area now!) Then there is the content. His letter to me says things about not wanting immortality and makes some comments about his children as well as literary critics. In other words, it's not just a thank-you note. It's handwritten on yellow foolscap, has two spellings errors. The dealer says a hair product no longer manufactured is what I first took to be a third spelling error. The letter is also written to somebody who has some reputation (finally) himself. The letter is in good shape with the original envelope and three-cent stamp, despite being missing all those years. There probably is no copy of it in the Steinbeck archives, and it's one of the few still uncollected private letters the man wrote. Value: $3250, minus the dealer's twenty percent. (Maybe I should have hung on to it and kept it in my own archive? Hmm.)

Have read several books about and by CHRISTOPHER ISHERWOOD recently. I have gotten over my resentment a bit, though I still think he was dead wrong to think I was trying to exploit him by getting publicity for Tennessee Williams, as he had asked me to do. Maybe his mind was going.

He seems to have had a painful death. I'm sorry for that. I'm also sorry I said a nasty thing here about Don Bachardy's hair. (I removed the comment, so you'll never know!)

Isherwood's diaries are slowly being published. I imagine my name will come up in the 1974-1976 period. Some people have been upset by his now-published comments, what he really thought in spite of the Nice Isherwood he presented to the world. I'm steeled for what he might say. But the worst would be not being mentioned at all!

DAN TURNER's niece called me a couple of months ago and said that Dan was appearing to her in dreams, insisting that she rescue his works. She also said that her eleven-year-old son, Danny Turner, is named after and a reincarnation of Dan. . . . Okay. Little Danny Turner was born the year Dan died, and he has shown musical and acting talent. In fact, his mother told me to watch him in a skit on the *Tonight Show*, and I did. I'm a complete atheist and don't believe there is anything after this life, but I also know Dan Turner wanted fame as much as I do, and so I can imagine his energy out there somewhere trying to rescue what he can from the Void. How ya doing up there, Dan?

In 1997 I tried to rescue Dan's music, in particular the music that we wrote together, some sixty-five songs in three musicals, because I felt it was just lying untouched in the Gay Historical Archives in S.F. I got tapes of everything, and in recent years I have had professional demo recordings made of some of these songs. I have also branched out and started writing some melodies to go with my own lyrics. I "sing" them into a tape recorder and have somebody else do a lead sheet and produce and sing the songs better than I can since I can't play an instrument or sing very well. But I have done perhaps twenty-five songs on my own, over and above the Curzon-Turner songs, and co-written a few with some new musical partners. I am happy to report that "Just As I Am," which Dan and I wrote in 1980 in our musical about a transsexual (*Comeback*) and later sung at Dan's funeral, has been optioned by a musical producer in London for one of his singers. Other songs of mine have won or placed high in song contests, and this seems to be opening up as a whole new creative area for me. It's a tough business, but country songs, Celtic songs, pop and rock songs don't encounter the same problems as anything gay does, or did. I always ran hard away from the hillbilly side of my mother, but country has "come out" in some of my songs!

Some plays I've written in the past few years have won prizes. Maybe I just write better now, but I also believe it has a lot to do with the subject matter. I have won prizes for non-gay scripts, notably the 1999 National New Play Contest for *Godot Arrives*, a sequel to *Waiting for Godot*, also at the Actors Theater Ensemble of Hollywood for "So Middle Class" (1998), at the Actors Theatre of Santa Cruz for "Sour Grapes" (1997). Mine was one of four scripts ("A Fool's Audition") selected out of four hundred entered in the University of Nebraska Great Platte River Playwriting Contest in 2001. What I'm saying here is that being a "gay writer" has been both a blessing and a curse. You have a built-in audience on the one hand, but on the other you have a lot of people who are upset and hostile or uncomfortable or resistant to that topic in and of itself, no matter how well it may be presented. I think this was Oates' problem with me and my first book back in the bad old days. Perhaps she has matured.

I feel vindicated having been successful writing other things, both musically and theatrically. Little Danny Brown, who used to put on "shows" in his broken-down garage in ugly old Detroit, Michigan, is grown up now, living well, full of revenge.

My Unknown Son, my play which did not succeed off-Broadway because of an inconsistent actor (boyfriend of Julie Andrews' daughter) had a successful production in Los Angeles in 1997. An actor who had seen it in New York remembered it and called to ask if he could play the role of the son. Of course, my boy. How many offers was I getting on this script?! Yes, the first cast walked off, the second cast wasn't as good, it was August in Los Angeles, theater is secondary to movies there, but it was better than the Equity production in New York. It didn't make a star of the actor who asked for permission to do it, but he did a good job. It was a good show. It's a ruthless profession.

ROBERT PATRICK moved out of his sister's home and went to Los Angeles. I've sort of lost track of him. We used to correspond, but every time I sent him a Christmas card I got back a complaint about gays promoting oppressive religions. Well, I couldn't agree more about oppressive, homophobic religions. It's hard to find one that's not, but, hey, a Xmas card is just a social convention. One of the best songs I've written on my own is called "An Irish Blessing," which invokes God's name. I don't mean it literally. You can listen to it for free on

YouTube, where I have placed some IDA VANOLA MUSIC cuts, named after my mother, born down in "the holler" in Tennessee. [It has been on YouTube since 2006.]

TOM AMMIANO ran for mayor of San Francisco, and lost, but he put a scare into the current mayor, Willie Brown. I voted for Ammiano, more out of gay solidarity than out of commitment. He represents that politically correct side of the city I live in that can be so mind-numbing. I am neither liberal nor conservative. I pick and choose on each issue.

N. A. DIAMAN – Somebody told me recently that he or she had met Diaman and my name came up and he said that he'd always liked me.

Shucks.

Now I feel guilty about him.

ARTHUR EVANS writes letters to the newspapers all the time, often complaining about the druggies and the dirties in the Haight. Well now, does this always happen to the Righteously Left when they get up there in years? (Actually, he's right. The Haight and other parts of San Francisco are a disgrace. You don't have to be an old fart to notice.)

EDMUND WHITE has beaten me out as the gay writer that the media notice. I don't think he's better than I am, but he certainly gets more press. He also has a regular publisher and I don't. When Knights Press closed up, it took away anything approaching a committed publisher for my work. The last I heard BETTIE GERSHMAN was being sued for sexually harassing a gay man on her staff, a gay man who later went straight. Then she became part of the Kennedy Clan because her daughter married one of the Kennedy boys.

(Could I possibly make this up???)

DAVID LAMBLE and I don't speak anymore. I let him speak his mind to me on the phone in our final days, but the fact that he abused a credit card that I co-signed for him and injured my credit rating ended our long friendship.

This year David's roommate Marty Liebman was killed by a car in downtown San Francisco. Another roommate, who was drunk and killed another driver in a car accident earlier, is out of prison now and working in computers. Is life strange, or is it me?

RANDY SHILTS already I can hear people saying "Randy Shilts? Who was Randy Shilts?"

Alas, they say that about almost everybody sooner or later, except Hitler.

ARMISTEAD MAUPIN broke up with his boyfriend, and I don't know if he's gotten another one. His books have been made into several so-so mini-series. (He's even fatter than I am.)

DEAN GOODMAN is in his eighties now, not acting quite as much. But, as I've long said, the ego is the largest organ in the human body, and the last to go.

DAVID BERGMAN is someone I've run into since I wrote this. I mention him only because he's an editor at a press that I am sending these memoirs to. I believe it was an MLA convention where we met. We both went to Wayne State University for our Ph.D.s. We talked about a professor we both disliked, Professor Rumble, and Bergman mentioned receiving a D from this teacher and yet somehow surviving.

Indeed, David Bergman started popping up everywhere as an editor. I don't know how he managed to accomplish this. No one ever asked me to edit anything, except student essays.

Bergman was writing poetry then. Maybe he still is. He sent me a book of his poems, and I think I said the appropriate things. But maybe I didn't.

Later I sent him a couple of stories to consider for an anthology he was doing, thinking I was a lock because one of the stories had been published in *The Kenyon Review*. Bergman was rather dismissive, and I felt no urge to send him anything else. Don't go into the writing game unless you are STRONG.

RICHARD EYRE has not been mentioned in this book before, I think. I mention him now only to remind myself (as if I need it!) of what a difficult task indeed it is being a writer. My London agent, who has now retired, sent my neo-Shakespearean play, *The Third Part of Henry IV*, to Richard Eyre when he was the head of the National Theatre in England. He didn't do it. No one did it.

Later, when I was attending a theatre course in London, Eyre was a guest speaker. I decided to speak to him as he left, though I had only a few seconds to do so. I mentioned the Shakespearean-style play and he remembered it, saying "a noble effort." I suppose I should have left it at that, but I am so committed to not being as shy as I was as a lad or as shy and afraid as my father was that I decided to write Eyre and sent him another copy of the play and some other scripts, urging him to give them a look or to pass them on to the incoming head of the National.

What I got was an insulting letter back, saying in effect to stop bothering him and that he simply didn't care for my work.

I've had many rejections over the years, both for gay work early on (merely because it was gay) and for other things, but I must say the animosity to anything gay is matched by the animosity to anyone, especially an American, *daring* to attempt to match William Shakespeare. Shakespeare, after all, is not just a man, not just a writer, but ENGLAND itself.

Believe me, I'll inform you when my Nobel arrives too.

FELICE PICANO hangs in there. Well, good for him. I guess he's even written some good books. I wrote some Juvenalian satires of him and Rita Mae Brown and Edmund White and some other of my writerly kin under the pseudonym of The Saint in an Alyson book a couple of years back. Rita Mae Brown now writes cat mystery novels. I guess that is an improvement over feminist rant.

WILLIAM DICKEY, the poet, died. Did I note this before? Of old age, I believe. His nelly lover (LEONARD SANAZARO) now teaches in the same English Department I do and thought I insulted him at some meeting or other. I certainly didn't intend to insult him, but now we barely speak. I really don't think it's my fault this time. Maybe I don't really know myself as well as I think I do?

DONALD ALLEN is a really old, frail man now. My partner and I see him from time to time in a restaurant that we go to. He always has a male companion. I haven't noticed him snapping his fingers at the waiters anymore. I pretend not to see him.

STEVEN SAYLOR always hated my books, or most of

them, and gave them bad reviews. He thought them too dark, bleak, or whatever. Now he is a writer himself. He writes, for the mainstream press no less, porn (semi-porn? it's so difficult to tell these days) novels about Roman gladiators and their sadistic man-sex. (No, I'm not laughing.)

TERRENCE DAVIES directed a well-received movie based on Edith Wharton's *The House of Mirth*. I didn't see it, but I noticed in an interview that Terrence is still bitching about being ugly and being sexless. (Honey, it's not going to get any better. You'd better hurry.)

CHRISTMAS LEUBRIE never had a child, just as I predicted in the novel I wrote based on my experiences (fictionalized) in fathering a child with a lesbian couple via a midwife. I teach this novel (*Only the Good Parts*) in my English 1A classes, and I get a lot of unsolicited compliments about it. They are on the order of, "I haven't read a book since I was seven, but this one I finished in two days!" Make of that what you will about today's educational standards. However, I have long believed that novels should tell stories. I could tell stories about the conflicts I've encountered with the non-linear school of gay writers, as illustrated by people like Robert Gluck and that crowd. But I won't.

Anyway, thanks to Christmas, I have a son, by the name of Zack Johnson. He graduated from high school in Oregon on June 6, 2001 at the age of eighteen. He was just a gleam in my eye a few minutes ago! Zack has turned out to be a good-looking, strong, tall young man who plays rugby and also likes the theater. (It's in the blood.) He played Juliet's father in *Romeo and Juliet*, which I went up to see. He also played Don Pedro in *Much Ado*. I didn't catch that one. My partner and I did go up to Oregon to see the graduation ceremony. His mother's first lover and her daughter and the current lover along with me and my lover all came together to support Zack. Funny thing, now it's almost "cool" to have gay parents, and Zack, who is straight (Sorry, we do what we can) wanted to introduce us to all his friends and they wanted to meet us. He has a very pretty girlfriend that he took the prom, and now he's going off to a nearby university this fall. I wrote him a letter welcoming him into the world of the grown-ups. Just as I guessed in my play *My Unknown Son*, he is turning out fine.

I have made a few friends in recent years. For all the ones I lose I seem to gain some new ones.

DAVE WALL is a friend now. He was the co-plaintiff with me in the lawsuit against the hate site against poor old teachers being told how to teach by remedial students. Welcome to America at the end of the twentieth century! He is a saint, coming in and helping me when few others dared to be so brave. He took me out to dinner three nights in a row during the darkest days because he was trying to stop me from killing myself. (It worked.)

NINKI MALET I met in a theatre course in London in 1997. She had black hair then, a white South African with an upper-class British accent, and we became close that summer. Such friendships tend not to outlive the occasion, but this one has. She lives in Los Angeles and she is the one who took me to walk along the beach at Malibu, a life-long ambition of mine, when she lived there several years ago. Now she is blonde and has permanently tinted eyelashes, has various troubles with her three children, but manages to travel the world much of the time. She's the only person I've ever met who actually has sold a screenplay (for $350,000, no less), even though it was never produced.

Ninki and I traveled through England in 1999 by car, and survived the experience, including a fender bender for which I took responsibility since the car was rented in my name. She had a born-to-the-manor habit of changing her mind ever other day about our itinerary and whether she in fact was going and for how long. She knew that I was irritated. But we have become good friends. E-mail is great!

A couple of little anecdotes about Ninki: When we first met, a group of us in the theatre course wanted to go to the Ritz for tea. Well, when someone called for a reservation, no reservation was to be had for six or so mere Americans. So Ninki called and made a reservation for Lady Malet. Guess what! There *was* room for Lady Malet and her party. What a laugh we had at the Ritz on how we had fooled them.

Well, it turned out that Ninki really *is* Lady Malet, a descendent of one of William the Conquerer's right-hand men. She pointed out the Malet coat of arms high up in a law library we visited in London. I am aware that titles sometimes come from thuggery, long forgotten, as well as from nobility.

But it didn't taken a coat of arms to prove the point. There is something in Ninki's voice and demeanor that makes the British pay attention. She doesn't use her title, but it apparently oozes out in a way only a class system can truly divine. One time when we dined at the Savoy one night before a performance, there were no tables to be had. I know since I asked and asked and was refused and refused, even though there were some empty tables in sight. "Oh, you may sit at the bar, if you wish, sir." You American you!

When I returned from the restroom, Lady Malet had been seated of course at one of the tables. We dined like the royalty I was not. Coming from the lower orders myself, I confess to a certain hankering for the glitter of that higher social world. But I'm not an ass-kisser there either. The upper class has its charms, more than the lower one does usually, but it's all sort of deeply disappointing, upper or lower, at the core of cores of things.

DANIEL CURZON

I'm alive and well.

Forgive me. I want to include a couple of sexual episodes. You can skip these if you think you'll be offended. I believe it was Eleanor Roosevelt who used to write a column called "My Day." Well, let's update the practice and be a lot more forthcoming than Ms. Roosevelt could be.

Here's just one of those times I have to tell you about. I tell it not because it makes me look good. It doesn't. But I probably will never write an autobiography, and biographers, provided there are any for me, always seem to neglect the actual sexual side of people. I mean, what they actually do.

I take Viagra now that I am sixty-three. I look younger, everybody says, but my dick says sixty-three. I have a partner of twenty-one years, but our sex has become pretty much an annual affair. Alas. At first he didn't want to. And now I don't want to. *C'est l'amour*. We've always had an open relationship.

Now it's very, very open. We don't fight as much anymore, but the sex is all but gone. But the sex drive is forever. As that wise old lady Gertrude Stein once said, Every once in a while men have to empty themselves.

I went out to the a Certain Area of a Certain Park in San Francisco. The ocean is just a stone's throw from the cruising area, which has trees and bushes. Cypresses, I think. They remain despite the best efforts of the landscapers and moral squads to tear down everything they think we can hide behind in our nefarious nightlife.

Anyway, I went out for sex. My song may get made into a record in England. I won second prize in a play contest, in Nebraska but still a win. It's a life, as they say. And an orgasm can never be bad either. I went when it was still light, and didn't see anybody interesting, nor did anybody express overwhelming desire for me. So I went across the street to the Thai restaurant I go to, often between orgasms. I guess I'm tight, trying to get two ejaculations on half a Viagra pill. I had half a carafe of white wine and fried rice with chicken. That much wine gets me high and slows down my orgasms, which tend to be too easy, too quick.

I stood along the now darkened fence, hoping somebody "into blowjobs" would come along, so I could come and move along. I was eventually approached by a bearded man with what seemed to be a turban. A Sikh? Only he didn't look Indian, more like an American. He seemed to like me, or at least my full chest. He had a long cock, inside his pants. He fellated me, and I hoped I'd come, but he stopped before I was able to. Suddenly the Sikh went away. I think he'd been drinking too. Several others came up and stood near me and seemed interested. But I wasn't. Several I thought erotic were not interested in me. I usually prefer to be "desired," but occasionally I can go after someone I fancy, though never very aggressively unless I feel a mutual attraction. I stood there, hoping that someone would go for my dick, which wasn't so bad once the Viagra kicked in, thick, a nice mouthful. But nobody wanted to suck.

Finally the Sikh came back. Should I seek the Sikh? Would the Sikh seek me out again? Most of all, would the Sikh suck me off?

I am happy to report that he came back over and rubbed my chest again, unbuttoning my shirt buttons, and groaning complimentarily. He sank to a squatting position and then to his knees, and had a go at my organ. This attracted others, who came closer for a looky-look. He was quite slippery, and in a matter of moments I shot forth my load, as they say in the porn magazines. I think I caught him by surprise, because he began coughing and choking on my sperm. I helped him up and patted his chest and prepared to leave. (You know how men are after they come!) He, still coughing, said, "1 just got a new job and I'm sort of short of funds. I'm not a prostitute or a hustler or anything, but do you think you could . . . ." I said, amused and annoyed and philosophical, "I don't bring my wallet with me . . . . But here's some change." I handed him what felt like thirty-eight cents and left to drive home. He was still coughing a bit when I passed by where he was on the other side of the fence. What can I say? An orgasm is an orgasm is an orgasm.

This was real sex in a real life. (June 18, 2001)

ANOTHER TIME

After my honey (John) decided he didn't want to go out to dinner, and because I had taken a Viagra pill for later in any eventuality, I went out to the Certain Area of a Certain Park. A cold wind was blowing in from the ocean. I parked my car, trying to decide whether to have some food first, with wine, and then go for the orgasm. Or should I be greedy, that is, have an orgasm first, hopefully mind you, and then dinner and the wine, followed by a second orgasm. Hey, it's not greedy; it's just thrifty. Half a Viagra costs a pretty penny even on my medical plan. I opted for the early-bird orgasm and circled the cruising area. Alas, the parks and grounds people are now starting to tear the wooden slats off the fence behind which a lot of us have tricked over the years. Can't stand the thought of someone having sex in a park, can you? Fuck you. I saw some old tricks, including The Hood, who always wears the hood of his sweatshirt up, day or night, hot or cold, probably because his head is malformed. Once upon a time I wouldn't have touched him because of what The Hood seemed to promise underneath, but once we got together he was actually good sex, with lots of touching and holding, not just the hard stuff. But this night we were not interested in each other.

After a bit and with the restaurant going to close if I didn't hurry, some skinny young thing with less-than-good teeth and bad posture sauntered over, grinning and smoking. "You want to party?" he asked me. I guess he figured because I was heavy-set I'd jump at his Chance. I wouldn't have had sex with him in any case. Not my type, never was. I'm so GLAD I've never been attracted to youth!

"No," I said.

He looked upset. "I just got here from Texas, and I don't know about this place yet. I was just trying to get a few dollars for something to eat."

Not from me, you're not. Jesus, that's the second time in a row someone has asked me for money. Well, I'm not *there* yet, honey. Is the word spreading among the hustlers about this spot? (If anything, they should pay me.)

Skinny grumbled his way off into the bushes. "Jeez, everybody's so cheap around here," he said.

A look here, a look there. I showed some underwear: my bulging underwear.

A man, sort of slight, not young, not bad looking actually, expressed some interest, perhaps catapulted into desire by the two guys making out nearby. He came closer. He reached out his hand toward my crotch. I allowed this to happen. I wanted this to happen, I'd rather go with someone who wants me than with someone who doesn't want me but will "put up" with me. He said, "Let's go somewhere, and I'll suck you." Nice words, but they always remind me of the Vice cop who arrested me years ago in Detroit. He too wanted to "go somewhere else."

"How about there?" I said, pointing to a spot maybe five yards away.

"Okay."

I unzipped.

He pulled down his pants and turned the baseball cap backwards on his head. He knelt down. My Viagra was working wonderfully. In no time at all as usual I shot my load. I think he was a little surprised at my rapidity. "Can you do it a second time?" he wondered as I patted my part with a handkerchief.

"Not right away," I demurred.

I hurried over to the Thai restaurant, but it was ten minutes to closing time. Damn.

I thought about ordering take out and eating in my car. Instead, I drove to the Safeway a few blocks away, bought an Italian-style chicken breast sandwich and a bottle of health-oriented peach-flavored ice tea. (Room temperature, but what the hell). I also got a chocolate cake parfait. Yum, yum. I've got to watch my weight, but when you'd just been sucked off, you tend to forget. In my car with the news on, I ate my sandwich and drank my peach tea, choking a bit from time to time. Of late my throat has been sticking a bit, either from allergies (which I never had before) or maybe from age. I'm sixty-three goddamned years old! But thank god I look about forty-nine. All right, fifty.

Then I went back to the cruising area, and the same gentleman who had asked me if could come a second time, was still there. I made an offer he couldn't refuse, and I stuck my dick into his mouth for the second time in just over an hour. "Suck it," I said. "Suck that cock!"

He was agreeable.

It took me a little longer to shoot this time. I thanked him. As Miss Manners says: "One should always thank someone after he or she has sucked your cock." (More straight men should learn this instead of insulting the very people who give them the greatest pleasure they will ever know in life. The greatest pleasures in my life have always been the sexual ones.)

When I got home, I ate my chocolate parfait and tried to forget the fact that I am growing old and that yesterday my new cat killed the lovely silver green hummingbird who used to fly around the tree in my backyard. He lived there for several years. He wouldn't be there anymore in the morning, darting around, curious, making bipping noises at the cat, coming up to the window of my bedroom to check me out. It's not the cat's fault. Though I scolded her. She's just doing what Nature tells her. And so am I. And so are we all.

It is no exaggeration to say that it was such sexual episodes that kept me sane during the enormous stresses of the lawsuit I was involved in. I'm not sitting home brooding about the sex I used to have, that's for sure. I didn't have any sex until age twenty-six. So I'm making up for it now. Meaningless, wonderful sex!

Of all the things in my life that have influenced me the most they are the following, as best I can understand: first, my homosexuality, which I used to lament and feel guilty about, but now I see that I get much more sex than most non-gay people do. Sex makes life bearable. (I also have a kid anyway. Ha, ha.) Having been raised Catholic, *without* my permission by the way, is another major factor in who I am. I finally rejected that noose at the age of twenty-one and have never been tempted to go back, not once. I could give you a long argument on "Why I Am an Ex-Catholic" (and in fact have published versions of this twice), but suffice it to say that I believe God is a yearning in the human race for significance, for immortality, only He does not exist, or, if He does, He doesn't have the petty mind and laws of human beings. You also can't save anybody by dying on a cross. Blood sacrifices are so non-twenty-first century! So good-bye New Testament. As for the Old Testament, have you ever noticed that it promotes incest, says that Almighty God in His Infinite Wisdom couldn't come up with a better method of reproducing the species than to have Adam and Eve mate with their children or their children to mate with each other. Any way you dice it or spin it, it's incest. Why was it okay for God then, but not now? Surely morality doesn't change! My, what people believe! This "holy" book should be banned!

The other thing that has shaped me is a life-long repulsion to a part of the human body that most people could care less about. I have the opposite of a foot fetish. I have been restricted in where I would go and what I would do because I did not wish to reveal this part of my body or see other people's. The fact that I can at least mention this intense phobia now shows some progress, I suppose. I don't mind telling you about my sex acts, but this is as much as I can say about this aspect of myself. When I was in the first grade and was about to be in a play at St. Rose of Lima School, I learned that I was expected to appear barefoot. I begged to be taken out of the show, and of course I couldn't tell the real reason. All my life I have had to find excuses to avoid this (for me) disgusting reality. I couldn't even say the word *foot* in its plural form, and I have rarely used it in my writing or speech. I don't even like the sound of the word in measurements and wince every time I hear it. I have no clue why I feel this way. Someone wise once said, "A neurosis is a secret we keep from ourselves." I am the only person I have ever known, or ever read about, who has this feeling.

UPDATE – 2004 – I

It's June 21.

LILLIAN FADERMAN

LILLIAN is someone I should have written about sooner, I suppose. Now it's wasn't because she's a woman! Oh, please, stop with all this Victimitis that plagues our times. Most people don't get anywhere close to everything they want, and it has much more to do with the Human Condition than biases and or targeting anybody.

She was on the hiring committee when I applied to Fresno State University in 1974, a dark-haired, regular-looking woman who was noticeably pregnant. I did not think immediately, "Oh, she must be a lesbian!" In fact, she was one of the early lesbian mothers – now become a flood of gay/lesbian reproduction.

Because I was "out" at that interview, even though I knew it could cost me the job, as it had other jobs, and I might have to go back to face the wrath of the U.S. military over having tried "to teach something gay" to our poor troops in Asia, Lillian Faderman and a closeted gay man on the hiring committee, along with some forward-thinkers, gave me one of the three one-year jobs. I think I interviewed well, but in this rare case being boldly gay actually helped. Believe me, it was not something easy to do in 1974. A student even soon wrote on his paper, "I don't know if I can accept being taught by a man who sucks cock." Why not? I had to accept a man who fucked pussy. (Or *hoped* to someday, more likely.)

The Zeitgeist is one of my favorite words. What you can do and what you can say is delicately controlled by the era. But you have to help the Zeitgeist along. I'm proud to say that I was a pioneer and helped change it to make the path much easier for gays who have followed.

There was no question then of Affirmative Action for homosexuals, or even now, those slots being reserved for the "approved" groups, true anti-white "racism" in action. Don't get me started. No, it was a matter of not being excluded from consideration for a job because of sexual orientation alone. It was "He's a HOMOSEXUAL!!!!" instead of "Is he a nice homo or not?" There is enough of this anti-gay attitude still lingering that people can feel what it was like back when. Even today people who are perfectly qualified are being kicked out of the U.S. military for being gay. People in even more benighted places, particularly where religious fundamentalism of any kind reigns, are actively persecuting My People this very minute. And by the way, a lot of the extremely numerous recent immigrants to the U.S. come from homophobic cultures. WATCH OUT, especially for the fundamentalists of all stripes. This is not crying victim when there is no victimization. It is a fact. I care a whole lot more about gay job equity and gay physical and social bashing than the flavor of that month, gay marriage. (Besides, my partner and I now have a traditional marriage. I pay all the bills and we don't have sex anymore.)

Anyway, Lillian Faderman hadn't written anything discernible when I was in the English Department at California State – Fresno. She may have been working on something already. When the topic of my actually teaching a Gay Literature class there (*mirabile dictu!*) came up during my interview, I remember Faderman being insistent that I include lesbian material. She was pushing *Rubyfruit Jungle* and said she'd give me a whole list. I had no objection to lesbian materials, but later on all this became severe jockeying for power within the gay movement, which ludicrously went on to become the Lesbian, Gay, Bisexual, Transgender, Questioning, and Had a Untoward Sexual Episode Once movement, complete with parades and Give Me the Fucking Grant, not you.

She and her lover, also a dean, invited me to dinner, at which there was another gay man from the university, who had written his dissertation on who becomes police officers. I've always remembered his findings: folks of the lower-classes, "ethnics" rather than WASPS, people with rigid notions of right and wrong, ones not particularly bright. I've noticed the same things in the cops I've had as students over the past forty-some years. Indeed. There are plenty of stereotypes about students that happen to be true. You just can't say them out loud. The Zeitgeist. A lot of the problems with students likewise don't go away because the Zeitgeist won't permit honesty about the problems or the harsh solutions needed.

Maybe I was supposed to invite the co-deans back over to my place, but I've always hated to cook. I didn't feel any particular rapport either. So I didn't.

I did base a character named Georgia Lamb on Faderman in my novel *Among the Carnivores* (1979). I referred to her baby as ugly. Not a very kind thing to say, I guess. . . . Well, it was an ugly baby! I wonder what he looks like now as a grown-up.

I seem to recall some pressure to give graduate credit to some butch woman poet somehow connected with Faderman. I gave the credit. Years later I read that there was something romantic going on there. The butch poet was good, but I resented the pressure. I guess I pretty much resent the ways of the world.

As time went on, Lillian Faderman went on to have lots of books, very feminist, with lots of publishers eager for her wares, it seems. I read some of them. I thought they were well meaning, had some good insights to offer the world, and were as (yawn) dull as mud. I even reviewed one in the late 1990s for the *San Francisco Chronicle*, hoping I'd like the book and be able to make up for calling Faderman's baby ugly. But the book was so Lesbians Are Saints that I couldn't refrain from saying it was admirable and (my God!) boring as hell. I didn't really have any reason to have an animus against this woman. Yet every time I write about her I feel this urge to knock her work.

Now she's more famous than I am! And she just won a Lambda Literary Award – a Lifetime Achievement one! I've never won one, not even been nominated! (No doubt you probably are merely kissing the ass of the Zeitgeist is you do win one – he said grumpily.)

Anyhow, GOD BLESS LILLIAN FADERMAN and her BEAUTIFUL, BEAUTIFUL BABY!!!!

JOYCE CAROL OATES keeps sailing along. I remember her saying once that Balzac wrote a hundred novels and she was going to equal that. *Mon Dieu*, she's probably surpassed him by now.

I believe Ms. Oates tossed out a whole novel that she wrote based on our relationship, if I'm remembering her biography correctly. I appear in some other stuff of hers apparently, but the parody of me in *The Assassins*, alas, occurs in one of her poorest books. I have not gone searching for evidence that I have impinged upon her work, though I hope I have. I wrote three short stories based on her, plus these memoirs. They'll serve. I hope literary ghouls will find this all at least a little interesting. I've also long believed you should get at least something lasting out of life's pains.

The final five or six lively "feud" letters that Oates and I exchanged in 1974 are part of my literary archives, which seem to be headed for the San Francisco Public Library. I donated the first half to it about eight years ago and got a small tax write-off. The second half was catalogued by ROGER WICKER and finally appraised at $58,500 in 2004, but it took three years to finish the job, and the economy went from boom to bust in between. Both the San Francisco Public's Hormel Collection (JIM VAN BUSKIRK) and the U of Michigan Labadie Collection (JULIE HERRADA) expressed interest in and made offers for my archives three years ago, only to renege on any money after all, because of the current hard times. I tried to get both to buy some of my collection and wound up with no money from either. Sigh. (I refinanced my condo instead and will buy back my remaining out-of-state college teaching credits and hopefully be able to retire one of these years. I will not be a Victim!)

I could take out the Oates letters and sell them separately.

I've had an offer. But I've also been advised not to divide my collection. At least the SFPL wants my papers because of my career, not Oates', and I may have to settle for the satisfaction of knowing the archives are somewhere other than in my garage.

Of course if I sell the Oates letters separately, she might buy them and destroy them! Or no, you don't, lady!

Somebody named Raphael keeps leaving urgent messages on my answering machine at school that I must call him because we need to "talk" about Oates. He keeps saying that he has reported her to the police for tax evasion and homicide, including the possible murder of her husband, and other crimes. And I thought she was just mean to me! Joyce, I hardly knew ye! (This caller seems to be suffering from delusions of some kind or other. I actually think it may be somewhat I met as a "fan" years ago and even had sex with! Somebody else wrote me a letter recently saying that the rumor around the University of Windsor campus, where Oates taught, is that I was the only man she ever loved and that she was pregnant with my child and had to abort it to save her marriage. I wrote back that it was, yes, possible that Oates and I once "did it," only I can't *remember*.

. . . Is this what being famous means? Most people in the world have never heard of me or Joyce Carol Oates, and the ones who are interested are crazy!

Why be famous anyway? For whom? Human beings make heroes of the oddest things – people who hit balls with sticks and throw them again and again through hoops! They get upset because people endanger themselves with marijuana (which I do not smoke) and yet pay to watch them go round and round race courses in fast cars and maim and kill themselves and others while using up precious gasoline. People cite ancient texts to justify their horrors and claim they were created in God's image: food in at the top, shit out at the bottom? And they all think they're going to Heaven, which doesn't exist! Who needs human beings and their weirdness!

. . . And yet . . .

MY LAWSUIT ABOUT THE HATE SITE

I became rather well known, for all the wrong reasons of course, during my fifteen (make that sixteen) minutes of fame. I was interviewed by Matt Lauer on *The Today Show*, appeared on Fox News, CNN, in *People* magazine, on the front page of the *San Francisco Chronicle*, and on umpteen radio programs.

The upshot of it all? We lost the lawsuit, but we won the war, because the website was thoroughly discredited. If it still exists, it is no longer connected to the college's website, has no flyers promoting it on campus, is ignored and not used. It's no longer possible to extort a grade from a teacher this way. I have fought for two main causes in my life, gay literature and teacher integrity. I feel good about both fights.

I also wrote a 714-page "non-fiction narrative" book about the situation (*What a Tangled Web*), adding humor. It was not funny at the time. This book, I am happy to report, is being represented by super-agent JEFF HERMAN. (Oh yes, I want the last word on this topic.)

ANN SHAY

As I write this, my friend Ann, according to her doctors, has six months to a year to live. Her cancer has returned. I've lost so many friends over the years, from natural causes or because of my own spiky personality; now I'm getting worried that I won't have any friends at all in the so-called Golden Sunset Years. Her body is going, and she can barely walk half a block without panting. The doctors have hooked up a urine-drip bottle to her leg as well. No, it's not pretty, but she handles it with her usual equanimity.

Ann is a play producer, hardly big time, but we've become close ever since she picked my sequel, *Godot Arrives*, to go to the Edinburgh Theatre Festival in 2000 as part of the bill for the California Travel Troupe. The play had won the 1999 National New Play Contest right in the midst of all the anxiety over the lawsuit over that hate website. Yay!

The California Travel Troupe is run out of a couple of World War II bungalows on my own campus, City College of San Francisco, but I didn't even know it existed until my play was passed by Don Cate of the Theater Department to Ann Shay. She probably picked it largely because I am a faculty member. That kind of alliance can only help a tangential theater company. She is a pragmatist. Most producers are pragmatists. I suppose you have to be to put up with all the frustrations of putting on plays. The California Travel Troupe has more than its share of dysfunctional members, people with attention deficits and borderline psycho personalities – I mean even more than the usual theater types! Its work is spotty, some of the children's shows hilarious, whether intentional or not. People forget their lines, the houses are small, the scripts are selected in some hodgepodge order that doesn't necessarily include actually reading the scripts! I've wound up directing several of my own plays and one other short one, as well as re-directing another director's play that wasn't working. Needless to say, I earned my Purple Heart with the company that time because nobody likes being told their work is so bad somebody else has to re-do it.

I don't like directing in general, because you have to coddle actors and spend a lot of time going over and over details to get everything right, but I have done it. I'm even pretty good at it. I guess I've become something of a pragmatist myself. You do what you can in this life. It's better than a kick in the head. (Is it better than a kick in the head? I've never had a kick in the head.)

Last week, however, as John Gettys and I (reconciled after ten days of not speaking) were leaving the campus bungalow following the opening night of a bill of one-acts in which I have a piece called "The Hit" (which won a prize in L.A. in 1997), suddenly I was confronted by a tall gentleman in a sport coat in the school's parking lot. He asked John to move away so that he could speak to me alone. I thought he probably was a playwright who wanted to have a script considered, since I am now the dramaturge.

John stepped away, and this man proceeded to identify himself as a "friend" of Susan Jackson, the recent chair of the Theater Department, a cadaverous, seemingly malnourished woman over fifty with short, bleached-blonde hair. He said that he had heard that I was saying negative things about Ms. Jackson and that they had better stop. "What things have I been saying?" I asked, amazed at the nerve. He couldn't or wouldn't say.

I should mention that Susan Jackson had introduced a rival course to the one in play and novel writing that I created over twenty years ago and still offer at the college. The Curriculum Committee of the English Department voted unanimously on two occasions against authorizing her rival course in the Theater Department because it was felt it could cut enrollment in our course and thus neither course would go, since you need twenty bodies, living or dead, to have any course. Jackson had enlisted the Dean (a former theater teacher) on her side, and he went over the head of our department and got Jackson's course approved. It so happened that both classes made their enrollments the first semester, but if they hadn't it would have been just my tough luck. "Oh, we can fix it some other semester," the dear Dean had said.

I felt Jackson had been duplicitous in several ways, misleading the new chair of the English Department about the true status of her course besides not being qualified to teach others how to write plays since she had very little experience in the craft herself. She was a director (indeed we'd done the school's fiftieth anniversary show together in 1985). She had also cast herself as an actress in any number of campus productions, all rather embarrassing in their display of egomania and limited-talent self-aggrandizement. I hadn't said anything about Ms Jackson behind her back that I hadn't said to her face at the Curriculum Committee meeting.

The confrontation outside the bungalow in the parking lot turned into a shouting match. Her gentleman, British it seemed, was defending "his woman," as I said to my partner.

"You had better stop the comments," he repeated. "And what if I don't?" I said. "Then I'll take care of it," he replied.

"You'll take care of it? What does that mean?"

"I'll take care of it."

"This man is threatening me!" I shouted. If he thought I was going to stand there in a parking lot next to a crummy bungalow on a second-rate community college campus and keep it "just between us" the fucker didn't know me. I called to John for us to go back inside the bungalow and tell Ann Shay, the producer, and anybody else still around what had just happened.

The man followed. More shouting took place. I wanted everyone to know that he thought he could threaten me about what I could or couldn't say. The tech man told us both to be quiet and to leave, separately. I left at once, having made my point. According to Ann Shay, the gentleman angrily paced back and forth, held back, but then eventually left the bungalow after me. Fortunately I had gotten away just in time.

Maybe he thought that I, as a gay man, was easy pickins, that I wouldn't fight back or resist. Wise up, asshole. He wasn't pushing me around. I thought about it for a week, then decided, on Ann's advice, to tell the chair of my department what had happened. He suggested that I write it up and give him a copy, to which he would add a note and send it on to the Dean in question and to the Provost for good measure.

The last I heard in America we have free speech, as long as it's not libelous. Maybe this gentleman needs his passport examined. You don't do me dirt and expect me to take it. I wouldn't have dreamed of sending my boyfriend to tell Susan Jackson to stop saying the disparaging things she has been saying about me.

And you bet I play the Gay Card now. God knows it's taken years to get it!

UPDATE – 2004 – II

June 23, 2004

JOHN GETTYS, my partner, is fifty-one, still no grey in his head hair, though the beard needs assistance now. We have been together for twenty-four years, through thick and a lot of thin. No "Ahh, how sweet's," please. Real relationships, like real life, are not what the formulas say they are. That surely is the message of this book – and of my life. It's much more irregular and inchoate than that.

We maintain separate residences, but we spend a good deal of time together. Evidently I want this relationship, frustrating as it has been. We've both have tried to end the connection at various times, but we never do. It's sexless now, though we had an "accident" not long ago; it's companionate but not that cozy. We don't touch as much, yet I can tell John anything. That's a big plus. There are so many things you aren't allowed to say in this old world, and I say more than most. Maybe John's appeal is that he requires me to be generous and nurturing, not usual everyday strengths of mine. You see people filling out ads for partners and saying, "I'd like someone who prefers long walks on the beach" or "I want a man with a sense of humor." But those may not be what you want at all. It seems to me that people don't usually know themselves very well and don't, deep inside, know what they want in others, just what they *think* they want. Maybe you actually want someone who makes the first sexual overtures, gives good head, and causes you a lot of grief. And most people, let's be honest, don't have that many choices. They think they do, but they don't, about anything.

John said, "Why don't you put my name on the back of your memoirs with the others." I said, "Okay – if you let me write about your recent problems." Employment problems. Legal problems. He said no. So I can't. His name will not appear on the back. He does get a photo credit, though, for the front cover of me taken in the 1980s in his apartment.

JOYCE CAROL OATES – Joyce Carol who?

LILY TOMLIN – She's around. She's one of those gay/lesbians who waited until it was safe to come out. The rest of us did the hard work. Did she come out yet or not? Rosie O'Donnell also waits and waits ands waits, and then gets all the publicity. And she's not even nice, like Ellen DeGeneres.

DAN TURNER – His songs are probably his only lasting legacy. I am trying to market the ones we wrote together through Broadjam.com and such.

HARRY BRITT ran for the California State legislature against Supervisor Mark Leno. According to the polls, many, even in the Castro, didn't know who Harry Britt was.

ROBERT PATRICK is in an online theater chat group I belong to. I was worried about him staying in too much, but he's had a couple of play productions of late and flying high on those. He even contributed a nice blurb for the *Collected Plays of Daniel Curzon* that I did through BookSurge.com: "Daniel Curzon is indeed an important, influential, enlightening, and entertaining author." Bob's a generous guy.

DORIC WILSON and I have never met in person, but on this same theater chat line we've communicated. He said even unkinder things about Allan Estes of Theatre Rhinoceros than I did. He too gave me a blurb for my seven volumes of plays: "Daniel Curzon is central and essential to the history of our community's culture." Aw, shucks. Little old me?

TOM AMMIANO is too "progressive" for my taste. I rail against the politically correct of the Left. I despise the Right. They are both simple-minded. There's no hope for me.

EDMUND WHITE is teaching at Princeton. I read in an interview that he and JOYCE CAROL OATES have become buddy-buddy. The circle is complete. (I hope she at least lets him be out of the closet around her.)

SALLY GEARHART and I marched in the Gay Whatever Parade in San Francisco in 2003. We were in the contingent remembering the activists who fought against 1978's Proposition 6, which – can you believe this? – actually to ban gays from the entire teaching profession. Sally saw me, but we didn't speak. You know what? I didn't care.

DEL MARTIN and PHYLLIS LYON are having a baby! Well, not really. But they were married in the Gay Marriage flurry of recent memory, at City Hall by the Mayor of San Francisco himself. Those gals sure know how to milk it.

HARVEY FIERSTEIN has been starring on Broadway in the musical *Hairspray* in the role drag queen Divine played in the original movie by John Waters. He has gone out of his weigh (oops, out of his way) to clarify that he has to put on tons of padding to become the 350-pounder the part calls for, when he's only a petite 250. (I sympathize. Really I do.) He's become this gay Jewish mother figure now.

ARMISTEAD MAUPIN is huge, in every sense. I'm not

envious. I'm not. I'm not! He gives candy. I give it not. He's also pretty nice.

WILLIAM DICKEY's ex-lover (LEN), with whom I taught and fought at City College, committed suicide by hanging himself in his basement earlier this year. I had nothing to do with it, I swear. (But Joyce Carol Oates probably did!) I'm kidding! I'm kidding!

. . . The pains of the past are fading.

DEAN GOODMAN is still around. I thought that because his Christmas cards had stopped coming he might have stopped coming himself. But I bet he hasn't. It's amazing how strong and long the sexual drive is.

STEPHEN SONDHEIM replied to my request for us to collaborate on a musical called Heaven, based on Studio 54, a show I had major interest in for a time from a multi-millionaire in S.F. as well as from a Russian émigré composer. (They dried up.) Sondheim reply was that he was too busy. But he was very nice about it. The beat goes on.

ROBERT CHESLEY has a play contest named after him. I suppose his or his mother's money funds it. I think I need a building or something named after me. A real cruisy park?

DONALD ALLEN is ancient now, but he's around. We haven't held hands for centuries.

JEANNE BARNEY got all huffy because some of her friends hadn't sent her Christmas cards, including me. It's become perfunctory after all this time and I don't send many cards at all anymore, but what the hell. I sent her another one.

TERRENCE DAVIES is still directing films. I doubt that

he has had a Big Epiphany and is happy and saturated with glorious, meaningless sex. People, I've noticed, change only in novels. In life they usually just become fatter, uglier versions of themselves.

CHRISTMAS LEUBRIE, the midwife for my son, is around town. She called me once to say that she had read *Only the Good Parts*, the novel I based on siring a child with a lesbian couple. She made the same mistake many readers make about fiction when she said "My, what happened up there in Oregon!?" When I said that I had made up most of it, she said, thoughtfully, "I could tell you some stories about the inseminations I did that would be even more extreme." I'm sure she could. But they aren't any more extreme than the results of heterosexual reproduction! Couldn't be.

It's a novel! It's got to have excitement in it. I'm glad I made the character based on Christmas Leubrie sympathetic. (It cuts down on the screaming when you meet up.) But no writer can censor himself too much over what he needs to say. Or why say it?

I am grateful that this "midwife" helped give me my son, Zack. He's finishing his junior year of college in Oregon, tired of school. When he turns twenty-one this July, he wants to try the "bar scene." I, good father to the bone, said, "Don't get AIDS – and get that college degree. You can do a whole lot of things with it that you cannot do without it." I even offered him a free trip to Europe with his old man if he completes the Bachelor's degree. (Something tells me traveling with your old man is not cool these days.) (Note: He agreed to go in 2005!)

THE KUCHAR BROTHERS are not much in my world,

and I don't see or hear of them at all. I think JOHN WATERS learned everything he could from them and made the money that was to be made from camp. Except of course for *Beach Blanket Babylon*, created by a gay man (named . . . ? I remember now – Steve Silver). That's still selling to the straight world after thirty years.

ROGER AUSTEN's self-drowning still bothers me.

TOM AMMIANO is in the news a great deal, though a shade less of late. I almost never agree with anything he says, such as providing translators to non-English speakers at Board of Supervisors meetings. Jesus, learn English! All this crap about the Beauty of Diversity. As a teacher I'm on the front lines of Diversity. It's at least as annoying and harmful to society as it is "wonderful." Some people's ideas simply do fit together and lead to terrible conflicts and turf wars. Christian Asians have already been out protesting Gay Marriage. That's just the tip of the iceberg. I haven't struggled in my Just Cause just to see if overturned by tons of bigots from other places.

TIM WOLFRED has dropped out of public life, and my prediction that he would become a major player was totally wrong. This either shows that I am a terrible judge of people or that Life Has Its Own Agenda. What do you think?

GEORGE BIRIMISA, body-building playwright, threw a party to celebrate his eightieth birthday, and I was invited, mainly because I contributed to the funding of a film based on his life. He was hearty, with many friends in attendance. (I couldn't hold a candle to him on friendships.) Apparently he's still active sexually, though living on not much money. For some reason I felt very uncomfortable there and could barely talk to anybody.

SEAN PENN, as you know, has won an Academy Award for Best Actor and presumably has stopped beating people up. I promise to stop beating people up if I can have an Academy Award too.

TERRENCE MCNALLY is quoted on the back of my collected plays, from the post card he sent me about my novel *The World Can Beak Your Heart*. I didn't ask formal permission. I presume he doesn't mind. CHRISTOPHER ISHERWOOD once told me never to say something in correspondence if you don't want it quoted later. It puts you in the difficult position of having to take back what you supposedly meant.

Lately I have been asked to give some blurbs myself for various book jackets. I gave one for JOSEPH ITIEL for an unsentimental book about elder sex. What a horny old bastard!

ROMANOVSKY AND PHILLIPS –

(Romanovsky and who?)

HAROLD NORSE is way up there in years now, despite the heart trouble and the swollen ego. He called me once and asked me to help get him a part-time teaching job. I did try but couldn't do it. It was quite sad.

But then some theater in Chicago did some of his poems as a play, so his Beat goes on too, I guess.

SISTER BOOM BOOM is still dead. Jack Fertig, however, actually took my writing class a few years ago. I encouraged him to write his memoirs as a member of the Sisters of

Perpetual Indulgence instead of what he was writing, but he said that time was all behind him now.

I mentioned Sister Boom Boom to my classes a few times. And they said, "Sister who?"

QUENTIN CRISP played Elizabeth I in a movie, and then he died at ninety. Rest in peace, sweet queen.

But, hell, why does the world still think all of us are queens?! Some of us are not.

JON SUGAR is still out promoting himself and giving a "Sugar rush" to everyone around him. I have not seen him in person for years, though. I still remember his line about somebody coming up to him and applying dough to Jon's big, wide, homely face. "Why would anybody do that?" you'd ask. "Because they wanted to make gorilla cookies!" he'd say.

He was funny – but exhausting.

LEE BRADY – She's a straight woman friend. I have had lots of straight women friends, as a matter of fact. But she pissed me off in Edinburgh in 2000 because I felt she treated me like one of her lesser friends when I needed a friend over there during the Fringe Festival. So I didn't speak to her for four years.

I know, I know! I'm trying to change. Recently I made an overture by going to see a revival of her musical here in S.F., and she made an overture. I gave her a good copy of the video of "An Irish Blessing," a song I wrote, which I made with her and my son as actors almost six years ago. I wasn't sure she had ever gotten a good copy of the video, which isn't bad for an AVI.

I thought: You know, Dan, it's time for you to stop always breaking relationships and even repair at least one. Of course when I put her in my one-act "The Hit," she got pissed and we did not speak for years. But then we *did*. I'm improving! I am!

Doug **H**olsclaw left a long, angry complaint on my telephone answering machine about the way I wrote him up in these memoirs. You know what? Tough shit.

ANN SHAY

On Christmas Eve, 2004, my friend Ann died of ovarian cancer at the age of sixty-seven. She was not ready to go. In the hospital she thought they were bringing her clothes so that she could "get married." They weren't. She sat on the edge of the bed and saw me weeping. She didn't know it was for her. She took a napkin from her food tray and offered it to me. She was dying, but she was thinking of me. "Oh, god, I wish I could help you, Ann!" I said.

She was one of the few people in my life who actually *loved* me.

DANIEL CURZON was once DAN BROWN. He changed his name because you couldn't put your real name on gay anything when his writing career began. And DAN BROWN seemed so ordinary besides. Now DAN BROWN is a famous best-selling novelist and it's not me. No matter. Bestsellerdom is the antithesis of what I and my work have been all about. Don't you see that, Danny Boy? Have you learned nothing about life or your own life?

You have turned sixty-six years old. EEK! You still doesn't look that old, but you can feel and see the changes. How can anybody believe in a God that would do this to His people?! You weigh two hundred fifty pounds, but you're planning to have some of the fat liposucked out fairly soon. You had liposuction when you were forty-nine, but new fat keeps on rolling like Ole Man River. (Why has sucking gotten such a bad name? There is absolutely nothing better in life than being sucked, lipo or cock though it be.)

You've also had Lasik surgery on your left eye and could see anything for about four years without glasses. Now that's wearing off and you need reading glasses once more. How about more Lasik in Heaven? (*Where?*)

You had a double chin cut out after you saw yourself on Fox News during your lawsuit. It left a scar on the lower chin, but that's better than a bag of fat there.

You have an enlarged prostate with all the attendant troubles, like urination urgency and having to get up often during the night, to say nothing of shrunken testicles and flaccid penis, and you were in a government study to see if saw palmetto might help. It didn't help you, but the prescription drug Flomax seems to be the answer. Yay! It's a hell of a lot better than the rotor rooter and microwave operations the doctor brought up. Your genitalia are back in full working order and saying "Howdy to the world."

You have some allergies now, never before a problem, plus repetitive stress syndrome in your right hand from writing on the computer. But you are reasonably healthy. The woman in the condo next to yours is dying of lung cancer and can barely breathe. The nurse says it's just a matter of days. All the more reason to live, live, live!

So you're packing your bags for six weeks in England. You really must stop thinking you've had such a hard time in life. How many times have you been to Europe now? How many books have you written? How many are coming back into print, even some that never saw print earlier? (So you had to do them with a POD. At least there are PODs now.) So your unflagging efforts at immortality in a hostile world will perhaps not be for naught.

You've had a pretty good life, Daniel Curzon, despite the knocks and your complaints. You've done mostly what you've wanted when it came to sex and to your writing (once you got rid of the Catholic shit). If nobody reads it, or not as much as you like, you can take comfort in the fact that you spoke the truth as you saw it. And teaching college English, even in a community college with your hard-earned pretty-much-wasted PH.D., is better than most professions because you're the boss. And with the so-called review hate site gone you're in charge again. So don't retire. You've got some good years left. Your father had the same prostate problem and smoked a pack of Camel cigarettes a day and still lived to be almost eighty-three years old! You can do better than that.

Hey, you've just finished a good book about some famous or semi-famous people whom you've known (*Dropping Names*). You've managed to capture an era, the last quarter of the twentieth century, and – you sly fox you – you even sneaked in that autobiography you thought you'd never write.

So go to England, enjoy the Lake District, see some theatre, have an outdoor orgasm or two, a few glasses of wine, start a new play (on Jane Austen's possible lesbian longings for her sister perhaps?). Re-do your *Gay Etiquette* book. Your books don't have to stay out of print. Maybe your agent will call with good news about *What a Tangled Web*, the "narrative non-fiction" book you've concocted out of the Internet lawsuit you endured, or perhaps a new edition of your gay etiquette book.

Or maybe you shouldn't come back at all. Fade away in a Lake District fell, be eaten by the last remaining wild beast in Cumbria? It's up to you, Daniel Curzon. It's up to you. Who wants to live forever?

Daniel who?

UPDATE – 2014

FOSTER CORBIN

I kept seeing these nice reviews of my books on Amazon.com and had no idea who H.F. Corbin was. I made no effort to contact this person. Finally I couldn't take it anymore -- here was somebody who seemed to be my perfect reader. He GOT it. So I tracked him down online and discovered that he lived in Atlanta and was a lawyer and a fair housing administrator. He had even taught college English. I was tentative at first, but we became great pen pals, and in the two visits we had in San Francisco I found him to be a Southern gentleman. He validated my work, and I was, as I grew older and older, very grateful for his efforts on my behalf. Foster Corbin's reviews seemed to correspond to something in the gay literary movement: we moved into the mainstream at the same time when only one or two gay bookstores remained.

Did the movement die from its own success?

AARON FRICKE

Who says Facebook is all bad?

I've actually met some new friends there, people I have come to know and admire.

And then there is Aaron Fricke. In case you don't know,

Aaron made headlines in 1980 when he sued his high school for the right to take a male date to the prom. It was an historical first. He detailed his exploits in his book *Reflections of a Rock Lobster* (1981). When he was promoting his book, he was a very cute, slender, boyish charmer. I believe I even reviewed Fricke's book, for IGNA (the International Gay News Agency), which I had helped found and then run.

Even though both gay writers, we had never met. Then I learned from seeing a posting on Robert Patrick's Facebook page that Aaron Fricke was living in San Francisco. How neat, I thought.

I had lost several friends or my friends lived in other cities and we rarely visited in person. (E-mail is okay, but sort of cold. And Facebook can be like Thoreau updated – where the mass of men live lives of PUBLIC desperation.) Perhaps, I thought, I could gain a new friend, a local, a writer. What could go wrong?

I ignored the warning signs in Aaron Fricke's posting to Robert Patrick. He seemed far too insistent on cornering Bob on some point or other, absolutely unwilling to let it go. I messaged Bob and asked if he had met Aaron in person. He had. As I recall, there was some sort of a warning from Bob. I chose to ignore this as well. What we won't do to have a friend! Let's face it, it's hard to make new friends when you're old.

Anyway, Aaron Fricke and I met for lunch and a movie in downtown San Francisco, at the very Mel's where my partner and I had been gay-baited by the sons of a woman blabbing away loudly on her cell phone. Somebody had told her to quiet down and have pity on other customers. Who, *me*?!

Aaron was late, and I barely recognized him. He was around fifty then, wearing a baseball cap, short pants, and had gotten humungous. I think he was eating something when he arrived. Maybe that was later. He ate through every movie we saw, and this was *before* we went to lunch. Now let me hasten to add that I myself have gotten a lot heavier in my senior years. And I resent it like hell when people comment on it. So I certainly did not comment on his size to Aaron. He himself commented on it very soon after we met, saying that he made a decision to get super fat on purpose to spite the people who thought he had been getting a little fat. What?? I was not looking for a boyfriend in Aaron. I have never been sexually attracted to twinks, so fat or thin, I just wanted a friend! Jesus! Is that too much to ask?

We had planned to see the new Batman movie on opening day, the very day when yet another gun-crazy American shot up a movie theater somewhere. So we changed plans and saw something else. I don't like violent movies anyway. I can get violence out on any street in America!

Our luncheon conversation was fine, though I recall Aaron saying that he didn't think he was a good speaker. He was good enough. What took me aback was that almost immediately, when Aaron found out somebody I knew was on an illegal drug, he asked me to get him some and he would trade some of his food stamps for it. Yikes! At least wait until the third "date"!

This was followed by umpteen emails and phone calls begging me to supply his needs. Even if I could have done so,

I wouldn't have. I think all drugs should be legal and up to the individual, like alcohol, but I don't use them myself and I am definitely not supplying any to others. When I introduced Aaron to a friend later, he began badgering the friend for drugs too. Oy.

Soon I had my new "friend." A movie with lunch began a regular thing, overall quite enjoyable.

Yeah, Aaron, ran from one movie in the complex to the next to see what he could squeeze in for free, went back and forth to the candy counter like a nine-year-old, and talked out loud during the movie, and made flamboyant sexually explicit remarks to handsome passersby inside and outside the movie theater. All in all, quite a "character."

It turned out that the Children's Theater of Boston had done a stage production of his gay-goes-to-the-prom book. How times had changed! Now the audience was rooting for the queers! Aaron had been invited to attend rehearsals and the performances. His partner had gotten him some airline deal, and the theater in Boston paid some of his expenses. But Aaron was full of complaints about the script and some of the performances. I've had complaints about some things done in my plays too. But Aaron was not content just to complain. He loaned me a tape of the live performance, and then told me how I was expected to react to it. I thought it was pretty decent actually, maybe going on too long. I don't really like "criticism," of my work, just praise, so I treaded very lightly here. I caught a typo in the program and pointed it out to Aaron, to show that I was attentive but not too judgmental. Well, his response was, "Don't ever point out typos in things I can't change."

What?!!

Furthermore, I was supposed to agree that the Catholic fanatic mother was over the top, the man in the wheelchair was a mistake, and so forth and so on. Whether I personally felt these to be shortcomings did not seem to cross Aaron's mind. I thought, Oh, God, this friendship is going to be a chore.

Aaron didn't seem to have a clue about my take on things, and admitted that he had never read a word of my work, and seemed to think I was being a pussy. Umm, I have been known to be crusty, snarky, and not the least bit afraid to give my opinion. In this case, I was simply trying not to be offensive too early in a new friendship. You can say a lot more to old friends. You can say anything to old boyfriends!

When Aaron just kept pestering me to say what he wanted me to say instead of what I wanted to say, or didn't want to say, I finally blew up and told him off. I assumed that was the end of the friendship and was prepared to drive him home and say goodbye. He surprised me by apologizing. Maybe it was just his way of testing my limits. Whatever, his skin was a lot thicker than mine.

When it turned out that Boston Children's Theater was going to do a second production of the prom book, a new problem occurred. Aaron now wanted to play the abusive Catholic fanatic mother character himself – in drag! He ran the idea by the director. I thought it was a terrible idea. But I didn't say so. I think you can push people's tolerance only so far before they push back – hard. Yeah, yeah, go to the prom with your boyfriend. But don't come out screaming in a frumpy dress and then be introduced as the author of the play that I've just applauded. For God's sake!

I was solicited to look after Aaron's three cats while he and his partner were away in Boston. The apartment building had a no-pets policy, the superintendent had smelled them after they capered in the hallway, and was on the lookout for them. The apartment itself was not even a studio. It was miniscule, barely bigger than a prison cell, with a box of dirty cat litter in the kitchen and three locked-up indoors cats. Aaron said he was thrilled to have the place, since he had been living in an SRO until he had managed to snag this one at a price he could afford. I think cats shouldn't be confined to a large place, let alone a virtual cage.

But I agreed to feed the kitties and give them a hug or two while the owners were gone. I came for a preliminary visit, and of course the cats ignored or hid from me.

I had a bad knee at the time, since fixed with a knee replacement, and this jewel of a San Francisco apartment was up three very steep flights of stairs. But I love animals. I also wanted to be a good friend. I was offered what I considered an insulting amount to look after the cats. So I said I said I didn't want the money.

I climbed up those stairs at least once a day for eight days – Aaron and the boyfriend deciding to stay over to "see some sights" while on the East Coast. I was tempted to set the cats free, but they probably would have been run over by cars. That seems to be like most of the real choices people have in life, not "Shall I marry the Sultan with the oil wells or the pilot with the nine inches?"

I even took pictures of the cats and e-mailed them to Aaron, who got all gushy about his babies.

He didn't come back when he had promised, however.

Eventually the cats and Aaron were reunited, the play had not done as much business as the first time, and I was feeling a bit exploited. Even the can opener for the cat food didn't work!

Then Aaron learned that I had published some of my books through Createspace of Amazon.com. He asked me to help him get *Reflections of a Rock Lobster* back into print. I really thought he should write a new book, but that didn't seem too likely, so I set out giving him detailed instructions on how to prepare a manuscript, design a cover, and upload it to the Amazon website.

Lord, it was like getting your granny to use the computer. I won't bore you with all the back and forth about everything. Let's just say eventually I had to go over to the squalid little efficiency apartment and see what was wrong. It had something to do with Aaron not knowing what Open Office was, or indeed any word-processing program, even though he was somehow using one. We both got so frustrated, we dropped the project. (I believe he got it up there many months later, somehow.) He kept saying that he had re-read his book and it sounded like "a child had written it." Probably. I advised him not to re-write it, to let it live in its time.

We continued with our "friendship," such as it was, but Aaron proved to be so argumentative, so poorly educated, and so borderline nuts that it was proving to be more of a chore than a delight. The last straw was some silly argument about whether most non-American parents would put up with disobedience and even verbal abuse from their children the way American parents do. It's one of my pet peeves that Americans think kids in the rest of the world act like they do, that they "rebel." They wouldn't dare, as any number of my foreign-born college students confirmed when I asked about this topic over many, many years. "We would be kicked out of the house," they said. "Or beaten." They clearly would never dream of saying, "Shut up! Fuck you, Mom!" or anything close to it. I wasn't even saying that I approved of the difference, only that it was so.

I don't think this difference in cultures is even disputed, except by Americans, who mistakenly think the whole world acts like they do. Oh, and of course by Aaron Fricke, who said to me, "Oh, that's something only an ignorant bigot would say."

And he wouldn't let it go when I said where I had gotten my information, besides my extensive travel in numerous other countries in Europe and Asia! Then I said, "I think it's time for our friendship to be over." He said, "Really?" I said, "I would think somebody who says 'you're an ignorant bigot' doesn't want to be a friend any longer. And I certainly don't want to be friends with somebody who is clearly an argumentative, ignorant asshole who doesn't know what he's talking about."

And there the "friendship" terminated, as I guess it was doomed to do from the beginning.

(But, ha, ha, at least I got a play out of it and this memoir!) And I can see now why Aaron Fricke got to go to his prom!

MICHAEL JOSEPH ARCANGELINI

Joe Archangelini wrote to me on Facebook to say that a book of mine, *The Misadventures of Tim McPick*, had helped him with its comedy during a dark period of his life. Who can resist a compliment? See, I'm not an old sourpuss!

I thought maybe we could meet up for a meal in San Francisco. He said he came down from his place near Santa Rosa from time to time.

One has to be careful with Internet friends, or so I've heard. They can turn out to be serial murderers or Jamaican scam artists.

But Joe and I met and the conversation in the restaurant was good. He turned out to be a highly literate, self-described poet who worked as a paralegal with workers' disability claims. He was bear-like, close to sixty, with some on-going medical problems. These problems soon turned into a triple by-pass and a kidney operation, leaving him with scars and a sense of the fragility of life.

It became apparent that he, of Catholic Italian heritage, had had more than his share of guilt dumped on his head while he was growing up. A serious case of alcoholism was the result, but luckily he had been sober now for many years. As I recall, he had functioned as a bisexual with physical ease, if not mental, until finally accepting his truest orientation.

He sent me his book of poems, *With Fingers on the Tips of My Words*, and I liked them. I liked his clarity, his confessional style. You never know if you're going to enjoy the work of somebody who compliments your work. It must be easier for people who don't mind lying. I mind lying very much indeed. I told him that I liked his overtly leftist political poems less. Secretly I like to hang around super-liberals. I basically sympathize, but I sometimes feel superior because I find them naïve about people. I don't like to hang around the overtly rightwing, except when I agree with them – on the occasional Tuesday or Friday.

Joe is fantastically knowledgeable about music and poets, and I can only admire his enthusiasm.

His little house in the country is packed with related goodies. It's nice to know that somebody is reading books! Even I read less than I used to! What's wrong with us?

Joe is a good son and visits his elderly mother in Cleveland every August. No greater love hath a son! Sing this to the tune of "April in Paris": "August in Cleveland . . ."

At a play we attended, Joe introduced me to his former lover, a former ballet dancer, a very nice-looking man whom I talked to easily. I thought maybe I had insulted him when he said he was from Detroit like me but then said it was really Bloomfield Hills, which is a very rich suburb of Detroit. "That's not Detroit!" I said. This same man committed suicide a few weeks later, hanging himself. According to Joe, the threat had been around for years. He'd had three hip replacements and was generally fed up with everything. But gays DO NOT COMMIT SUICIDE anymore. It's very bad form and very bad for our Cause. (Of course some do, and we can't bury our heads in the sand about the dark side of life.)

Joe, I think, would like more literary recognition than he

has had so far. He has held back from promoting himself and his work. I hope he will do more in that line. God knows, you can't wait for other people to do it for you. (Even I do not have a literary executor.)

If there is a flaw in this very kind and generous new friend of mine is might be his participation in wild boar hunts, followed by butchering and feasting. I'm such an animal rights guy that I simply don't understand such actions. I confess to watching Mixed Martial Arts on TV and even wild animals attacking others on nature programs. But I think hunting should only be allowed if the wild boar, or whoever, is given a gun too!

LADY MALET

I believe it was the very next month after the falling-out with Aaron Fricke that I went to stay for a month in Palm Springs. I could be off by a year. (It happens at my age). This was at the invitation of my closest friend. Let's call her Lady Malet, shall we. After all, that was her real title. We had been very close, traveling together, keeping in constant communication even after she married again, this for the second time. It was a Match.com made in Heaven. Well, not quite. Lady M. admitted to me that with her children grown and without a romantic partner she had been very lonely, even resentful of the couples she saw everywhere. I even arranged a get-together for her and the man who had joined me a lawsuit. But that didn't work out in the end. Then suddenly she was married!

I had never been to Palm Springs. I had just completed a new novel, called *Saving Jane Austen*, and thought it would be relaxing and glamorous to stay with a good friend in the famous resort.

Wrong.

The plan was for Lady M. and me to work separately on any writing projects we might fancy. She had recently translated a screenplay from Italian to English for an old Italian movie director she had worked with in the past. She sent me the screenplay to read and asked for feedback. I thought it was incoherent, all lovely imagery but missing a coherent plot. I even suggested a way to make it hang together better. But Lady M. didn't want to be too critical, so she didn't pass on my suggestions. Now she wanted to do some of her "own" writing. She had written and sold some screenplays of her own previously. Good for her.

I didn't have a laptop to bring with me, but there was to be a computer at the rented condo, plus two bedrooms, a large living and kitchen area, extensive grounds, a tennis court, even a pool.

What is wrong with this picture?

Well, certain restrictions had been put in place before I arrived: Lady M. was to have primary use of the computer. Not a problem. I could use it when she wasn't using it. Fine. We'd share food costs and I'd take her out to dinner whenever we both wanted to. Great.

Even with air conditioning, Palm Springs, it turns out, is a Hellhole. Resort, my ass. It gets to one hundred by eleven in the morning. You have to draw the blinds before noon to be able to stay alive.

I had grown up with awful Detroit summers (and winters), but Palm Springs was supposed to be ritzy.

I hated it.

Lady M. was not doing any writing. Instead, she signed up at a club to play tennis every morning, She is a very good tennis player. She even beat me. But I claim a pass because of my knee replacement. Besides, a guest should always be polite enough to lose at tennis!

But my hostess wanted me to come and watch her play and beat the pants off old retired millionaires and such. Well, of course I'd come. It was, after all, "at the club."

So there I was in the morning heat walking onto the tennis court about to take my seat on the sidelines to watch my good friend of royal blood. Little Danny Brown of Farmersville, Illinois, was living the high life! Except that Lady M. suddenly noticed a sign that said: No Visitors on the Courts. There were empty places to sit, next to the jackets and extra equipment. "Oh, Dan, you can't stay here!" I was told. What?! Why not? "Oh, no, it says no visitors." So fucking what? I had been invited – no, more like commanded – to come and watch Her Ladyship on the field of play. "You had best go and watch from over there!" She pointed to a spot four or five courts distant. What?!! I did not say anything, or much, but went off to my appointed place on the far, far sidelines. The match went on without me. Naturally, Lady M. won. "You couldn't see?" she queried. "I gave up trying," I said cryptically.

Then other things began to irritate the idyll. Lady M.'s husband drove down from their home to the north to spend a weekend. He was, shall we say, not of royal blood. He, in fact, was a bit on the "common" side, not quite Lady Chatterley's lover, but close enough. He and Lady M. were actually close to a divorce. Preliminary papers had been filed. I had comforted her in e-mails and on the phone and in person almost from the moment that marriage had begun. The husband was unfaithful, insensitive, trying to cheat her out of her money; on and on went the complaints. I let Lady M. cry on my shoulder as much as she wanted to. I always took her side, always. What are friends for? I even told her *not* to get a divorce, to bear with it. You have to pay a price for a relationship, I believe.

As we were eating a pizza with too many peppers on (her choice, not ours), the husband out of the blue said, "I used to have nine inches, but now I think it's less." What does one say to that? Is one expected to help measure to confirm?

The husband also came out of their bedroom that night in his underwear as I was using the computer. He wanted to sleep on the sofa because it was so damned hot in their bedroom. I offered to leave the computer, but the husband said it was okay and went back to bed.

The next morning I was informed by Lady M. that I should not have tried to use the computer when the husband wanted to sleep on the couch. I bit my tongue. After all, it was a free vacation!

But all good things, it would seem, must end.

Eleven days had transpired since my arrival. I had not written a word, though I had done some publicity for *Saving Jane Austen*. I have never suffered from writer's block and certainly was feeling no guilt about not writing anything in

Palm Springs. There I had a fuzzy TV in my bedroom, but I decided to watch the better one in the living room. I thought an educational program would be a good choice. Lady M. was off playing tennis yet again.

When she returned, she said, "Dan, you're watching television in the middle of the day!" What?!! All television is not the same – I wanted to say. She added: "And why aren't you watching it, if you must, on the TV in your room!?"

Yeah, it's nice to have a royal friend, but you can be more royal than the royals! And an imperious royal pain in the ass!

"I'm not six years old! How dare you tell me when and where I can watch television!" I said.

"But you're just sitting around all the time!"

"I just finished writing a novel!"

I think there may have been a dismissive wave of a royal hand.

"You're out playing tennis every day!" I said.

"Well, at least I get some exercise!"

"Good for you. But you are not talking to me like I am a child being told how to behave!"

"I think this visit may have been a mistake!" said she.

"And I understand your husband a *whole* lot better now!' said I.

Naturally I then stormed off to my bedroom and took a nap. It was out first quarrel, and I thought we both needed some time to cool off – if you can cool off in that damned place!

When I rose from my nap and went out to the living room, Lady M. was at the computer with her back to me. She was checking on the time of a real estate viewing that she had scheduled earlier.

"Do you still want me to go with you?" I asked.

She turned to look me in the eye. "I want you to leave."

I am not one to beg, not even a little beg. "All right, I will leave right now." I hurried back into "my" bedroom and called the airline I had flown in on. It was too late to get a flight that day.

I came back to the living room and informed the Lady of the House that I couldn't get on a plane that day. I offered to spend the night in a hotel.

She said that wasn't necessary, that the next day would be good enough.

I went back to the bedroom and booked my return flight for the next day, paying a penalty of course for changing the flight.

Lady M. then went off to look at the house that she was thinking of purchasing, without me.

We ate dinner and watch a bad movie together, a pall settling over the rest of the day. I thought time would heal the rupture, since we had been close friends for fourteen years by that time.

But Lady M. did not say "Let's forgive and forget" in the morning. She drove me to the airport.

On the way, she even invited me to look at the house that she was considering to add to her real estate holdings. It looked a little run-down, but she had a talent for refurbishing properties and raising their value. I said, "Let me know if you buy it."

"Oh, I will," she promised.

Inwardly I sighed in relief. I had worked to save this friendship. I'd had enough broken friendships to last a lifetime. Whew! See, Dan, you can learn a thing or two.

She even gave me a kiss on the cheek at the airport. And a wave.

However, she un-friended me on Facebook immediately, and we haven't spoken since. What will be will be.

PAUL SAGAN AND BILL NEVILLE

I had to travel two and a half hours to find some new friends, all the way to Ukiah, California.

That's where Paul Sagan and Bill Neville lived, after they had left the unliveable, creep-filled Tenderloin section of dear old San Francisco.

Again is was the often-maligned Facebook that provided the conduit by which I met them. (Mark Zuckerberg can send me a check anytime!) Paul "liked" some little comment I made on a friend's page, and soon we were joking back and forth. Paul thought we had actually met in some playwriting group connected with Theatre Rhinoceros, but I didn't recall any such meeting. Paul was a theatre director, so I probably would have remembered. You can never know too many directors. They are willing to go through those tedious rehearsals one has to in order to mount a play.

It didn't matter really if we had met before. We were meeting now. In fact, I arranged an in-person get-together by scheduling my annual trip to the Shakespeare Festival in Ashland, Oregon, so that my partner and I would pass through Ukiah. Let's face it, Ukiah is not some place you go as a tourist. Another one off my bucket list: I've seen Ukiah, California! It's hot as hell and suitable only for living someplace cheap and free of crime.

The first time, Paul and I met for lunch without Bill. It was pleasant, but not especially memorable. Nobody threw a chicken salad at anybody. We gossiped about the characters at Theatre Rhinoceros, and that was fun and purging. Paul and I were on the same page about the many sins of Theatre Rhino. (Now that this early gay theater seems all but dried up and blown away, its characters are taking on a more nostalgic, if phoney, charm. Funny about that.)

Paul, it turned out, was a literary executor for playwright George Birimisa, who died in 2012. Hey, you can never know too many literary executors, right? Especially once you hit seventy. He made his living writing scripts for travel companies. His partner was a retired government worker. (You don't see people at their best that way). Bill and Paul were one of the early gay couples to get legally married.

The retired government worker, Bill, did not appear until my second visit, a year later. His health was obviously precarious, and he was younger than me! He had many, many ailments and could barely walk. Evidently all the bad health had descended upon him since coming to Ukiah. It wasn't Ukiah's *fault* – I think. He seemed to have no self-pity and toughed it out.

I even met up with Bill in San Francisco when he came down to see a doctor or two. He mistook me for a celebrity, and I didn't have the heart to disabuse him of that illusion. It was still obvious that he had major mobility problems. I'd had a knee replacement myself somewhere in this period and thus appreciated the simple ability to walk where and when you wanted (The handicapped placard is very nice, however!)

I sent them some books of mine to read. Happily they both appreciated the fierce yet funny truths contained in *Halfway to the Stars: Cable Car Tales of a Grumpy Gripman*. They had lived the dark side of San Francisco, even worse than I put into that book. When I encounter people who don't live here, they always gush about how wonderful San Francisco is and how much they want to see it. They are in for a shock if they go downtown. My book is sort of the anti-*Tales of the City*. (People don't like you to destroy their illusions, I've noticed. But somebody's got to do it!)

Bill Neville was not able to make it out of the house during my third visit to see them. He waved from the doorway. Jesus! Boys and girls, *carpe diem*!

On my fourth visit, he was pretty much confined to a wheelchair. I went by the house and we all chatted away. He loved Audrey Hepburn, had sort of a shrine for her in one room. Who knew? Paul seemed dignified, resigned, a little sad.

I was a little sad myself.

I hope things are better during my next visit with them. I do sad in my books. I do it less well in life.

ZACK JOHNSON

So few things work out well in this life, at least if you have high ambitions. Haven't you noticed? So it is with relief and some pride that I report on how the child I sired with a lesbian couple anonymously many years ago has turned out. I did not see him until he was seven. Was that unfortunate? Yes, environment matters, role modeling less so – there are plenty of male role models in the world, by the way, many of them mean and nasty – but biology, it seems to me, is much more important. I also did my best to expose him to life's variety: the circus, a cabaret, theater, a baseball game, etc. I even starred him in a music video when he was fifteen, of a song of mine called "An Irish Blessing," now on YouTube. (He was a teenager and hard to direct, but now we have the music video.)

Zack is thirty-one years old now. (That is odd since I claim to be only thirty-one myself. But then math has never been my strong suit.) He is 6'4" and a big guy, black-bearded. His passion is rugby. He is straight and has married as woman, Crystal. What can you do!!? You have to love them anyway, right?

Fortunately, Zack is very loveable. It seems to be liked and sought out by just about everybody, from old ladies in a theatre course I took him to in London when he was turning twenty-two, to all his many relatives from parents and co-parents and their endless relatives. He's just a great guy.

Actually, he has an *edge* to some of his comments, observations. Where could he have gotten *that* from?! However, people don't seem to notice it the way I do. His aura is more benevolent than mine, I suspect.

I was especially impressed with Zack when my sister, a virtual skeleton, was on her deathbed. She and my son quite independently and accidentally had moved to Phoenix, and like many young people, he struck me as uncomfortable around the enfeebled and sickly. I didn't exactly seek them out myself. But Zack came through along with my dying sister's daughter, Debbie, and was kind and helpful to all of us, very much a man in the best sense, a grown-up, my son the non-Jewish mensch.

If I have a complaint about my baby, it's that he lacks his father's drive. Zack, we're still waiting on that Bachelor's Degree! I attribute his overall comfort in his skin to his being heterosexual and having been raised middle class. Those of us working class and gay probably felt an overwhelming desire to protect ourselves from the vicissitudes of life. I certainly never felt the world was looking out for me. I knew that I had better do it myself. (And I am doing just fine at age seventy-six: nice pension, reasonably good health, mind still clear. Maybe the legs are less steady than they were, but I just put in four life-alert buttons in my condo.) Hey, I have fallen before, but I always managed to get up!

Was my boy harmed by being conceived by a consenting

gay and two lesbians and a midwife?

Hardly. He told me once that when he was in high school he was afraid to tell his buddies that his mom was a "lesbian" and didn't for a long time. When he finally "came out" as the child of gay parents, his buddies said they already knew about his mother and it didn't bother them one iota. I don't think it's a bad thing at all to be a bit "different." It makes you strong.

Now Zack dines out on the fact he has not just one gay parent but *two*! See, if you push the envelope on the Zeitgeist you can help change things for the better. All this new biological planning is absolutely better than the shame and secrecy and frustration of the horrible past.

CHARLES KRUGER

Once again I have Facebook to thank for providing me a friend. I don't need a ton of friends, just a few I can see in person and talk to honestly.

Charles Kruger mentioned that he had read some of my books but that I hadn't "been on [his] radar" for a while. Well, it sure as shootin' wasn't from me not trying to be on the radar! You have to dismember a puppy to get noticed in America's media these days.

Charles was running a blog called TheatreStorm, wherein he wrote reviews of plays, operas, and so on to a small but probably appreciative audience. I thought he wrote quite well, clear, not jaded. He was even a member of the Bay Area

Theater Critics Circle, an organization I had belonged to myself back when I was clear and unjaded. (!!) To be frank, you can see too many shows. It can get very tiring always to have An Opinion and put it into words, just to get a free ticket. I went to several things, of varying quality, with Charles on his press pass. It was a relief. I seem to remember an elderly pupeteer couple doing energetic things for an audience of seven in somebody's living room.

And an unrelenting, one-note "Three Penny Opera" in San Jose. (Oh, but I didn't and don't have to have an opinion about any of it.)

Charles even drove. He had become one of those Lyft "taxi" drivers, the ones whose cars are outfitted with a pink mustache on the front bumper. I have no great sympathy for traditional taxi drivers; they are often pricks. I bought Charles a dinner or two. He bought me one or two. It was all very civilized. The taxi job had even lifted Charles out of debt.

He was a rather short man, from the Boston area, bearded, given to saying he was "sixty" when he was only fifty-seven. Hey, you don't go adding years when you don't have to! He was now also running a reading series called Generations, where people a generation apart read together. I was half-heartedly interested in reading there to promote my new books from my new publisher (Wisehouse of Sweden, the one publishing this very book), but I didn't really want to "apply" and go through all that crap. Mostly I didn't want to sit through other people reading their work. It tends to be either badly mumbled or shouted by angry black lesbians. Been there, done that.

I think I started a bad habit with Charles, bantering a little too much, a little too snarkily. It's fun for a while, but it wears thin. It's probably best for a long-term friendship to keep it sparkling but not overly contentious. (And I am *the* expert on friendships!)

Charles intrigues me because he often speaks of his many failures in life. Apparently he was once a drunk. So many gays of a certain generation have or had substance abuse problems, no doubt from the immense social pressures laid on them. I abuse *others*, not substances, so I don't have to drink to excess. Yay me!) Charles' mother was a successful actress and he felt her presence to be very strong, perhaps too strong. He had acted himself but seems to have put that behind him. I gave him a book of my plays to read anyway, just in case. (I have discovered that people rarely find your plays and coming running to you contract in hand. You have to coach them, coax them, sometimes club them over the head and force their hand to sign the contract.) (Interestingly enough, while Googling myself recently, I discovered that there was a production of my play *Godot Arrives,* which won the 1999 National New Play Contest, (shameless plug) at the University of Dhaka in Bangladesh – a good year and a half before the time I learned about it. The folks there had not bothered to ask permission or pay a royalty. I was half-flattered and half-annoyed. I don't think they noticed that it's really an atheist play. But maybe they did and sneaked it in. Good.)

Charles Kruger also told stories of his teaching experiences in high scools in various mid-sized cities in California. He confirmed what I know to be true of the teaching conditions in American schools. Teachers are treated like shit. They are paid pitifully and expected to be the police, wardens, and uncomplaining victims of rudeness, threats, and violence. Exterminte the brutes! I say. Every liberal should be thrown alive into an American high school. The major problem is not bad teachers. It is bad students – not every single one, no, just too many – indulged, over-praised, lazy, mean, arrogant, and ignorant. They can't or won't read, either. (If you want to know what I really think of American secondary school students, just have me to lunch.)

My friendship with Charles is my newest one and thus an on-going project. He came to my reading at the Commonwealth Club of San Francisco on August 21, 2014, where my most memorable comment was "Despite what you may have heard to the contrary, I have always found cocksuckers to be very nice people". I was grateful for that. Hope it works out.

JOYCE CAROL OATES

In my 2012 novel *Saving Jane Austen,* in which I have Jane Austen's head and neck survive into modern times, I cunningly use events from my experiences with Miss Oates written in Austen's style, as if they happened in 1812.

Almost nobody seems to have noticed, or care.

JOHN W. GETTYS

My partner of thirty-four years (with an open sexual relationship) still doesn't want me to write him up in this book. Damn!

Let's just say he has made my life "interesting" for the last thirty-four years.

Yay?

DANIEL CURZON

Cyber-bullying is everywhere these days. The author feels strongly that if he had won his lawsuit against what in effect was cyber-bullying of teachers it would not be such a problem now. The law can still be changed, for god's sake!

The author donated the third and final collection of his manuscripts, reviews of his plays and novels since 1971, letters, and so for forth to the Hormel Center of the San Francisco Public Library in September of 2014. It was bittersweet, both a beginning and an end. And a professor visiting from Spain is doing research on me there and planning a monograph. What's not to like about a monograph about your work?! (And, hey, if I don't see you again, well . . . goodbye!)

www.ingramcontent.com/pod-product-compliance
Lightning Source LLC
Chambersburg PA
CBHW021827220426
43663CB00005B/154